ƒP

ALSO BY DAVID K. HURST

Crisis & Renewal:
Meeting the Challenge of Organizational Change

LEARNING
from the
LINKS

Mastering Management

Using Lessons from Golf

David K. Hurst

THE FREE PRESS
New York   London   Toronto   Sydney   Singapore

THE FREE PRESS
A Division of Simon & Schuster, Inc.
1230 Avenue of the Americas
New York, NY 10020

THE FREE PRESS and colophon are trademarks
of Simon & Schuster, Inc.

For information regarding special discounts for bulk purchases,
please contact Simon & Schuster Special Sales:
1-800-456-6798 or business@simonandschuster.com

Designed by Katy Riegel
Manufactured in the United States of America
1   3   5   7   9   10   8   6   4   2

Library of Congress Cataloging-in-Publication Data

Hurst, David K.
Learning from the links : mastering management
using lessons from golf / David K. Hurst.
p. ; cm.
Includes bibliographical references and index.
1. Management.   2. System analysis.   3. Golf.   I. Title.

HD31 .H822 2002
658—dc21   2002019740

ISBN 0-684-86501-7

For my grandparents,
whose love of the game lives on

Acknowledgments

There are many people to thank for their support in writing this book. The Center for Creative Leadership believed in the project from the outset and supported me unstintingly during my period in residence with them. In particular I would like to thank John Alexander, Stan Gryskiewicz, Susan Rice, and Tom Bridgers, who organized my stay, as well as all those who made it so pleasant, especially Barbara Demarest and Lynn Fick-Cooper, Mike Lombardo, Bill Drath, David Horth, and Chuck Palus. The gang of card players at the center sustained me through the inevitable ups and downs of writing a book and made sure that I retained a sense of humor at all times. And there are so many others in the library and other support services at the center who went out of their way to help me, especially Carol Keck and Peggy Cartner.

Then there are my golfing colleagues, many of whom I met on the first tee, had a great game with, and never saw again. But they sustained my belief that there was a real need for such a book. My Canadian golf coach, John Cochrane, has been an ongoing source of inspiration and sound advice, both in golf and in management. Maarten Asser in Amsterdam, Jean-Francois Duchaine in Quebec, George Barnes in North Carolina, and Jim Womack in Boston have been continual sources of encouragement and have been tireless readers of manuscripts. Jeff Dotson, Finn Hovland, and Creston

Shields read early versions of the book, and I am much indebted to them for their comments.

Annie Graham and the editorial staff at Strategy+Business have been continual believers in my perspectives on management and have published much of my more recent writings. Annie Graham herself has been tireless in her support of the whole project. My colleagues at the Richard Ivey School of Business, especially Rod White and Mary Crossan, have been longtime sources of stimulation and assistance.

I would also like to thank Dominick Anfuso, my editor at The Free Press, and his assistant, Kristen McGuiness, as well as my agent, Joe Spieler.

Lastly, but most important, there is my family—my wife, Di, and our sons, Nick and Jeremy. My wife has been a constant source of encouragement and a supplier of editorial advice, reading every draft of this book. I thank them all for their love and support.

—Oakville, Canada
January 2002

Contents

Introduction

AN INVITATION

Golf is life and life is lessons.
> —JOHN UPDIKE'S TEACHER, GOLF DREAMS

I think the happiest moments for a golfer are those that he spends in study and experimentation.
> —BOBBY JONES*

Comedian Jackie Mason tells a story about some wealthy boaters who bought luxury power cruisers without realizing that the engines weren't installed. They liked to party with their boats tied up to the dock and never noticed the motors were missing! Management books are a bit like those boats—it's very difficult to tell at a casual glance whether they have any "engines" in them.

This book has "engines." There is power. It asks you to read it, to go on a journey with the writer. I have an ongoing fascination with management and a long-standing passion for golf, and as far as I am aware, this is the first time these two activities have been brought so closely together. This book is for all those managers who have ever launched a change effort with high hope of success, only to stand by powerless as the initiative drained away into the

---

*This and subsequent quotations from Bobby Jones are taken from S. L. Matthew (ed.), *Secrets of the Master*, a collection of Jones's syndicated columns from the 1920s.

sand. It is also for all those golfers who have ever stepped onto the first tee brimming with confidence, only to end up hacking about in the rough.

Many managers are skeptical about what they can learn from management books. I share that skepticism. As a former manager who has spent twenty-five years in a variety of industries, I know that no book can tell me exactly what to do. How could a writer on management possibly know that? They may have a lot of information, but they don't have on-the-ground knowledge. They have no idea of the contexts in which I work, of my skills and abilities, of the people and personalities I have to deal with, of the subtle dynamics of my industry. I doubt if many managers listen to speakers or read management books to be told what to do. I know I don't. I look for perspectives and experiences that will help me frame what I am currently doing. If I can make sense of my own experience, then I will know what to do. This book will help you do that—to coordinate your experience across several fields, especially golf and management.

There's another problem with books on management. Knowing *what* to do is not the same as knowing *how* to do it. Golfers share this problem; I have been playing golf since I was twelve. Like many fellow fanatics, I have taken scores of lessons and hit thousands of practice balls. I have also read (and been given!) a lot of books on golf. No activity, other than management, has more books on advice about *what* to do. And yet, as every golfer knows, improvement is a real struggle. If it were a question of theory, we would have no trouble, but when it comes to performance, that's another matter.

Maybe "how to" books are misnamed. They are really "what to do" books that leave a whole lot unsaid about implementation. When we were kids the instructions were simple: eat your carrots, say "please," always flush. When we get into more complicated tasks, our tribulations mount quickly. It's no wonder that many people don't bother to read computer manuals. They rarely tell you what you want to know, and they often assume the very knowledge you are trying to gain. As a result, you understand the instructions only after you no longer need them! When it comes to complex activities like golf and management, as the book makes clear, the whole instructional model starts to fall apart. Improvement comes only from well-structured experience and perfect practice.

Only recently have I understood why this should be and been able to change things for the better—hence the book in your hands.

This book is about getting things done, about implementation. More precisely it is about the problem of execution. It is about the gap between ideas and action and how to bridge it. It is written for all managers who have an interest in improving their own effectiveness and the performance of their organizations. Ideally they should also have some experience with the game of golf and be interested in improving their golfing performance. Knowledge of golf is not essential, however, for throughout the book there are illustrations drawn from many forms of artistry. It is something of a leap to see both managing and golfing as forms of art: we tend to see managers, in particular, as intensely practical people who deal with the world as it is. My argument, however, is that expert managers and top golfers are just as much performers as any other artists. They are designers and makers of their worlds, not manipulators.

So if golf is not a source of excitement for you, just skim through those sections until you come to a more congenial image. There are examples drawn from music, athletics, swimming, art, and, of course, the management of organizations of many kinds. In the process you may even come to appreciate the subtleties and delights of golf!

Throughout the book I use the theory of complex systems as a discipline to focus and concentrate on golf and management. The introduction of a conceptual lens between the two activities helps us to select features and relationships to study. On the surface, golf and management seem to be two very different activities. The systems lens allows us to see their underlying similarities and to look at each of them from the perspective of the other.

I will be supplementing the complexity framework with some

of the latest results and thinking from teachers of golf and management and from the fields of sports science, artificial intelligence, neuroscience, and cognitive and evolutionary psychology. In the process we will get a better understanding of all three components of the framework—golf, management, and complex systems.

Readers of this book will learn

- *how to look at themselves, their organizations, and their golf swings as complex systems* with dynamic processes that are layered in space and ordered in time.
- *the important difference between hierarchies of command-and-control and hierarchies of control* and the advantage of systems that are built up in modular fashion.
- *the central importance to learning as well as control in all complex systems of timely, effective feedback and why ineffectiveness is often due to our inability to pay attention*—to sense a situation accurately and understand the context in which we are operating.
- *why so much depends upon self-regulating processes and why focused attention is the scarcest resource in all such systems.* Indeed, the ability to pay attention may be the single critical difference between top performers and also-rans.
- *why the differences between top-level and other performers in business and sports are due to qualitative rather than quantitative factors:* that is, top performers don't just practice more, they practice differently, with both focus and effective feedback.
- *why intellectual knowledge of the need to change behavior is insufficient to trigger the change.* The need to change must be felt viscerally, not just appreciated conceptually. This is achieved by complete immersion in the problem situation.
- *why the biggest barrier to change in golf and management is our reluctance to give up power—top-down power.* For until we give up this unilateral, effortful, coercive power, we cannot experience the other kind of power—bottom-up, effortless, synergistic power.

- *how an exclusive emphasis on final outcomes in management and golf can destroy the practice of the skills necessary to produce top-level performance.* Using financial results as your only measure of management performance is just as helpful as thinking about your golf score during the swing. It's a desirable outcome of good performance, but a very poor guide to right action!
- *how to practice at management and golf in ways that promote the development of repeatable skills at many levels.* In both activities this means the use of drills and simulations that mimic conditions encountered in the real world. In contrast, the annual budgeting process in many companies, when looked at as a vehicle for practice and improvement, is almost totally dysfunctional.
- *how to coach and mentor individuals so that they can improve their performance by providing timely, specific feedback* at the appropriate levels of the systems involved. This feedback must be supplied in a language that the learner can understand and use to change behavior.
- *how to integrate multiple skills across levels to produce sustainable improvement in performance in management and golf.* In golf it's the rhythm and tempo of a swing that flows effortlessly, with the ball flying toward the target as if it had been pulled there. In management it's the ongoing integration of sound disciplines with continual experimentation via the creative process we call leadership.
- *why imagination is so critical to both management and golf because it allows us to build systems based on "pull" rather than "push."* Imagination is not just an adjunct to reason, it underpins it and is shot through it. Imagination is woven throughout our physical and mental existence. It is the mediator of perception and the catalyst for action, the primary instrument of our will.
- *the central importance of stories in focusing attention by helping individuals, teams, and companies to organize their experiences in the physical, biological, and psychological worlds in which we live.*

Thus my objective in writing this book was to help us reorganize our experience: to connect what we already know in a new way. For it is by organizing experience that we turn ideas into action and make meaning of our lives and those around us. In short, it gives us power to go on the journey.

Come with me—it's time to step onto the first tee. . . .

Important Note About the "Course"

The book consists of eighteen chapters of varying length, each of which has a "par" and a nominal distance in yards. Think of it as a long (over seven thousand yards), old-fashioned, links-style course with a slightly quirky layout but a generous par of 73. There are four par-5s but only three par-3s! To get a quick idea of the "course," read chapters 1 and 2 and then 17 and 18. If you have time to look at only one chapter, read chapter 17—it is, in effect, an executive summary.

Good luck!

NO. 1

Making the Links

Par-4	307 yards

Is there a connection between athletic skill and management ability? The June 1998 issue of *Golf Digest* contained the first ever ranking of the golf handicaps of the CEOs of America's largest corporations. The magazine surveyed the three hundred publicly traded corporations in the Fortune 500 and succeeded in obtaining 110 handicaps sanctioned by the United States Golf Association. Top of the list was Scott McNealy of Sun Microsystems with a handicap index of 3.2 (the index is an adjusted handicap to reflect the relative difficulty of the courses played). Jack Welch of GE followed him closely with a handicap index of 3.8. The list continued all the way down to William Steere of Pfizer, whose handicap was 34.0.

Shortly after this, *The New York Times* commissioned the well-known compensation expert Graef Crystal to correlate the handicaps with the performance of the corporations. He found that over the previous three years the corporations that generated the best returns were led by the CEOs with the lowest handicaps. The results were statistically significant, and the *Times* article speculated as to why this was the case. Were natural leaders also natural athletes? Did time on the golf course build social skills and contacts that allowed golfers to make better deals? Perhaps the years spent caddying developed golf skills and exposed young people to business jargon early in life? And so on.

Some nongolfers viewing these statistics might argue that the time the golfing executives spent on the golf course kept them out of the office, allowing their subordinates to get on with the job more effectively! This argument may have merit, but it need not reflect badly on the golfers. After all, the selection of effective subordinates and the creation of contexts in which they can get on with the job is an essential part of management. No organization can be effective for long if it depends upon the continuous presence of one person. So the question remains, why did this correlation exist? Although this book was begun long before *The New York Times* published its findings, I hope to throw a good deal of light on this question. For continued success and improvement in both golf and management require a deep understanding of how complex systems function, and there is a great deal to be learned by comparing the one activity in terms of the other—systematically.

Golfonomics

If you have picked up this book looking for a humorous piece written about golf and management, you may be disappointed. There is humor in it; for often things happen in both golf and management where all one can do is laugh! But this book is a thoughtful attempt by someone who is serious about both golf and management to understand the parallels between the two activities, particularly as they apply to learning and improvement in performance. For many years I have been struck by the similarities between the two activities, but I have never been able to explain what they were or why they existed. Now, with the help of a framework developed from the emerging study of complex systems, it can be done.

Organizations are incredibly complex, and they can be understood only by analogy with things and processes with which we are more familiar. My central analogy for this book is a complex system that we all know well—our own bodies (and brains) engaged in one of our more enjoyable diversions, playing golf. The complex, systemic nature of our bodies is, however, well hidden from us. They regulate themselves so well that in the normal course of a healthy life we are rarely aware of them. It is only when our bodies are stressed, less pleasantly by disease or injury and more pleasantly by physical activity such as sport, that we realize how complex they really are. Golf in particular, as a target sport that engages the whole body, is especially demanding. In fact, some might argue that golf is closer to a disease or an addiction than a sport! Writer John Updike calls it a "narcotic pastime" and a "non-chemical hallucinogen." As such it holds its sufferers in a condition somewhere between sickness and health. A few years ago this charge was featured prominently in an article in *The Economist,* which blamed the collapse of the Asian economies on an "obsession" with the game. Titled "Asia in the Rough" and appearing under a section headed "Golfonomics," the article was published in the often tongue-in-cheek year-end issue of 1997:

> Golf fanatics often find it hard to put the reasons for their addiction into words. They talk of the camaraderie of the course, the striving after a sort of perfection, and the joys of the fresh air, exercise and natural beauty. But the game can be seen in another way, too: as a symptom of a social, political, economic and environmental malaise whose effects are only just beginning to be felt. Many theories have been put forward to explain why the economic progress of South-East Asia has so suddenly left the fairway: the forces of globalization; mis-

guided economic policies; exclusive and unresponsive political systems; a pursuit of growth at the expense of everything else, including the environment and the livelihoods of the poor. The phenomenon of golf unites all these hypotheses.[*]

The article went on to describe the growth of golf in Asia as "cancerous" and accuse the game of embodying "a clubbish elitism, an almost feudal social order." Golfers were not amused, and the article attracted apoplectic letters from Peoria, Tokyo, and Karachi that the magazine's editors felt compelled to publish under the heading "Golfing Humour"!

The Economist article may reflect the current confused state of economic theory and our inability to predict such major events as the meltdown of an entire region, but from a systems point of view it may have been on to something. After all, this was not the first time that golf has been accused of having dangerous consequences for the social "body." In the fifteenth century a succession of Scottish kings tried to outlaw the game, culminating in the ban of 1491:

> It is statute and ordained that in na place of the realme there be used Fute-ball, Golfe, or uther sik unproffitable sportis contrary to the common good of the Realme and defense thereof.[†]

Apparently golf and football interfered with archery practice, putting the safety of the nation at risk. As precision sports requiring considerable practice, golf and archery have a lot in common. In England this was underlined three hundred years later when, at the outbreak of the Napoleonic Wars, the British army gave serious consideration to sending companies of bowmen to fight with the forces of General Sir Arthur Wellesley (later the duke of Wellington) in their campaigns on the Iberian Peninsula. There was no doubt that the longbow, with its thirty-inch "clothyard" arrows, was a superior weapon to the musket. It had equivalent

---

[*]*The Economist*, December 20, 1997, p. 85.
[†]Robert T. Sommers, *Golf Anecdotes*, p. 12.

range and accuracy, with a much greater rate of fire and higher reliability. The problem was training. Interest in archery had declined over the centuries (perhaps owing to golf—we know that the bow makers diversified into the manufacture of the early wooden clubs!), and the archers would have to be taught from scratch. A raw recruit could be trained to use a musket effectively in a day: the training of effective bowmen took years and required regular weekly practice at the butts. The plan was dropped.

Golf as a Shared Experience

I don't believe that understanding the golf swing is any simpler than understanding organizations. But at least, as golfers, we are familiar with it. Every day we act in systems that we don't completely understand, often with quite successful outcomes. These activities range from driving a car to maintaining interpersonal relationships to managing in global markets. While we may not have an intellectual understanding of these complex systems, we do have some kind of knowledge of them. This knowledge is best described as an intuitive "feel," or knowing-in-action, as it has been called: it is a knowledge that is embodied in our motor and perceptual skills, enhanced by training and experience.

The golf swing is an activity like that. It is also a shared physical experience that all golfers have and can serve as a common platform of knowledge on which to explore ideas about habits and about change. For golf is one of the most demanding individual sports, and all golfers know how difficult it is to maintain a consistent standard, let alone improve at the game. The reasons for this are systemic. They must be, because everyone experiences them! And if we can understand the systemic reasons golf is such a difficult game, perhaps we can understand why managing and improving business organizations can also be so challenging. For the fact is that, at least as measured by popular financial standards such as economic value added, many businesses score worse than "par" for most of their lives. Getting a business to perform at par or better is a significant achievement.

The Head-Down Theory of Knowledge

Historically the teaching of both golf and management has suffered from what I call the "head-down theory of knowledge." This theory of command-and-control assumes that the head or the brain is the most important part of the body, the primary container of knowledge, and the "boss" of the rest of the components. All that is required for excellent performance is for the head to tell the rest of the organization what to do and for them to obey immediately—then it will happen. In golf this takes the form of long lists of instructions:

- Try to make a big turn.
- Keep your left arm straight.
- Tuck your right elbow in.
- Drive your legs for power.
- Keep your head down.
- Etc.

David Leadbetter, one of the best-known teachers of golf, describes these kinds of instruction as "an unhealthy diet of myth and folklore, which seems to exist wherever the game is played. . . . Though there may be some truth behind the principles upon which these clichés were originally based, taking them too literally or out of context, can seriously inhibit your ability to swing a club with a free-flowing motion . . . these tired expressions get you thinking too much."*

The head-down theory of knowledge is deeply embedded in management theory and practice, and its lineage can be tracked back to antiquity via the military and religious institutions that are the ancestors of our modern organizations. It is difficult to distinguish, for example, between the management philosophies of Frederick the Great (1712–1786), king of Prussia, and the founder of modern management thinking, Frederick Taylor (1856–1915)!

Positive Practice, pp. 37–39.

"No one reasons, everyone executes," was the first Frederick's famous dictum, reflecting his sole responsibility for situational analysis and the development of strategy. His relatively small forces, with their professional officers and press-ganged soldiers, were eventually swept away, however, by Napoleon's massed columns. Napoleon had discovered that huge masses of men could be managed using ideological means in addition to the basic disciplines. Napoleonic armies could forage for food and live off the land without deserting. They could take cover from fire and still move ahead and inflict severe losses on a fleeing enemy without loss of control. The powers of mass and maneuver proved devastating. None of these actions was open to Frederick the Great or commanders who built armies on his model—the human material with which they worked was just too unstable.

Perhaps it was the composition of the workforce that explains, at least in part, Frederick Taylor's management philosophy. For it was developed on the shop floor at a time when the workforce often consisted of new, unskilled immigrants. Taylor viewed them as ox-like—"heavy both physically and mentally," whose work could be performed by training an "intelligent gorilla." "All possible brain work should be removed from the shop and centered in the planning or laying-out department," wrote Taylor, ". . . leaving for the foreman and gang bosses work strictly executive in nature. Their duties should be to see that the operations planned and directed from the planning room are promptly carried out in the shop."*

Although Taylor's management philosophy was complex and more subtle than that of his disciples, his methods were embedded in all modern mass-manufacturing systems, where they performed effectively for many years, notably in the automotive industry. The whole system would be swept aside in the 1980s, however, by the emergence of the Japanese "lean" manufacturing systems developed by Toyota and Honda. As we shall see, this system, with its roots in Japanese religious and cultural thought, is inherently not a head-down approach.

In North America the professional schools' view of knowledge

Scientific Management, pp. 98–99.

has been overwhelmingly head-down. In the teaching of management, this perspective has been most prominent in the field of business policy, where the formulation of strategy has been taught as being prior to and separate from the implementation of that strategy. In management practice this led to the illusion that plans could be developed at the "head" office and then handed down to the "branches" for implementation. Although its proponents have argued that this split between thinking and doing was made for teaching purposes only, in the classroom the head-down theory results in the use of what longtime Harvard Business School professor Fritz Roethlisberger called "verbal wands":

> At the drop of a hat the students would reorganize the company and provide it with all the standards and controls it needed. If the management did not know its costs, for example, it should install a cost-control system; if management did not know what the consumer wanted, then it would do consumer research; if foremen were not supervising well, foremen training should be introduced; and so on and on. . . . Not only were the students well equipped to make an organization into a perfect organization, they were well equipped to change people's attitudes, motivations and personalities into the proper ones. At the stroke of their verbal wands, they could change deviant employees into conforming ones; untactful supervisors into tactful ones; autocratic supervisors into democratic ones; apathetic workers into highly motivated ones . . . and so on and on.[*]

The use of the "verbal wands" that Roethlisberger complained about was, unfortunately, not restricted to the MBA classroom. It is still widespread in management, especially in the consulting community, where it has become so common that we hardly notice it. A recent article in the *Harvard Business Review* entitled "The Smart-Talk Trap" lamented the gap between *knowing* and *doing* in contemporary business and explained, "Managers let talk substitute for action because that's what they've been trained to do. . . .

[*]*The Elusive Phenomena*, p. 128.

Smart talk is the essence of management education at leading institutions in the United States and throughout the world. Students learn how to sound smart in classroom discussions and how to write smart things on essay examinations. . . . They don't actually have to implement the recommendations or act on the insights that emerge in the conversation."*

Now the head-down approach is great for teasing out the priorities, the great issues and questions that an organization must address. But for effective performance, these "good questions" cannot be answered on the same level at which they are asked: they must be addressed on many levels throughout the organization. The "head" conducts the inquiry, but it's the "hands," the body of the organization, that has to respond.

An Embodied Theory of Knowledge

Throughout this book I will be using a very different theory of knowledge—the idea that knowledge as well as "mind" is best seen as a quality that is distributed throughout our organizations and our bodies. It is an evolutionary view of the mind as consisting of myriad special-purpose mechanisms, each of which has been honed over evolutionary time to deal with recurrent challenges to our survival and growth. These mechanisms are buried so deeply within us that we are rarely aware of them—we don't know what we know. I will argue that improving effectiveness in both golf and management depends upon surfacing, developing, and transferring this tacit knowledge that is buried deeply within all complex systems and organizations.

This concept of knowledge is also buried in our language. The roots of the word *know* are the same as those for the word *can*, with the Scots *ken* (as in the question "D'ye ken?") being a neat blend of the two. True knowledge is always about personal experience: it is "know-how" and deals with our capacity to act, to get

---

*Jeffrey Pfeffer and Robert I. Sutton, *Harvard Business Review*, May–June 1999, p. 136.

things done. Knowledge, therefore, is about competence. This implies that our knowledge of most of golf and much of management is subjective and practical, rather than objective and theoretical. In the case of golf, knowledge is embodied—it exists in our bodies *and* our brains, and not just in the conscious part of our brains. In the case of organizations, knowledge is embodied everywhere. It is encased in the systems and the technologies: it exists within and between individuals as well as in larger groupings inside the organization such as teams, departments, and divisions. Knowledge also dwells among organizations—between a business and its customers and suppliers, for example.

Teaching and Learning Embodied Knowledge

It is the tacit, embodied nature of knowledge that makes it so difficult to teach and transfer. In real time we are largely unaware of how complex systems such as our bodies and our organizations function. We cannot access what is happening, let alone express what is going on. So we always know much more than we can tell. For this reason, while tacit skills can be acquired, they are extremely difficult to teach. And even the acqusition of tacit skills in complex systems is not easy. All the evidence is that they can be learned only through personal action and continual practice. All golfers know this (even though they may not follow its implications), but somehow the message has only just started to trickle through to the field of management. It is over forty years since Peter Drucker described management as a practice, yet we still don't understand what that entails. Drucker himself has never really explained what he meant:

> Effectiveness . . . is a habit; that is, a complex of practices. And practices can always be learned. . . . Practices one learns by practicing and practicing and practicing again.*

*Peter F. Drucker, *The Effective Executive*, 1966, p. 23.

But how do we practice management? What kinds of habit are desirable? What activities are required? *How* should they be performed?

Drucker has always emphasized the need for managers to be organized and systematic:

> Strategic planning . . . is the continuous process of making present entrepreneurial (*risk-taking*) *decisions* systematically and with the greatest knowledge of their futurity; organizing systematically the *efforts* needed to carry out these decisions; and measuring the results of these decisions against the expectation through organized, *systematic feedback.**

It's difficult to disagree with this advice, but it does beg many questions. What does it mean to be "systematic" and "organized"? We can be systematic only if we understand the relationships among the variables in a system and know what activities lead to which results. To be organized we have to know the logic of cause and effect, so that we can do "first things first." But how do we obtain such knowledge? And what exactly is "systematic feedback": what is its role, and how do we arrange for it to be present? In short, what are the essential qualities of a system? These questions raise a host of other issues. How do individuals learn in organizations? How do we transfer knowledge from experts to novices? How do we turn information, "know-what," into knowledge, "know-how"? How do we transform ideas into action?

There is plenty of explicit knowledge (sometimes called "information") around on how to play golf and how to manage, but there is relatively little written about how to turn information into behavior, to turn "know-what" into "know-how," to create practices that are effective. This book takes up the challenge.

---

*Peter Drucker, *Management: Tasks, Responsibilities, Practices* (New York: Harper & Row, 1973), p. 125, original emphasis.

Summary

At one level this book examines the systemic similarities between golf and management using the theory of complex systems as a lens between the two activities. This approach promises to deliver a number of valuable insights in how to improve performance in both activities. At a deeper level the book is about the relationship between thought and action, the brain and the body. The traditional Western head-down theory of knowledge stresses the primacy of reason and logic. It pervades our culture and is particularly noticeable in the teaching of both golf and management. This book takes a different perspective and tries to redress the balance with a more "body up" view. It stresses the primacy of the body, both in the evolution of thought and in the control of the behavior of complex systems.

The reader may well be skeptical that a close relationship can be developed between activities as apparently dissimilar as golf and management. In the next chapter I will outline some aspects of the curious parallel between the two.

No. 2

A Curious Parallel

Par-4	433 yards

The golf swing is a most complicated combination of muscular actions, too complex to be controlled by objective conscious mental effort. Consequently, we must rely a good deal upon the instinctive reactions acquired by long practice.
—BOBBY JONES

Much of the error of historians, economists and all of us in daily affairs, arises from imputing logical reason to men who could not or cannot base their actions on reason.
—CHESTER BARNARD, FUNCTIONS OF THE EXECUTIVE

The par-4 18th at Harbour Town on Hilton Head Island in South Carolina is one of the finest finishing holes in all of golf. Set beside the waters of Calibogue Sound, it measures up to 478 trouble-filled yards in length. From the air it's shaped like a crawling snail at full stretch, tail on the tee and head on the green. On the right-hand side, along the flat underbelly of the snail, it's out of bounds all the way. The landing area for your drive is on the broad hump of the snail, which swells out into the dense sea marsh that fringes the sound.

The line to take is toward the famous red-and-white-striped lighthouse, but depending on the location of the tees and direction of the wind, you may not want to hit a driver. For at 270 yards out from the back tees, the sea surges in to take a big bite out of the fairway and it's easy to run out of room. In any event, the second shot is almost always a medium to long iron over the marsh. Par is a good score.

It was a lovely, bright afternoon when we came to the 18th, but there was a steady breeze into our faces and I knew that I would have to keep my drive low to stand any chance of getting home in two. Par on the 18th hole would see me break 80 for the first time on this tough course. I teed the ball low, put it a little back in my stance, just as the pros say you should, and tried to punch it into the wind. To my horror, I hit a sharp snap hook to the left and the ball dived like a rabbit into the tall grasses of the marsh.

"Bad luck," sympathized one of my golfing partners.

"It looked like you came over the top," suggested another, trying to be helpful.

But I was too shattered to respond. It wasn't bad luck, it was the same old story: just as things were feeling right, I had managed to mess them up. I hit a provisional drive and, too disgusted to watch its perfect flight, set off to hunt for the first ball. Why? I asked myself, Why, why, why?

Struggling with Golf

I have been playing recreational golf for over forty years now. I began at the age of twelve, when my grandfather, who was a keen golfer, undertook to teach me. Twice a week he and I went out to practice and play golf. We had a wonderful time and I improved steadily, eventually playing to a single-figure handicap. Over the years I have always been able to hit the ball solidly, but like all golfers, I have struggled with my inconsistency. I think I have been more erratic than most, for my problems went beyond the usual bad shots—the wayward drives, mishit irons, blown chips, and erratic putting.

From time to time my swing just seemed to "fall apart." Usually "it" happened between games, but sometimes "it" happened between holes. The difference was dramatic. On those occasions the movements that had worked so well the previous week or even on the last hole just wouldn't produce the same results. I was using the same swing and the same swing thoughts, but the results were now terrible: hard pulls and vicious hooks (sometimes in the same shot) spiked with the occasional sh——k (I hate to use that word). And I never knew which one of them was coming next! If there is any other combination of shots more destructive of a reasonable score in golf, I cannot imagine what it is. That low hook, in particular, seems to have a mind of its own. "You can talk to a fade," said Lee Trevino, in a philosophical mood, "but the hook won't listen." The legendarily taciturn Ben Hogan was more visceral about it: "I hate a hook," he once said. "It nauseates me. I could vomit—it's like having a rattlesnake in your pocket." I've never had a rattlesnake in my pocket, but I know what he meant. That hook can bite you at any time.

I would go home in despair and fling my clubs into the basement, vowing never to play the game again. But sooner or later, usually within the week or so, a thought would come to me about what I was doing wrong. It would just come straight out of the blue, usually when I wasn't concentrating on anything in particular: the early morning shower was an especially fruitful time for such notions. Even though my conscious mind had forsworn thinking about golf, apparently my unconscious mind had been plugging along all the time, living with the problem. Hmm . . . that's right, I would think. I have been doing that. Let's see what Hogan has to say about it. And as soon as I had finished my shower I would open my well-thumbed paperback copy of *The Modern Fundamentals of Golf* searching for the appropriate section. Sometimes it was the arrival of my subscription (which I had meant to cancel) to the latest golf magazine that triggered the process. There would be a full-page photo spread of the swing of the latest, hottest player and perhaps an article entitled "How to Cure the Sh——ks." I would pore over it, searching for clues to a remedy for my malady. Before long I would find myself rummaging for the clubs in the basement, preparatory to heading out onto the lawn, where I could catch a glimpse of my swing reflected in a window. Hmm . . . let's just take a look at this. . . .

The next step would be a visit to the practice range. There it was easier to get into a rhythm, and sometimes, very occasionally, the whole swing would snap back into place, reappearing as suddenly and mysteriously as it had left me. Before long I would be bouncing balls into the boundary fence with my driver. But more usually the practice tee would be as frustrating as the course: I would seem to have lost all feel for the game. It's difficult to express that feeling of helplessness and anguish, when the familiar is lost and the new cannot yet be grasped. Poet Matthew Arnold could have been thinking of struggling golfers when he described people as "[w]andering between two worlds, one dead, the other powerless to be born." Frantic, I would go home to ransack the past issues of golf magazines and review all my books, enlisting Palmer, Player, Nicklaus, all the saints, and whoever else I could find.

When all else failed and things were truly desperate (usually after I had dinged some of the household glass!), I would visit a professional for a half-hour lesson. These were the days before the introduction of videotape, so I'm not sure what was happening technically during those sessions, but usually the pro would put me back on track. After some initial discomfort with the modified moves, things would improve. With the new swing thoughts and a better tempo, the ball seemed to fly straighter and my scores would get better. My confidence grew, and with that, the terrors of the hook and the sh——k seemed to recede. Slowly the feeling would grow that "this time I've really got it!" And sometimes, on the strength of that feeling, I would acquire some shiny new sticks, trading in my old weapons. "You can always bring 'em back if you don't like 'em," said the pro.

Fantastic! Now I could hit it longer and straighter than ever before. There would be crisp mornings and golden afternoons, when all was right with the world; the hot streaks on several holes in a row and those elusive moments when my swing would feel silky smooth. At these times the ball would fly off the clubface without my realizing that I had swung at it. One got a fleeting glimpse of what was possible: absolute mastery, total control—draw . . . fade . . . high . . . low—no problem! I loved the people I played with . . . the club championship loomed ahead—anything was possible.

And then . . . and *then* . . . suddenly, out of nowhere, just as I was trying to hold, against the wind, a high draw to a hidden pin, I would produce that low, mean, vicious hook, the kind that turns your knees to jelly and your bowels to water . . . and it would all fall apart again. Pull, hook, shank—there, I said it—the full cycle of misery and despair, this time deeper than ever before, because I knew what it could be and I'd lost it. And then the trip back to the basement, this time to take the clubs back to the pro; the humiliating deal to redeem the old sticks and credit the new ones; and back to the beginning all over again.

It wasn't a question of practice; I would spend hours on the practice tee, "grooving" my swing, but as soon as I got out on the course the feeling would mysteriously disappear. Somehow I just could not break the cycle. Looking back, I wonder whether the books and magazines really helped. Sometimes I would try to copy swing elements from several players—Player's stance and Palmer's swing, for example, and that definitely didn't work. For the advice of the pros was often contradictory and just plain confusing. I'm still not quite sure what Ben Hogan meant by "supinating" the left wrist at impact, and I'm quite sure I never learned how to do it. Hogan had fought a hook throughout much of his golfing career, and at times, his view of what was important seemed quite different from Jack Nicklaus's. And people don't agree with Nicklaus! Some teachers say, for example, that Jack's recommendation that golfers play all shots with the ball aligned with the left heel has been a major source of short-iron problems for many players. It seems that Ben, Arnold, Gary, and Jack have each developed his *own* thoughts for his *own* swings, and none of them helped me!

Struggling with Management

I have spent over thirty years in management now, first as a manager and more recently as a writer and consultant. I started my career in the late 1960s, in the golden era of the great conglomerates. The American business schools were just beginning their rise to supremacy, and those were the days when it was thought that a good general manager could run anything. Executives like Harold Geneen of ITT, Royal Little of Textron, and Tex Thornton of Litton Industries were held up as examples of people who could do it. ITT, which was the darling of Wall Street, had grown rapidly through acquisitions and ran a polyglot of companies in a highly decentralized structure. The only commonality was money, so the language of the head office was the language of finance. Geneen was famous for his search for "unshakable facts" and his no-nonsense, by-the-numbers approach to management. His cadre of financial analysts, attached to the head office, was feared by all the divisions, and woe betide an operating manager who appeared unprepared at one of Geneen's famous planning meetings. There must have been hundreds of corporations around the world who aspired to be like ITT, Textron, or Litton. All one had to do was make a number of acquisitions and group them together to garner the synergies that were thought to flow from that structure. It didn't matter if you knew nothing about the actual businesses; the use of calculation and financial technique was all that was necessary.

Although running a business is a vastly more complex activity than striking a golf ball, it seems to me that there are some deep systemic similarities between the two activities. Take the cycle of triumph and despair, for example. Every business operation that I have ever been involved with, whether it was a single unit, division, or conglomerate, seemed to go through phases when everything worked, interspersed with periods when nothing would work. It wasn't just me—the phenomenon seems to be universal. Just like many of the companies featured by Tom Peters and Bob Waterman in their 1981 book, *In Search of Excellence*, the turning point was usually right after the companies had been proclaimed to be excellent. For example, their list of corporations that passed all hurdles for excellence in the period 1961–80 included the following:*

---

*The figures in parentheses show the corporation's 2000 relative rank within the largest companies in its industry in *Fortune*'s lists of "America's Most Admired Companies."

Amdahl (not ranked—owned by Fujitsu)
Avon (7/10)
Delta Airlines (4/10)
Digital Equipment (not ranked—owned by Compaq)
Fluor (7/11)
Kmart (10/10; filed for bankruptcy in 2002)
National Semiconductor (5/10)
Revlon (10/10)
Wang Labs (not ranked—owned by Getronics)

The specific reasons each of these corporations lost ground relative to its industry are probably as varied and as difficult to figure
out as the loss of form by a struggling golfer. It's true that each of
them failed in some way to adapt to technological, social, and political change, but this is no more enlightening than saying that
Retief Goosen "choked" on the 18-inch putt on the last hole of the
fourth round of the 2001 U.S. Open. It's a description, not an explanation—an explanation would require a much more detailed
systemic account of cause-and-effect relationships.

The woes of many of the firms featured in *In Search of Excellence* have been well documented. I raise the topic here to underline the dangers of the practice, common to golfers and managers,
of following exemplars of "excellent" performance without knowing the unique conditions responsible for their apparent success.
The subtitle of Peters and Waterman's runaway best-seller was
Lessons from America's Best-Run Companies, and one wonders how
far one would have got following the examples just listed.

Of course, the practice can be much more dangerous for firms
in industries too small to attract many large-scale Fortune 500
companies. In the early 1980s, when I was working for a medium-
size Canadian conglomerate, the building supply division justified its aggressive acquisition strategy (I still shudder when I
recall it) by referral to the apparently successful expansion of
Wickes in the United States. At that time, Wickes was a fast-
growing chain of hardware and lumber stores whose performance
had attracted a wide following on Wall Street. It was spoken of

in the same breath as Hechinger's and Lowe's, two highly successful do-it-yourself hardware chains of the era. The division's strategies were conceptually elegant, and their logic was unassailable. They made eminent sense to the board of directors. The idea was to buy up regional distributors, pool their buying power, and blow the competition away with lower costs and superior value. The whole system was to be coordinated with a customized version of wholesaler-specific software produced by a third-party supplier.

There was just one problem with the strategies—we couldn't execute them. For it seemed that our strategic reach exceeded our operational grasp. We would conceive of ambitious strategies—to capture this market or implement that service—but our ability to make the strategy work on the ground, our capacity to execute, was woefully inadequate. Perhaps if the directors had gone out to visit the operations on the ground, they might have understood why. Regional wholesalers are unglamorous businesses that don't usually attract huge amounts of management talent, and the necessary operational capabilities and disciplines did not exist. Many of the physical facilities were run-down and totally unsuited to housing modern streamlined distribution systems. Every outfit we had acquired seemed to have its own idiosyncratic way of doing things, and none of them was well constructed or internally consistent. The software design house never did meet any of the delivery deadlines, and the software, when it arrived, was clunky and expensive, with far more "bells and whistles" than we needed. Converting the business processes of a variety of small regional businesses to such a system turned out to be a nightmare. Our competitors feasted on our lapses, and by the time our stores were on-line we had lost a great deal of ground to them.

The division's strategies turned out to be just like those high, floating one-irons that I can see so vividly in my mind's eye but couldn't hit if my life depended on it. Then, in an alarming development, our role model collapsed! In 1981 Wickes entered Chapter 11 bankruptcy, at that time the second largest corporation ever to do so. Apparently they couldn't implement the strategy, either!

Our own building supply business, perhaps in tribute to our faithful mimicry of them, collapsed a year later.

But even in perennially successful businesses, the formula for prosperity can be fickle. Just as is the case in golf, stress or adversity of some kind often precipitates problems. Downturns in the business cycle, like high winds on the course, have the effect of magnifying mistakes and revealing operational flaws whose existence one might never have suspected in normal times. Even prosperity can have the same effect. The health maintenance organization Oxford Health Plans Inc. expanded at a breakneck pace from 1992 to 1997, but in the process it first overloaded and then destroyed its basic billing and costing systems. We'll take a closer look at them in chapter 5.

During such tough times in a corporation's life, the strategies and activities that had been so successful in the past just don't seem to perform anymore. Indeed, they may never have functioned in the way they were explained. I'm not sure that our conglomerate's strategies ever "worked," at least in the way we formulated them for the board and the investment community. Too often the strategies stayed on the pages on which they were printed: just so many black marks on white paper. The implications of what we intended to do never reached the levels in the organization where they could be examined, improved upon, and actually implemented.

Golf and Management: Side by Side

The cycles in business are longer and bigger than they are in golf, but as practitioners, golfers and managers often seem to respond to adversity in the same way. When earnings came under pressure, for example, our senior management team, led by the CEO, would begin to fiddle with the organizational setup, shuffling the managers of the strategic business units, changing responsibilities, eliminating some activities and starting others. Often we would canvas our colleagues in related businesses for their ideas, pay visits to firms that seemed to be doing it right, and sometimes call in the consultants for advice. We would begin to thumb through the back issues of the *Harvard Business Review* in search of frameworks and perspectives and scan the business journals for examples we might follow.

We would also look to the practices of the leading companies for strategies we could copy and programs we could duplicate. Just as the building supply division looked to Wickes, so each of the other divisions had its own icon of how to run the business. Even the conglomerate head office kept (and published) its own list of corporations against which it ranked itself and whose success it hoped either to emulate or surpass. Our responses to pressure for results were typical of many firms. The imitation of strategies of apparently successful firms is widespread in business, although managers rarely admit to the practice. The acquisition by the Big Three auto manufacturers of European "boutique" brands in the early 1990s happened in a sudden burst of activity, when it was the "thing to do." Chrysler bought Lamborghini, Ford snapped up Aston Martin and Jaguar, and GM invested in Saab and decided to bring out the ill-fated Cadillac Allante. All paid significant premiums for these businesses. The familiar "herd" tendency in bank lending, which usually ends up with the banks being overexposed to one sector or another of the economy—commercial real estate in the 1990s—is another example of the same process.

Management fads, such as Zero-Based Budgeting, Total Quality Management, and Business Process Reengineering, seem to travel on the grapevine in much the same way golf tips do. However, these tips don't travel on just the grapevine: there's a vast publishing industry poised to disseminate them. And whether it's golf or management, these magazines use almost identical styles.

Put a copy of *Fortune* magazine and an issue of *Golf Digest* side by side, for example: look at their tables of contents and skim the major stories. The topics may be different, but the intellectual approaches are identical. Both magazines share a cheerful simplicity in their attitude toward complex change, together with a breezy, uncritical acceptance of the latest tools and techniques: "It's Hot, It's Happening, It's Now: Reengineering the Company," trumpeted

Fortune in 1993, on a cover replete with blueprints and plumb bobs. "One Smooth Move," assured *Golf Digest* on another. And then there are the stories of the secrets for success delivered by the stars of the hour, their professors and teachers, coaches and caddies. "Jack Welch's Secret Weapon," "Michael Porter on Strategy," "Nick Price's Swing Keys," and "Jim Flick's 24 Surefire Tips," which will "take strokes off your score today." The more tips there are, it seems, the better the magazine will sell—"44 Pages: More Tips than Ever," blares the cover on a recent issue of *Golf Digest*.

The stories in these publications are usually well written, sometimes brilliantly so, and they are fun to read. One gets a sense of vicarious pleasure, learning of the exploits of the stars and seeing them in their glossy surroundings. There's a feeling of being part of it all, as if we are personally "in the game" and a member of the same community. And that's great—the articles just aren't necessarily much help in improving either one's golf or the performance of one's organization!

None of this seems to slake our thirst for advice. The demand for and supply of management books seems to rise sharply during difficult times—their number has exploded since *In Search of Excellence* came out in 1981. In the decades prior to that, management writings had been far more conceptual, spearheaded by the rise of strategic planning in the 1960s. But in the late 1970s the abstract concepts of strategic planning had proven helpless against the Japanese onslaught on American enterprise. The leading Japanese firms like Sony and Toyota seemed capable of producing coherent, effective performance without using any of the concepts that guided us in the Western world. In fact, they seemed to turn many of our prescriptions upside down! We, for example, had emphasized fast decision making at senior management levels to be followed by implementation at lower levels—the "head" told the "hands" what to do. Unfortunately, our decisions seldom got executed—the strategy was fine, but the implementation failed, we would say to ourselves. The Japanese decision-making process worked the other way around, and it took forever. Via their famous *ringi* signing-off process, the "hands" were involved early and continuously in the development of the decision. All the "head" had to do was announce the conclusion that the "hands" had reached. And by then the decision was well into being implemented.

But the advice contained in the new generation of management books, like their golfing counterparts, has often been contradictory and confusing. Should we develop a vision or downsize the workforce? Reengineer our business processes or empower our people? Consider the recommended first step of one formula for transformation:

> A commitment to eliminate upward of 50 percent of the workforce while maintaining current revenue levels, with no excuses accepted for failure, forces an organization to relax restrictive management principles and practices associated with functional hierarchy. . . . This shock works much better to overcome organizational inertia than would a series of 10 percent cuts; inertia dissolves immediately.[*]

Wow, I'll bet it does! But I wonder what it does to customer service and trust within the organization. And how does one square that with W. Edwards Deming's point number eight of his famous fourteen points, which made up his principles for transformation? He wrote: *"Drive out fear.* No one can put in his best performance unless he feels secure."[†]

The situation is no better within strategy development, that well-established bailiwick of senior management. Canadian management maverick Henry Mintzberg, a respected writer on strategy, has now identified ten schools of strategy formulation. The early approaches are typically rational and analytic, requiring a great deal of data gathering and conscious thought, while the later schools emphasize learning, openness, and flexibility. To make matters even more confusing, there are now schools that combine different approaches!

So what is a struggling manager to do? Following the practices of individual "excellent" firms does not seem to be any easier than

---

[*]Richard L. Nolan and David C. Croson, *Creative Destruction*, p. 26.
[†]*Out of the Crisis*, p. 58, original emphasis. Deming doesn't even mention downsizing.

following the advice of expert golfers. Are the "secrets" of Microsoft, Disney, Wal-Mart, and Flavor-of-the-Month Inc. any more applicable to the ordinary organizations than those of Gary, Arnold, Jack, and Tiger are to golfing mortals? In the teaching of both golf and management there has always been an implication that "one swing fits all," that lessons can be learned from the experts and transferred across to others. At best this leads to a great deal of confusing advice being given. At worst it encourages the learner to borrow indiscriminately parts of swings from different players in a Frankensteinian attempt to construct a perfect swing! In golf the "one swing fits all" theory is clearly suspect, as all people are not built physically in the same way. And the same is true of business organizations—each is unique. Perhaps every organization has its own "swing," the key elements of which are peculiar to it and not transferable to any other.

Struggling with Technology

To this list of similarities between golf and management one must add the general struggle for improvement through the use of technology. The claims made for the efficacy of new information technology in business are rivaled only by those made for the raft of medieval torture devices now appearing on the Golf Channel! Evidence of their effectiveness is often anecdotal. Despite the advent of titanium drivers, graphite shafts, and sophisticated golf balls, the USGA says that golf handicaps have been stable for the past fifteen to twenty years. Golfers may be hitting the ball marginally farther, but they aren't scoring any better. It is a seductive thought that a piece of hardware available at your nearest pro shop can substitute for long hours of toil and effort, but it is clear that the magic is in the wizards, not in their wands! Of course, almost two-thirds of golf shots are played from one hundred yards or less, so it would take a major improvement in driving to make an appreciable difference to the score of the average golfer. Golf Research Associates estimate that an extra ten yards on every drive is worth less than half a shot per round—even if all such drives are in the fairway! Despite this evidence, the average golfer is much more interested in the highly visible improvements in power on the long shots than in reducing his or her score by a few strokes. As we will see, there are performance counterparts to this in business.

In business organizations the productivity of new technology is by no means automatic. Indeed, getting new equipment to do what it was designed to do can be notoriously difficult. In the early 1980s, General Motors under CEO Roger Smith spent $40 billion on capital equipment and facility upgrades with negligible improvement in GM's competitive position. It wasn't just problems with the hardware, although some of the state-of-the-art robots did fail spectacularly. In one famous incident, which gladdened the hearts of many technophobes, painting robots sprayed each other rather than the cars! The root of the problem was the inability of GM's managers to create an effective system, where people were trained to program, use, maintain, and repair the robots so that the production lines could flow effectively. They seem to have completely underestimated the on-the-ground know-how required to tune and integrate the technology. They may have been victims of the head-down theory of knowledge embedded in their education. The economist's concept of substituting capital for labor is valid only if we think of labor as muscle power.

The situation is no better with information technology, where managers too often think that they can easily substitute computers and software for people. It's easy to confuse information, disembodied knowledge, with the embedded know-how required for systems to run effectively. Vendors of information-processing machines whose aim, like that of golf equipment makers, is to sell more hardware often compound this confusion. The individual pieces of hardware may work fine, but their integration into a system is the problem. Witness the problems so many firms have had implementing enterprise resource-planning (ERP) systems.

It seems that improvement in the performance of any complex system may be difficult to achieve.

Golf and Management: The True Connection

These similarities may sound superficial, but what if there was a systemic connection between improving performance in business and in golf? I contend that there is. Golf and management do have a deep connection: success in both activities requires a mastery of the dynamics of complex systems.

Consider the following list of injunctions:

- There are no quick fixes.
- Work on only one thing at a time.
- Focus on execution, not outcomes.
- Always get feedback on your actions.
- To develop skills, use drills.
- Things may get worse before they get better.

Good advice to golfers wanting to improve their games? Certainly. These items come from some of the top professional teachers of the game. But they are also excellent advice to managers who are serious about improving their businesses, and I will show why this is the case.

Now consider another list of injunctions:

- Do simple things first.
- Learn to do them flawlessly.
- Add new layers over the results of the simple tasks.
- Don't change the simple things.
- Make the new layer work as flawlessly as the simple.
- Repeat, ad infinitum.

This too could be a list of advice to golfers (and managers). But it isn't. It comes from the world of artificial intelligence, where scientists are trying to build mechanical and electronic devices that will replicate human behavior. That is, they are trying to build robots that behave like complex systems. Ooh boy, you may be saying to yourself, I'm not built like a robot, so why would I be interested in instructions on how to play golf [or manage] like a robot?

But these robots are not the special-purpose automatons that work at painting and welding in auto factories; neither are they the robots of science fiction like C3PO of *Star Wars* fame. They are the result of a new approach to building what have been called "artificial creatures." As we will see, this approach is diametrically opposed to the traditional way of building robots. Instead of using a top-down "brain first" framework, this approach uses a bottom-up, "behavior first" perspective. The artificial creatures built in this way exhibit behavior that is strangely lifelike. Many of them look like large, weird insects as they scurry around in natural environments, avoiding obstacles and searching for resources, and they learn as they go. Speaking more technically, they behave like complex adaptive systems. And it has been argued that the approach employed in their construction is valid for building complex systems of any type. In some uncanny way, these artificial creatures seem to behave rather like us! This is the reason that the second list sounds as though it might apply to both golf and management.

Summary

In this chapter I have pointed out some of the similarities between the activities of golf and management and the problems in performance encountered in each of them. I have suggested that our responses as golfers and managers to these unpredictable changes in performance have a good deal in common. We tend to reach for the similar tools and techniques and look for models to follow. The assumption behind these "solutions" is that the "head" can tell the "hands" what to do. This implies that it is relatively easy to copy someone else's "swing." Copying someone else, however, is no guarantee of success. His "swing" will be unique to him, reflecting his own situation and developmental history, and it may be difficult to emulate. In addition, the advice we receive is often contradictory. Even the use of technology does not seem to bring any guaranteed improvement. I have suggested that the reason for the uncanny resonance between golf and management is that success in both activities demands the mastery of complex systems. In the next chapter I will describe the nature of these systems and what we know about them from the emerging study of complexity.

No. 3

Bodies of Knowledge

Par-3	250 yards

(I)n the brain-vs.-brawn arguments, it is inescapable that our bodies are often smarter than our brains, if we could only learn to trust them.
—JOHN JEROME, THE SWEET SPOT IN TIME

The basic function of management is homeostatic; it is to keep a system alive by making sure that critical variables remain within tolerable ranges constantly.
—JOHN KOTTER, A FORCE FOR CHANGE

The realization that the human body is a self-regulating system, which is itself composed of other self-regulating systems, is a fairly recent one. Although several physiologists in the nineteenth century had pointed out the body's ability to maintain an internal stability, it was not until the 1930s that Harvard physiology professor Walter Cannon put the whole picture together in his classic book, *The Wisdom of the Body.*

Cannon's work was to be a catalyst for the development of cybernetics, a new science of feedback and control. For it was he who coined the word *homeostasis* (Latin for "same state") to describe the body's ability to keep itself stable by holding critical variables within narrow ranges through feedback-based control systems. We now know that all the systems in the body have servomechanisms that operate in this way. They range in size from the myriad reactions taking place within the minute chemical factories that we call cells to the larger systems such as those that govern the cardiovascular, endocrine, and digestive processes.

Nature is a compulsive tinkerer when it comes to building complex systems and rarely discards anything. Our bodies are composed of layers and layers of systems built up over the billions of years since life evolved on earth. The systems that emerged early in our evolutionary history depend upon the circulation of liquids such as blood and lymph to carry chemical messages to the different organs. The mechanisms of self-repair and the operations of the digestive system, for example, are triggered by the release into the bloodstream of chemical messengers, which then activate the appropriate responses. The systems that emerged later in our evolutionary development are based on electrochemical communication within a web of nerve pathways. These faster-acting networks are combined with the slower circulation-based systems so that their functions overlap. Many of the systems may collaborate with each other to maintain key variables, such as our body temperature, within narrow ranges. It is the redundancy built in to us by this collaboration of a multiplicity of systems, using different communication processes, that ensures that our bodies don't break down very often. If we get too hot, for example, there are about half a dozen options that the body can use to cool itself and restore equilibrium.

The bottom line:

1. *Our physical existence depends upon self-regulating, feedback-dependent processes of which we are often not aware.*
2. *These systems and the processes that constitute them are a form of knowledge, which is neither taught to us explicitly nor retained in our heads.* We have acquired these survival-oriented systems through the process of evolution. Some of them, such as our endocrine, respiratory, and immune systems, operate automatically and require no intervention from us. Others, such as our neuromuscular system, are developed through experience, through trial-and-error learning, as we

interact with the world around us. And the competencies we develop in this way remain distributed throughout our bodies.

3. *Our brains are extremely flexible instruments, allowing us to turn our attention from balance to reading and myriad other tasks, but real-time capacity is severely limited.* For our conscious minds to be effective, all of our body's many systems need to run without the need for conscious intervention.

In this chapter I look at the nature of complex systems: we will learn how complex systems are constructed and why they are so difficult to understand, let alone change.

Complex Systems

Since the mid-1980s, the study of complex systems has been focused and popularized by the work done at the Santa Fe Institute by a group of researchers from many different disciplines. Here economists, physicists, ecologists, mathematicians, biologists, and other scientists have been trying to discover the systemic similarities that operate in all the complex phenomena they study. In the dynamics of systems ranging from the workings of the economy to the functioning of the immune system, they are looking for basic models that can give them insights into all such systems (as far as I know, they have not studied the golf swing!). Although there is a good deal of disagreement about how precisely to measure and study complexity, there is general agreement on the characteristics of complex systems:

- *Complex systems consist of many specialized agents interacting with one another in many different ways.* Our bodies are composed of numerous specialized cells, organs, and systems, each of which performs specific functions but is linked in multiple ways to other agents within the system.
- *Complex systems adapt to the environments in which they live.* Adaptation, or learning, takes place best on the edges of the

system, on the boundary between order and turbulence. This place, where the system is optimally stressed, is sometimes called the "edge of chaos."

- *Hierarchy is essential to the development and stability of all complex systems.* These are not hierarchies of command-and-control, where the subordinate parts are told what to do; they are hierarchies of control through constraint, where subordinate systems are restricted from doing certain things. I will have more to say about this in a moment.
- *In a multilayered complex system, stability is achieved by having the big and/or slow processes govern through constraint the smaller, faster processes. Sudden change can take place in a complex system when agents at one level escape the constraints usually exercised by agents in another part of the system.* In our bodies the fastest processes take place within cells. But the behavior of cells is constrained by the organs "above" them. The activities of the organs, in their turn, are constrained by larger, slower-acting processes such as the circulatory, respiratory, and nervous systems. When control breaks down, small causes can lead to large effects. Cancer is a classic example of the growth of certain cells within the body escaping the discipline usually imposed on them by the immune system.
- *Control of a complex system is highly dispersed, and cause-and-effect relationships are hard to identify.* Much of the control over our bodies is carried out below our level of awareness by myriad self-regulating, overlapping systems. When our internal systems malfunction, the causes of our malaise may be difficult to track down, for cause and effect are often not closely connected in space and time, and there may be "coincident symptoms"—variables that looked like causes but are not.
- *History matters in complex systems—so-called clean sheet designs cannot be implemented easily in well-established systems. Indeed, efforts to change a complex system can often have perverse outcomes.* Every golfer is familiar with the "worse before better" pattern that often follows a lesson from a profes-

sional—it takes some time for the new moves to blend with one's old habits and become second nature. Conversely, tips from golfing buddies often have a "better before worse" dynamic, briefly easing one's suffering before the malady returns in full force!

The Role of Hierarchy

Hierarchical organization is a feature of all complex systems and appears to be central to their existence. The best illustration of the reasons for this is management scientist Herbert Simon's story of the two watchmakers (watches are relatively simple systems, but the illustration works). Each watchmaker makes watches containing one thousand parts. The first watchmaker builds a watch at one sitting, connecting all the parts. If he is interrupted during his work, however, the watch will fly apart and he will have to go back to the beginning of the process, working with a heap of one thousand parts. His production of watches is likely to be low. The second (wiser) watchmaker builds watches by assembling modules, each of which contains (say) ten different components. First he builds one hundred 10-part modules. Then he takes these modules ten at a time and makes ten supermodules (each consisting of one hundred parts). Last the wise watchmaker assembles these ten supermodules together to produce the watch. If he is interrupted during his work, only the unfinished module that he is working on will fall apart. His production will hardly be affected. *So hierarchical, modular construction simplifies the development process and makes systems stable—resistant to disturbance and temporary setbacks.* This means that the only way complex systems can be built over time is layer upon layer—hierarchically.

Command vs. Control

This systems sense of hierarchy, however, is rather different from the management concept of hierarchy. Traditionally we think of management hierarchy as a system of command-and-control and of the organization as composed of positive connections that the upper levels use to instruct the lower levels what to do. In a strict command-and-control hierarchy the lower levels do only what they are told to do. But it is also helpful to think of a complex system hierarchy and the organization that accompanies it as a system of negative constraints. In such a system, the upper levels just set the ranges within which the lower levels can function. The lower levels can do anything that is not declared to be "off limits" by the higher levels. Such constraints allow freedom at all levels of the hierarchy, but within defined limits that broaden progressively as one travels upward. The resulting hierarchy is a hierarchy of control without command! The "lower" units control themselves through feedback, holding the ranges set for them. Change is achieved not by telling the lower levels to do different things, but by changing the settings that constrain them.

The Advantages of Modular Systems

One finds many golf swings and many organizations built in exactly the same way that the first watchmaker builds watches. This is particularly true of novices in each field—in beginning golfers and young, growing organizations before the basic routines have developed. For golfers, such swings feel as though they consist of a thousand different parts, each of which has to be thought about during the course of the swing. For managers, such organizations feel as though they cannot be left alone for a moment and that everything requires their personal attention and micromanagement. In short, such poorly functioning systems require a command hierarchy if they are to perform: every component continually has to be told what to do. Unfortunately, neither as golfers nor as managers do we have enough mental capacity to run such a system very effectively. And even if we had the mental capacity, this kind of control would not be desirable. For a command-based control system specifies the actions to be performed, and in the absence of omniscience at the top (or a very stable environment) that would make us and our organizations too inflexible to respond to local conditions and changes in the environment. The kind of control we want is one that specifies a range of outputs that produces acceptable outcomes using variable actions. Stable golf swings and stable business organizations deliver this kind of control; they are constructed in the same way as watches made by the second watchmaker.

Artificial Brains

The study of artificial intelligence (AI) is probably the most direct descendant of the development of cybernetics. Emerging in the 1950s, it focused initially on narrow planning and problem-solving situations like playing chess. These programs have always worked and have been improving steadily, as demonstrated by the triumph of IBM's "Deep Blue" machine over chess grand master Garry Kasparov. But that merely confirms, as *The Economist* put it, ". . . something that has been known for a long time: that chess is trivial." For chess solutions are in principle computable, and all IBM did was push the number-crunching power of its machine until it outstripped the performance of the human thought processes used in the game. IBM needed to apply brute force, because the human processes used for playing chess seem to rely on pattern recognition rather than calculation. Pattern recognition is something humans are very good at. We can, for example, distinguish hundreds, if not thousands, of human faces under many different lighting conditions without getting confused. Yet even the most sophisticated computer-based AI struggles to recognize a single face under anything but highly artificial conditions.

The traditional AI approach has been based on a head-down theory of knowledge rather like that used in the teaching of both golf and management! AI traditionalists have concentrated on building computers that can scan the environment, build a symbolic model of the world, manipulate the symbols, and then take action based on the outcomes of their calculations. In other words, traditional AI has used the conventional, reasoned, "see think act" logic familiar to all of us. In traditional robots, the "brain" of the robot sits between the inputs and the outputs and, removed from the world, mediates the robot's actions—it is a centralized view of intelligence. This approach has not been particularly successful: visual representations of the world have proved particularly difficult for computers to handle. AI's critics have, rather scathingly, labeled this the "brain-in-a-box approach" and have argued that intelligence and knowledge cannot be separated from subjective bodily experience. This is where Rodney Brooks and his artificial creatures come into the picture.

Artificial Bodies

Since 1984 MIT professor Rodney Brooks and his students have been building robots at the Artificial Intelligence Laboratory in a way that is quite different from the top-down method used by followers of what he calls "Good Old-Fashioned Artificial Intelligence" (GOFAI). In a groundbreaking paper entitled "Intelligence Without Reason," Brooks argued that human-level intelligence did not appear suddenly on the evolutionary scene, but emerged slowly over long periods of time: "Real biological systems are not rational agents that take inputs, compute logically and produce outputs. They are a mess of many mechanisms working in various ways, out of which emerges behavior that we observe and rationalize."

Brooks uses a bottom-up approach to build robots. He does not start by trying to design a brain. Instead he creates robots that are situated in the real world and have bodies that experience the world directly. For him the central aspects of human intelligence are development, social interaction, physical interaction, and the integration of information from all the senses. There is no abstract model of the world: his robots, like humans, start off with simple behaviors. These behaviors become more complex as the robots encounter increasingly complex situations. They use the actual world as they encounter it as their model: "The world is its own best model," as Brooks puts it. Thus his machines perceive and act *without* GOFAI's intermediate step of "thinking"! The links between sensors and actuators are as direct as possible and follow simple rules. In this way he has been able to produce amazingly lifelike behavior. For instance, a six-legged cockroach-type "mobot" built by Brooks walks without "thinking" about "walking." Here is a description of the process in an early mobot named Genghis:

> Genghis had six legs but no "brain" at all. . . . Each of Genghis's six tiny legs worked on its own, independent of the others. . . . Walking for Genghis then became a group project with at least six small minds at work. Other small semiminds within its body coordinated communication between the legs . . . walking emerges out of the collective behavior of the twelve motors. Two motors at each leg lift, or not, depending on what the other legs around them are doing. If they activate in the right sequence—Okay, hup! One, three, six, two, five, four!—walking "happens."[*]

There is no "brain" reading input, making decisions, and then sending output to the legs to implement the decision. Something is needed to initiate activity, but once the process is started, "walking" emerges as a coordinated activity. This is, of course, just how a centipede walks, and as the old joke goes, the process works fine until it has to "think" about it. It is also, of course, exactly how we walk—once we start the process, it continues automatically without conscious control on our part. I believe that solid golf swings and well-run organizations rely on the same kinds of deeply embedded microhabits.

Brooks achieves more complex behavior in his mobots not by adding a brain, but by adding additional layers of specific behaviors on top of the simpler levels below. These layers rely on the lower levels to do their specific jobs, which frees them up to do theirs, and everything runs in parallel. For example, the most basic level might be an "avoid collision" behavior that backs the mobot away from any obstacle detected in its path. The next level up might be a "track the wall" behavior that allows the mobot

---

[*]Kevin Kelly, *Out of Control*, p. 38.

to follow a vertical surface. Avoiding collisions always overrides tracking the wall so that the mobot can explore a maze without accident. Now, at a level above these behaviors, a simple memory can be added that allows sonar readings and places to be correlated—the mobot can "recognize" where it has been and can return to previous landmarks. Add another layer to this one and the mobot can be sent to places that it has not yet visited—that is, it can "imagine" what the sonar readings might be if it was there and search for that configuration! Every level makes use of all of the levels below it and never abstracts from them—*the processes used to sense and act in the imaginary world are the same as those used to sense and act in the real world.*

Brooks expects that the behaviors that we call "intelligent" will emerge from the interactions of the various layers as the mobot, like a young infant, builds experience moving around the real world. He believes that the development of human intelligence requires humanlike interaction with the world. He is currently working on building an integrated system that will incorporate vision, hearing, voice, balance control, and powered arms. This robot will be able to learn from social interaction with its "caregiver"—by reading and mimicking facial expressions, for example. It will also be able to integrate the information from senses such as vision and hearing. Whether it will be able to play the PGA Tour has not been announced!

Implications

Inspired by Brooks's work, Kevin Kelly, executive editor of *Wired* magazine, entitled his book on complexity *Out of Control*. In it he listed the rules for the construction of mobots:

- Do simple things first.
- Learn to do them flawlessly.
- Add new layers over the results of the simple tasks.
- Don't change the simple things.

- Make the new layer work as flawlessly as the simple.
- Repeat, ad infinitum.

Brooks's approach to building robots is significant for golfers and managers in that it helps us understand how complex behaviors can be built out of basic routines and sustained through feedback. If we want to change these behaviors, we have to look at the fundamentals, changing the lowest levels first.

In the case of our bodies, at the very base are the physical structures whose functioning has evolved over vast periods of time. Their dynamics may be very difficult to change, although their functioning can be improved through appropriate diets and physical exercise. Some levels above them are the layers of habits that we have acquired in our lifetimes. When we try to change the performance of the total system, many of these habits may have to change. Those at more fundamental levels will have to be changed before others, but all of them are quite immune to verbal instructions! This creates problems for the head-down theory of knowledge, which too often assumes that the transmission of information from one head to another is all that is needed to change performance.

Summary

This chapter has outlined the major features of complex systems, especially those in the human body. It shows the existence of skills embodied within every one of us of which we are rarely aware. They and myriad mechanisms like them constitute a vast, layered underworld of preexisting routines and habits that work in bottom-up fashion to support our existence. It is our lack of awareness that underlines the tacit, hidden nature of the knowledge contained in our bodies. After exploring briefly some aspects of complex systems, I emphasized their necessarily hierarchical and modular structure if they are to be robust. I distinguished between hierarchies of command and hierarchies of control. We also saw how in the field of artificial intelligence, the traditional head-down perspective on intelligence has been challenged by a promising bottom-up approach.

The next chapter looks at the golf swing as a complex system and applies the complex systems framework to the major components of the swing.

No. 4

At the Edge of Chaos

Par-4	393 yards

(W)hen everything seemed settled after I had passed the difficult part of the course . . . I suddenly lost all idea of how to hit a golf ball, and in the next five holes I lost seven strokes to par.
—BOBBY JONES, REFLECTING ON A ROUND IN THE
1928 U.S. OPEN AT OLYMPIA FIELDS

Reverse every natural instinct you have and do just the opposite of what you are inclined to do and you will probably come very close to having a perfect golf swing.
—BEN HOGAN, POWER GOLF

"Golf is man's most humbling diversion," wrote Sidney James, then managing editor of *Sports Illustrated,* in his introduction to Ben Hogan's *The Modern Fundamentals of Golf.* As we have seen, sudden change is a feature of all complex systems, so perhaps we shouldn't be surprised by the variability in the game. But the abruptness of the transition from success to disaster is often shocking. From the fluffed chip and muffed putt to the inexplicable disappearance of well-honed skills, every golfer has experienced the shock of sudden shift in the results they are producing. When Greg Norman blew a six-shot lead in the final round of the 1996 Masters, every golfer knew what it felt like.

How did that happen? No one knows for sure, certainly not

Norman—even to this day he cannot give a coherent account of the disaster. "I played like shit," he said. "I don't know any other way to put it." Many observers said that he choked, but this is a description, not an explanation. It tells us what Norman must have felt like, but it doesn't say anything about causes of the problem. And the problem must be systemic, because it happens to everyone at some time or another. And if it's systemic, that means that the chains of cause and effect are likely to be matted in a complex mess of physical and psychological factors.

Golf Swing as a Complex System

As the diagram shows, from a systems perspective the golf swing can be divided into three separate feedback regimes: the setup, the backswing, and the downswing. Now this is a fairly common division used in teaching, but the systemic rationale behind it is not always made clear. The phases of the swing differ from each other systemically according to the role that feedback plays in their con-

The Three Feedback Regimes of the Golf Swing

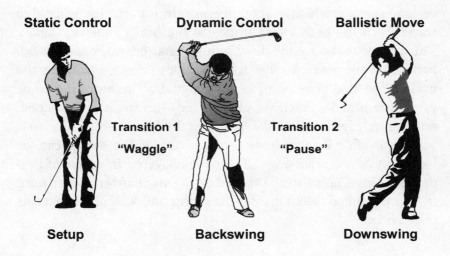

Static Control   Dynamic Control   Ballistic Move

Transition 1   Transition 2
"Waggle"   "Pause"

Setup   Backswing   Downswing

trol by the golfer—provided, of course, that he or she pays attention to it.

The setup, for example, can be thought of as *static control*. When the golfer addresses the ball and takes her grip, stance, and posture, there is plenty of time to listen to the observations of an instructor, look at oneself in the mirror, or use other sources of feedback to achieve a correctly aligned starting position. There is plenty of conscious mental capacity to handle the setup because it's being done in your own time.

The backswing requires *dynamic control*—the move has to be felt as it is executed. But now multiple moves are taking place in real time. Conscious mental capacity quickly becomes scarce, as the golfer's attention moves from one segment of the backswing to the next. The golfer can no longer observe him- or herself in a mirror without interfering with the execution of the move. Real-time feedback is still available, however, through the feelings of the muscles, tendons, and joints. Sometimes on the practice tee one sees coaches giving their players enhanced real-time feedback by setting physical "stops" to indicate the correct positions of elbows, hands, and so on. After-the-fact feedback is available either from an observer or a videotape.

The downswing is a *ballistic move*—that is, once it is launched, it cannot be stopped. The downswing takes from 0.2 and 0.25 seconds to execute, which is about the minimum time for a signal to travel from the body's extremities to the brain and back again. This means that once the downswing is started, no conscious adjustments are possible—the feedback loops are too slow for the brain to be able to respond to error signals. The move has to be preprogrammed—practiced and drilled—before it is launched, and the only feedback available is after the fact.

As the table below shows, each phase of the swing can be looked at as a cascaded set of activities, layered in space and ordered in time. This listing is based on the standard sequence used in many golf books that divides the swing into several distinct sets of activities:

AIMING AND SETUP*

Grip   Stance   Posture

BACKSWING†

Feet————————→
Legs————————→
Hips—————————→
Trunk——————————→
Shoulders———————————→
Arms——————————————→
Hands———————————————————→

DOWNSWING‡

Feet———————————————————————→
Legs—————————————————————→
Hips————————————————————→
Trunk———————————————————→
Shoulders——————————————→
Arms————————————————→
Hands———————————————→

---

*This is the sequence recommended in most golf books (this one is based on Hogan's "fundamentals"). Grip is almost always first, but the other elements can vary in order. This phase, however, constrains and governs the next phases.

†Most professionals recommend a one-piece take-away (David Leadbetter prefers to call it "move-away"), with the upper body coiling against the resistance provided by the legs and hips. In this way the legs and hips govern the movement of the other parts. The arrows show the simultaneous start for all components and how the smaller parts carry on moving for longer.

‡In the downswing events must unfold in the correct order. In this, the fastest and least conscious phase of the swing, there is consensus among pros on the order of events. Here too the big, slow variables govern the process, with each part of the body in turn supplying the context for the next member to do its job. Some pros describe the movement of the body on the downswing as a "twist" to distinguish it from the "turn" it makes on the backswing.

This diagram is only a simplified, partial picture of the system, but the broad outlines are clear. The three distinct phases of the swing—setup (or address), backswing, and downswing—are in a clear systems hierarchy, with each early, slower phase supplying the context for the next, faster phase. The architecture of the golf swing is layered a bit like that of one of Rodney Brooks's mobots. The effective performance of activities on any one level depends on the correctness of actions being performed on other, more primary levels. If the swing components on the primary levels are not correct, then actions on the secondary levels cannot be performed easily and effective contact with the ball will require an adjustment of some kind. Pros say that the majority of swing problems can be traced back to the setup, and the systemic reason for this is clear—it is the largest, slowest, earliest element of the systems hierarchy of the physical swing. Small mistakes in the setup can have large consequences later on. There is solid evidence that professional golfers set themselves up much more consistently at address than do amateurs. Even then, every golfer finds that, over time and without corrective feedback, errors can creep into these most basic parts of the swing. Thus the address acts as a powerful constraint on the next two phases of the swing—the backswing and the downswing—each of which contains its own hierarchy of physical activities within it.

Nested Hierarchies

The nested hierarchies in these two dynamic phases are clear, at least in theory! On both the backswing and the downswing, the big, slow muscles in the hips and trunk should constrain the smaller, faster muscles in the shoulders, arms, and hands. This is the systemic wisdom behind the advice of many professional golfers that the big, slow muscles be allowed to control the golf swing. "Let the dog wag the tail," as David Leadbetter puts it. The whole idea is that the center of gravity of the swing should remain as low as possible. On the backswing, the one-piece take-away is aimed at having the body start to move as a whole, with the larger body parts and muscles initiating and guiding the process in space and time. Ideally, like the wise watchmaker's modules, the larger, slower components of the body should constrain the activities of the smaller, faster elements. The smaller limbs and muscles move "naturally" within the contexts successively created by the larger ones: feet—legs—hips—trunk—shoulders—arms—hands. Because the smaller limbs and muscles can move farther and faster than the big, slow ones, the "turn" of the backswing results in their being coiled in tension.

This tension is increased by the bodily "twist" of the downswing, when the larger body parts and muscles again initiate and guide the process. Now, as the downswing unfolds, the smaller limbs and muscles can apply power, provided each stays within the spatial and temporal guidelines provided by the earlier stages. Problems develop when the smaller, faster processes escape from these guidelines. The net effect of a correct downswing on the club head is that, like the tip of a whip, it accelerates smoothly to reach its maximum velocity at impact with the ball. The "tip of the whip" is an accurate description of the club head, as research has shown that at impact the club head behaves as a freely moving object—that is, as if it were swinging at the end of a piece of rope!

Transitional Moves

Between the setup and the backswing, there is the "waggle," a small, critical movement that marks the transition from the slow, deliberate, structured setup phase, which can be performed in the player's own time, to the real-time dynamics of the swing. It is the first step toward implementing the swing in real time. As such it is a miniature rehearsal of the first *feelings* of the move away from the ball: "As ye waggle so shall ye swing," say the Scots. From a systems perspective, the role of the waggle is to remove tension from the body, particularly to relax the small, fast muscles of the shoulders, arms, and hands and allow the bigger, slower muscles of the legs and hips to guide both the backswing and the downswing. When the pros talk about "soft hands," they mean exactly that—the small, fast muscles are relaxed and taking their lead from the bigger, slower ones. "There is a definite chain of command," writes David Leadbetter, "your hands and arms must react to, not dominate the movement of your body."* Of course, from a strictly systems perspective it's not a chain of command that tells the muscles what to do, but a line of controls that sets limits on their actions.

The second transitional move is the pause at the top of the swing that is noticeable to a greater or lesser degree in all golfers. Like the waggle, it should probably be regarded as a transitional event that marks the "phase change" from one feedback mode to another. The top of the swing is the last moment at which dynamic control can be exercised over the swing—when the club can be manipulated in real time—witness Tiger Woods's amazing ability to stop his stroke if distracted during his backswing. Conscious dynamic control over the swing at this late stage ensures that the ballistic portion of the swing is as short as possible. But we wouldn't want the pause to preempt too much of our attention. The pause at the top of the swing may be a little like breathing. The diaphragm muscles that power our lungs are right on the boundary where conscious and unconscious control systems overlap. If we wish to use our diaphragms to breathe deliberately, we can do so and control the tempo and rhythm of our breathing. On the other hand, we can delegate the processes to our bodies' automatic systems and turn our attention to something else. When our timing is good we don't notice the pause at the top of the backswing; when our timing is "off" it helps to pay attention to it. Good golfers will often work on so-called stop-and-go drills, in which one stops the club at the top of the swing before swinging down through the ball. This helps one pay attention to the feelings at the top of the backswing as well as the feeling of the moves that initiate the downswing. Indeed, this drill is so effective that David Leadbetter now recommends that golfers use it even when they play.

*The Swing, p. 46.

Push and Pull

Some professionals emphasize the importance of the follow-through in the golf swing, not as a move that can be controlled consciously, but as an objective to be imagined and as a position to be felt and drilled. As we have seen, with real-time feedback ruled out, the downswing is a ballistic movement: the club head is like an unguided projectile whose trajectory we cannot change after launch. We can control it only by programming the path it will take in advance, a path that should be initiated as low as possible in the hierarchy of the body—in the feet, say many pros. As we will see in the chapters that follow, our primary method for programming all such moves begins with a process of imaging—creating pictures and feelings of the desired pathway. Compelling images, especially feelings of a good follow-through, are beneficial as a mental target that helps you practice and drill the component moves needed to produce it. Images of the follow-through have the added benefit of preventing us from trying to "hit" the ball. Instead of trying to "push" the club head through the impact zone, the feeling is one of pulling it through. Perhaps this is what the pros mean when they say that all we have to do is to execute the swing and just let the ball get in the way of the club head!

Complexity in the Swing

The diagram of the golf swing illustrates how all the aspects of complex systems listed in the previous chapter can be identified in just the physical activity of swinging a golf club. It's worth running through them:

- *Many "agents" have to interact with each other in many different ways to execute the swing.* Our legs, hips, trunk, shoulders, arms, and hands are all part of one system, but as all golfers know, they can also act somewhat independently of each other. From their many interactions there emerges a dynamic complexity that can produce spectacularly successful outcomes as well as dismal failures.

- *All golfers live at the "edge of chaos"*—that boundary between order and turbulence. If we are skilled and lucky, we may spend some of our time in the ordered region, but often, especially when we try to pull off shots that exceed our skills, we fall off the edge into chaos.

- *Control of the golf swing is highly dispersed,* and cause-and-effect relationships are hard to identify. Between the intention to play a particular shot and the actual outcome a host of complex actions has to take place. Pinpointing the root causes of a bad shot can be extremely difficult.

- *The golf swing is organized hierarchically—layered in space and ordered in time.* The high level of order that we call a "natural swing" emerges from interaction of the "building blocks" or basic disciplined processes at lower levels.

- *A repeatable golf swing is achieved by having the big, slow physical parts of the body such as the legs and hips control the smaller, faster parts such as the arms and the hands. Sudden change can take place in the swing when the smaller, faster parts, like the arms and hands, escape the constraints of the larger, slower parts.* This can happen easily because the constraints between the levels are not very powerful. For example, when we try to "hit from the top," the arms and hands move too early, which at a minimum upsets the timing of the swing.

- *Cause-and-effect relationships are often difficult to identify, and a problem may have multiple causes at several levels.* It may take an expert with access to slow-motion video to pinpoint all of these. In addition, bad shots that look the same can be produced by very different causes. Pinpointing the reasons for a poor result can be even more difficult when we are dealing with small-scale activities like putting.

- *History matters when we try to change our golf swings.* "Clean sheet" designs sound beguiling, but every golfer knows that they are extremely difficult to implement in mature golfers.

There is a limit to how many habits can be changed and the speed with which new routines can be adopted. Worse-before-better patterns of change are common, and every golfer knows the horror of being stuck out on the course with too many thoughts about what to do running through one's head.

Golf at the Edge of Chaos

Most athletes, whatever their discipline, agree that the physical activity of swinging a golf club is perhaps the most unforgiving action in all of sport and that the differences between a well-hit and a mishit shot are the most dramatic. From a systems perspective this is because the hierarchy of activities is so unstable, the action takes place so fast, and the target is perfection. If we compare it with riding a bicycle, for instance, it is clear why riding a bicycle is inherently easier. First of all, the bike itself is a robust platform that will not disintegrate under you except in extreme circumstances. The balancing skills required to stay upright are easily acquired, and within broad limits, the faster you move, the more stable the whole system becomes. Most important, the deviations from course that take place are slow enough for the rider to respond with the appropriate corrections. It must be noted, however, that these corrections are performed subconsciously, and it may be impossible to explain afterward "what we did" to remain upright. The key point is that the control feedback loops work in real time and corrections can be made at levels very close to where problems occur. As we will see in chapter 15, the just-in-time process made famous by the Toyota Production System works on the same principle—correcting problems at the place and time that they occur.

In golf, in contrast, the platforms, which are all parts of the body, form a tottering tower that becomes less stable as the speed of the swing increases. On top of our basic physical structure and motor skills we build layers and layers of movements involving our feet, legs, hips, trunk, shoulders, arms, and hands. All these layered activities have to work together in space and time with a high level of precision. An error of only one-sixteenth of an inch or a fraction of a second can make the difference between a good shot and a bad one. There is always a risk that the legs and hips that make up the base of the swing will be set up incorrectly or placed on an uneven footing. Small mistakes at early stages are greatly magnified at later ones and, when transmitted to the ball, can create enormous deviations from plan.

In contrast with a bicycle, our bodies are multipurpose systems. This means that the constraints between levels have to be flexible to allow a wide variety of actions to be taken in all kinds of circumstances. This is, incidentally, one of the reasons some golfers play better as they age—the stiffening in their joints actually reduces the variety of moves possible, making them more consistent and machinelike! Iron Byron, the famous golf-testing machine, for example, is a special-purpose system, and the constraints between the levels of its organization are rigid. Iron Byron's "hands" cannot "hit from the top" because they are rigidly constrained from doing so. In fact, the machine cannot do anything other than hit a controlled shot from a controlled lie. Only in very exceptional circumstances will Iron Byron hit an unplanned shot (when a control system breaks), but it can hit shots only in a tightly controlled context. In fact, the USGA is moving to a different testing process in part because Iron Byron machines are so difficult and time-consuming to set up.

Learning the Swing

When you think about it, it's amazing we are able to make contact with the ball at all. Indeed, this is precisely why we shouldn't be thinking about the swing as we execute it—it has to become automatic. We cannot execute a golf swing using explicit knowledge. We can do it only with huge amounts of tacit knowledge—tiers and tiers of routines and subroutines that can be invoked as required but will work without conscious intervention. This is not the case when we start the game. Even though we are relying on many general-purpose subroutines, we are acutely aware of the movements we make and of how awkward they feel. Too much is explicit, and our conscious capacity to focus is overwhelmed by the variety of the input.

Over time, however, and with practice, we start to learn. We break the swing down into segments. For the static setup, when we can take our own time, we build routines and checklists. For the dynamic parts of the swing, we group actions together into "chunks"—the take-away, the hip move, the wrist cock, and so on. Soon activities that used to require our conscious attention start to feel "natural"—they become tacit and habitual. After a while we may no longer be aware of the components of the swing, just as we are no longer aware of our efforts to crawl and stand as an infant. All the complex chains of cause and effect become buried. We start to focus on outcomes, on results.

Just because the swing feels natural, however, doesn't mean that we are doing it right. It's quite possible to produce a good result by using a combination of offsetting faulty moves. To some extent, every golf swing is an application of built-in corrections to built-in faults, but in the case of the top professionals, the compensations are minor. Their performances will fluctuate within quite narrow ranges. If the faults and the corrections are significant, however, the resulting swing won't be reliable and will tend to collapse under stress. Corrections made at one level to deal with a fault at an earlier stage of the swing will themselves become faults to be corrected at yet another level later in the swing!

Thus these compensating moves can cascade throughout the swing. A golfer may find himself flipping his hands early in the downswing to make up for a poor shoulder turn caused by a bad hip move that was in its turn due to an incorrect posture at the address. It is all he can do to make solid contact with the ball, let alone play the high shots and low shots, draws and fades, required to score well. The introduction of control mechanisms too late in the swing, using the "small, fast" variables, effectively preempts the flexibility a golfer requires to hit a wide variety of shot shapes. If, for example, the hands are consciously active on every shot to offset problems earlier in the swing, then it's much more compli-cated to use them to shape shots deliberately. *The more adjustments the golfer has to make, the less time he will find available to make the swing.* Conversely, the fewer the adjustments, the more time there will be.

The bottom line is that golfers with poor fundamental moves find themselves having to intervene consciously in their swings. Without the disciplined routines of the big, slow muscles, the smaller, faster elements of the swing cannot function reliably. This is a recipe for chaos, for it is just the opposite of what is needed for stability in complex systems. Under pressure for re-sults, the brain naturally resorts to using actions and habits that are familiar. The most familiar physical instrument of control in any right-handed golfer is the right hand. Thus it's very easy for the right hand/arm/shoulder to escape the guidelines placed on it by the rest of the swing hierarchy. When this happens early in the swing, look out! Anything can happen. No wonder such swings just collapse!

Summary

The golf swing is a complex, hierarchical system layered in space and ordered in time. It demonstrates all of the characteristics of complex systems, including the capacity for sudden change. The reasons for this are the hierarchical nature of the swing, the rela-tively weak constraints operating between the levels, and the speed with which the movements have to be executed. Our reac-tion times are too slow to make corrections once the ballistic move of the downswing is started, so all such activities have to be pro-grammed and practiced in advance. Images, pictures, and feelings play an important part in this process, both in the development of sound habits and in the execution of the swing. Better consistency requires that we layer the swing components correctly, so that the big, slow variables control the small, fast ones. Problems develop when we try to correct mistakes made early in the process by intervening at later stages. The more adjustments we have to make, the less apparent time there is in which to swing. There are systemic counterparts to these learning challenges in the management of organizations. For, as the next chapter shows, business organizations are also complex systems.

No. 5

Discipline and Freedom

Par-4	296 yards

To me, a great golfer illustrates two very precise pictures. One is proper fundamentals. The other is unencumbered motion. Without the first, it follows that the second is impossible to produce.
—TOM WATSON, QUOTED IN DAVID LEADBETTER,
THE GOLF SWING

If just some of the sensible principles that keep players out of trouble in their day-to-day affairs were applied to their golf game, their handicaps would drop drastically.
—GREG NORMAN, QUOTED IN DOWNS MACRURY,
GOLFERS ON GOLF

Monday, October 27, 1997, was a very bad day for the shareholders of Oxford Health Plans. The company announced it was taking a charge of between $47 million and $53 million as a result of problems in billings and claims that had recently "come to its attention." The stock price fell 63 percent, wiping off $3.4 billion in market value. *Fortune* magazine described it as "one of history's most sensational destructions of shareholder wealth in one day."* A few weeks later, the company went on to report a loss of $78 million for the third quarter, its first in its six-year history as a pub-

---

*Fortune, December 29, 1997, p. 238.

lic company. Oxford's chief financial officer resigned "to pursue other interests." And then things got worse: in the fourth quarter the company reported a loss of nearly $285 million, wiping out all the profits it had ever made as a public company. Six months later, the firm reported a further loss of over $500 million, effectively wiping out its shareholders' equity.

What happened? Oxford had gone public in 1991 as a health maintenance organization (HMO), with an innovative fee-for-service plan that attracted top physicians and a variety of health care options that appealed to young, healthy people. The so-called Freedom Plan was a scheme that seemed to delight both customers and suppliers. The business took off, growing from 105,000 enrollees in 1992 to 1.9 million in 1997; revenues surged from $151 million to $3 billion over the same period, an annual compound growth rate of 111 percent. The total return on a share of stock bought in early 1992 was 2,429 percent. Oxford was the darling of Wall Street, and its founder, Stephen F. Wiggins, was hailed as a wunderkind, making the *Forbes* list of "Corporate America's Most Powerful People" in May 1997. And then it all fell apart.

The proximate cause of the collapse was the breakdown in the computer systems that tracked revenues and costs, making the business unmanageable. The seeds of the disaster had been laid much earlier, however, back in 1993, when Oxford had only 217,000 members. HMO computer systems are complex at the best of times—they have to collect premiums from a membership that is continually changing jobs and health plans, while paying claims to a constantly mutating network of health care providers. Oxford's old system was forgiving and fault tolerant, but clunky and slow, and management set out to plan for a new one. Wiggins was a technology enthusiast, and he decided that it was to be custom-built in-house to accommodate all the flexible options that the company offered to its membership.

This variety had delighted the customers, but it taxed the system designers to the limit as they tried to accommodate all the choices. The system development costs, which included building a "backbridge" to link the old and new systems, would eventually exceed $100 million. Unfortunately, the new system did not come on-line until late in 1996, by which time enrollment had already swelled to 1.5 million. In addition, the new system was exacting, demanding a much higher level of precision in the structure of the data entered. Under the tremendous time pressure, the code of the backbridge had not been tested thoroughly enough, and when it was used it corrupted data as it transferred it.

To make matters worse, Oxford had tried to solve all of its problems at once, opting for the aptly named "big bang" conversion process. When it started to convert the bulk of the database at the same time, disaster was at hand. The messy data transferred from the old fault-tolerant system could not be processed in the new, unforgiving environment, and the entire conversion process broke down, with disastrous consequences. The new system rejected thousands of records, exposing Oxford's systems people to the full complexity of myriad transactions without the use of the hierarchical control and the processing speed provided by the computer. Like a struggling golfer who can no longer rely on his basic routines, Oxford's "swing" collapsed and its people found themselves caught between two worlds, a familiar past to which they could not return and a future that didn't work.

Organizations as Complex Systems

An organization, like a golfer swinging a golf club, is a complex system. As we shall see, an organization is much more complex than a golf swing, but the systemic properties still apply:

- *Organizations consist of many specialized agents interacting with each other in many different ways and across several dimensions, none of which can be ignored.* People are the most obvious examples of such agents, the rough counterpart of the cells in our bodies. As such they are aggregated together to form the functionally specialized "organs" of the body, such as marketing, accounting, manufacturing, and so on. In addition, unlike most body cells (and like some brain neurons), people can be used flexibly to form special project teams to deal with nonroutine matters. Oxford people became expert at forming teams to deal with many of the problems they encountered as a fast-growing company. The excessive use of cross-functional teams, however, can dangerously weaken the basic organizational setup—the functional skills. The challenge of changing large computer systems cannot be tackled in an ad hoc way—the functional disciplines have to be solid if the project is to be completed effectively.

- *Organizations adapt to their environments at the edges of the system, where they are exposed to the external world, while still maintaining the basic disciplines.* Organizations such as monopolies and government organizations that stay away from the edge tend not to learn very much. Many of Oxford's innovative ideas were developed at the edge, where they met customers and suppliers. The "edge of chaos," however, is a challenging place to live, and as Oxford found to the cost of its shareholders, it's easy to fall off it.

- *Hierarchy is essential to the development and stability of organizations.* The successful completion of high-level strategies and initiatives pursued by corporations depend upon the smooth execution of innumerable routines and technologies that are organized hierarchically.

- *In an organization, stability is achieved by having the big and/ or slow processes govern through constraint the smaller, faster processes. Sudden change takes place when agents at one level escape the constraints usually exercised by agents in another part of the system.* The policies and procedures, systems and routines, that characterize large, complex organizations have usually developed over long periods of time. Typically they change relatively infrequently, incrementally, and only after considerable experimentation and testing. At its peril, Oxford Health Plans management eschewed such traditional corporate policies and consistency in favor of freewheeling deal making with its health care providers and customers.

The "small, fast" executive decision-making processes were unconstrained, and the exercise of freedom without discipline led inevitably to disaster.

- *Control of an organization is highly dispersed, and cause-and-effect relationships are hard to identify. Efforts to change them can often have perverse outcomes.* Many control processes operate without managers being aware of them. We usually realize this only when systems break down, as they did at Oxford Health Plans. Pinpointing the precise reasons for such a failure can be difficult. The Oxford's management team's attempts to enhance its data-processing systems ended up severely damaging the business, because they were unable to anticipate the systemic consequences of what they were doing. A slower, more incremental approach would have been much better, although in all probability it would still have resulted in some significant, but perhaps acceptable, degradation in performance, before all the bugs were ironed out and the conversion completed. But many organizations "rush their swings." The classic example of this was in the aftermath of the *Challenger* disaster, when it turned out there were people in the system who knew there was a real risk to launching the vehicle on that cold morning of January 28, 1986. Unfortunately, that knowledge was swept away by NASA's need to "perform," to launch shuttles, and could not be brought to senior management awareness in time.

- *History matters in business organizations—"clean sheet" designs cannot be implemented easily in well-established systems.* Oxford could not escape the facts of its past and the consequences of the astonishing growth that had fueled its success. Redesigning data-processing systems from scratch and implementing them using big bang approaches is fraught with risk. Last, it should be pointed out that the big bang conversion process was a ballistic move. In fact, the decision to do the conversion all at once required a large part of the process to be completely ballistic and made it needlessly risky. Making such projects modular—breaking them up into smaller segments—keeps the ballistic portions relatively short and allows feedback to take place between them. It's exactly like a golfer playing three shots to a long par-5, instead of risking "going for it" in two! Without extensive practice—thorough testing of the conversion routines—the disaster at Oxford was inevitable.

Understanding Cause and Effect

The failure of Oxford's computer systems, like the failure of the infamous O-rings on the space shuttle *Challenger's* solid rocket boosters, was the immediate cause of its downfall. But it was only the last link in a complex web of cause and effect. Just as was the case in *Challenger,* the disaster did not come out of the blue—there were warning signs for months beforehand, but this was feedback to which the senior management was insensitive. Indeed, one investment analyst had picked up clues as early as mid-1994 that all was not well in Oxford's administration. When she voiced her concerns, however, Oxford management told her that her interpretation was "incorrect," and she was excluded from the corporation's inner circle of analysts.

How did things get so bad? As is the case in all human systems, it is a tangled mix of physical, developmental, and psychological factors. Founder and chairman Stephen Wiggins was a charismatic leader and talented entrepreneur with a flair for marketing. He had assembled around him an enthusiastic, fiercely loyal, but inexperienced team whose apparent success would see their self-confidence grow to an almost cultlike belief in their ability to get things done. The emphasis was on innovation, marketing, and growth, apparently to the exclusion of concern for basic routines. Not only was there no powerful voice within the organization to make the argument for the basics, but when things began to go wrong Oxford had no static control position to return to so that it could check itself. Through its continual use of cross-functional teams, the functional accountabilities had become blurred. Ironically, Oxford had proclaimed in its mission statement that it was a company that "disdains bureaucracy"!

Oxford management also appears to have been unable to exercise dynamic control over the conversion process. The feedback was there, but it appears to have been swamped by other issues. There is no doubt that Wall Street, the investors in Oxford and the analysts who followed its stock, played a part in this process. When a company goes public, as Oxford did in 1991, it obtains access to additional financial resources at the cost of splitting the interests of ownership and management, to create a much more complex system. Private ownership usually acts as a "big, slow" constraint on the performance of an organization, able to take, at least in principle, a long-term view of the organization's performance. As such, it makes for stability in the system. The Street, on the other hand, with its quarterly time horizons and activist investors, can act as a "small, fast" control mechanism on a public company. In newly public fast-growing companies in particular, aggressive young management teams in tandem with investment analysts and the investors that follow them can create "feeding frenzies," situations in which only positive feedback is present and negative information is either rejected or rationalized away. Stock prices can spiral upward to unsustainable levels, as the recent bursting of the Internet bubble and the shocking collapse of the high-flying energy trader Enron remind us.

Whether the short-term focus of public financial markets is a "good thing" or not has been a subject of great debate. From a systemic perspective there is no right or wrong answer to this—everything depends upon the situation. When a company has matured and stopped learning—when it has become too orderly, too far from the "edge of chaos"—then the introduction of a "small, fast" variable deep in a systems hierarchy may help the system move closer to the edge, where learning is possible. Here the public markets, activist investors, and even turnaround artists may all have useful roles to play. As I pointed out in *Crisis & Renewal*, natural systems have evolved so that they continually take advantage of naturally occurring disasters such as fire, hurricanes, insect attack, and disease—"small, fast" variables—to strengthen and renew themselves.

When, however, the company is already close to the "edge of

chaos," where the system is under considerable stress, it is easy for the "small, fast" investment component to run away with the system as a whole. Just as an addiction to hard drugs can sweep away concerns for personal health, so it becomes possible for concerns with quarterly earnings and growth to overwhelm longer-term considerations of corporate survival. This may indeed have been what happened at Oxford: the focus on growth swamped any concerns about the ability of the "big, slow," information management systems to keep up. In the absence of feedback, the entire conversion process turned into a single ballistic move with immense risk.

The Development of Competence in Complex Systems

We have seen that hierarchical structure is central to the survival of all complex systems: take away hierarchy and the system collapses. So what do the popular predictions by management writers of the "death of hierarchy" mean in systems terms? What the critics of bureaucracy seem to mean is that the disciplines in such organizations are being enforced at the wrong levels of the organization. We saw in the last chapter how a golfer who lacks the correct fundamentals is forced to introduce higher-level compensating adjustments. These high-level controls will tend to limit the variety of shots he or she can play. In the same way, firms that have poor routines and employ individuals who are not self-disciplined (that is, have bad fundamentals) will find themselves compelled to introduce controls at higher levels than optimal. Inevitably this will preempt the attention of managers, inhibit the creativity of their people, and hamper the organization's ability to adapt to changing circumstances. Disciplines that are embodied give people the freedom to respond and adapt to change. Disciplines that have to be imposed from above inhibit them from adapting to change.

The following diagram shows this relationship between discipline and freedom. Over its lifetime, the competence of a complex system (individual or organization) follows the classic S-shaped trajectory, rising from relatively low levels of competence at birth to high levels at maturity before declining in old age. Like the trajectory of a golf ball, this line is a constraint curve, along which the external forces exerted by the environment exactly balance the internal dynamics of the object—the object is constrained by its environment. In the case of a golf ball, the entire curve is ballistic, with its trajectory being determined by its initial design, velocity, and spin as modified by gravity, wind, and ground and by collisions with larger objects such as rocks and trees. In the case of human systems, actors can modify their own internal dynamics, as well as those of organizations, while they are "in flight." In their case, the constraint curve consists of a series of "flights and perchings," as psychologist William James called them. The flights—ballistic moves—are followed by periods of "perching"—periods of reflection, recalibration, and rehearsal, after which the next ballistic move is launched. So in human systems the constraint curve records the state of the boundary between the actor's own complex

Building Competence in Complex Systems

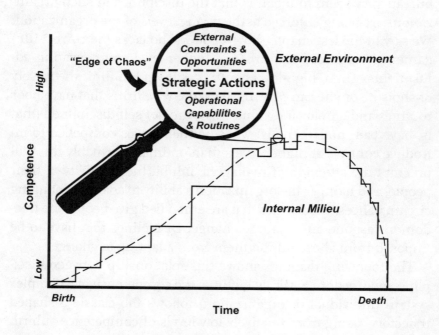

system—his internal "milieu"—and the complex system(s) within which he is acting—the external environment. This line is the so-called edge of chaos.

Competence improves when an actor develops skills or technologies that allow him to overcome constraints and exploit opportunities. The external environment poses the challenges to which the actor must respond: it asks the questions to which the actor has to find, or develop, answers. The effect of the answer, the new skill or technology, is to convert the constraint from an external uncertainty to an internal routine, to *incorporate* it within the body of the actor. Thus, when the teaching pro tells me that my wild shots are due partially to an inconsistent setup, I can overcome the constraint by introducing a consistent routine into the way I address the ball. Once the variability in shots is reduced, however, I may find that I have a chronic fault, like a slice. To fix this I may have to make a series of changes to my swing that will take considerable time and effort. Rather than change my swing, however, I might choose to buy a set of slice-correcting (offset) irons or one of the new face-modified drivers. If these work, I will have overcome a constraint on scoring (slicing) by incorporating into my play a new technology.

A similar "embodiment" of constraints takes place in organizations as they encounter obstacles in their environment. The bellows of the early coke-fired blast furnaces of the eighteenth-century iron industry, for example, were driven by water wheels whose continuous operation was threatened by summer droughts. In the early part of the century, this constraint was partially overcome by installing the newly developed horse-driven water pumps that were used to pump some of the water back uphill, where it could be reused. Later, when the horses were replaced by steam engines, iron production was freed completely from the constraints of the weather. In this way, these and other constraints were overcome by incorporating into the iron production system increasingly sophisticated technology.

Thus, by encountering constraints in the external environment and incorporating them via routines and technology into the internal milieu, an actor moves the boundaries of the edge of chaos "upward," increasing his competence and gaining the freedom to explore new territories. Thus discipline leads to freedom—provided it is embedded into routines and technologies where it does not demand continual conscious attention. We call the process "learning" in the case of individuals or "adaptation" in the case of systems.

Competence declines when skills deteriorate or, more usually, when the environmental constraints change, placing new demands on the organization. In the last few decades, for example, Toyota's development of its lean production system for automobiles has created new constraints for U.S. automakers by raising to new levels customer expectations for cost and quality. Chrysler, Ford, and GM have all had to respond by introducing new manufacturing systems and management philosophies that address the new demands.

When examined in detail, progress along the competence curve is made in stepwise fashion, with the actor experiencing both improvements and declines, peaks and slumps, along his path. The collapse of Oxford Health Plan's computer systems would be shown as a plummeting line in the graph of its capacity to handle customer transactions. The successful installation of a new system, on the other hand, would show a sharp increase in competency. In the diagram, the competence trajectory shows a steady improvement trend early in the actor's life cycle, peaking in maturity and declining rapidly thereafter. The shape of the S curves would vary widely, however, from activity to activity. The competence of female gymnasts, for example, typically peaks in their early teens, when their flexibility and strength-to-weight ratios are at their peak. Golfing skills seem to reach a maximum at a much later age and typically undergo only a gradual decline. But whatever the shape of the curve, competence is achieved only through the construction and maintenance of a system of routines and skills. And as the system grows, it is inevitable that the actor will have to spend more and more time and attention on maintaining the internal milieu that lies below the "edge of chaos."

The location of the strategist, poised on the blurry edge of chaos, underlines the critical position of the actor in a complex system. So much is unknown, and there are so many options. Constraints on competence can emerge from the external environment, from the internal milieu, or from the interactions between the two. *The strategist is concerned with identifying the key constraints, the important questions, and the challenge is to maintain the focus of all members of the organization on only those critical elements.* This problem of creating and maintaining focused attention is the topic of the next few chapters as we develop and refine the mantra:

- There are no quick fixes.
- Work on only one thing at a time.
- Focus on execution, not outcomes.
- Always get feedback on your actions.
- To develop skills, use drills.
- Things may get worse before they get better.

Summary

I have used the example of the collapse of the Oxford Health Plans computer system to show that business organizations are complex adaptive systems. They can be usefully viewed through the same lens as that we used to look at the golf swing—all the systems principles seem to apply to them. As shown by the systems breakdown, the patterns of cause and effect are complex and consist of a tangle of physical, developmental, and psychological factors. This allowed small, fast variables (daily transactions in the case of Oxford) to escape the control of the system. Hierarchies of control are essential to the stability and survival of complex systems organizations, but it is important that the disciplines be instituted at the lowest possible levels. Only then can discipline create freedom. If disciplines have to be imposed from upper levels, the flexibility of the entire system is jeopardized as attention is preempted and creativity stifled.

Last, we looked at the development of competency and how actors in complex systems learn at the edge of chaos, where their embodied skills encounter the constraints and opportunities in the environment. The strategic actor has to choose which constraints and opportunities to focus on and the routines and technologies required to address them.

The Mundanity of Excellence

Par-4	328 yards

If there is any one "secret" to effectiveness, it is concentration.
Effective executives do first things first and they do one thing at
a time.
        —PETER F. DRUCKER, THE EFFECTIVE EXECUTIVE

About the only identifiable across-the-board advantage that
good athletes seem to have over the rest of us is the quality of
their attention. They pay attention to the task in hand a little
better than you and I do.
        —JOHN JEROME, THE SWEET SPOT IN TIME

It's the nightly show on the Golf Channel, and everyone seems to
be selling their "secrets." There are the training devices that look
like instruments of torture from medieval times—great racks
upon which to stretch your swing and restraints for hands, arms,
body, and head that would have warmed the heart of the Spanish
Inquisition. There are the clubs: high-tech woods that will hit the
ball farther and straighter and extract it from any lie; irons that
will lift it up, hold it low, and reduce hooks and slices; putters that
will keep the ball rolling smoothly on its line, and so on. Then
there are the teachers demonstrating their drills and skills and dis-
pensing advice for the price of a phone call. It would take several
lifetimes and multiple fortunes to explore all the options.

Does any of this stuff work? Maybe. No one really knows. What we do know is that identifying the multiple chains of cause and effect in complex systems is extremely difficult, and teasing out what effects are due to which causes is probably impossible. So while Iron Byron may be able to hit the space age, multimetal, gas-injected, turbo-shafted, ceramic-faced driver farther and straighter than any other club, that's no guarantee that I will be able to use it effectively! Many professionals still miss their persimmon-headed woods because the ball stayed on the clubface an instant longer, allowing them to work the ball more effectively. Only hands-on experience on the golf course can determine whether a technological advance really works, and even then, it may be purely psychological rather than physical, the golfing version of the placebo effect. Some people may say: "If it works, who cares?" But we need to care, to understand what are the keys to excellence in golf.

The Roots of Excellence

What makes for excellence in golf? Talent, natural ability, hard work, concentration, confidence—the "usual suspects" are rounded up and trotted out. But I will argue that these words are descriptions rather than explanations. As we shall see, they tend to be recognized in athletes after they produce superlative performances rather than beforehand, and they supply no useful guide to action. The invocation of talent or natural ability suggests that either you have it or you don't. Being told to "work hard," "focus," and "concentrate" are head-down injunctions that are hardly helpful—at what, on what, how? And as for confidence, we know it when we have it but are often powerless to find it when it's lost.

Surprisingly, very little work has been done on the subject. If anyone has systematically studied the factors that top golfers have in common, he or she has been remarkably quiet about it. Even the physical factors such as build, height, weight, and strength are not documented in any comprehensive way. Perhaps it is because no one thinks that these factors matter. They may well be right:

top golfers come in all shapes and sizes—fat and thin, tall and short, muscular and flabby. It used to be argued that big people had a disadvantage in the short game, lacking "touch" around the greens, but the success in recent times of golfers like John Daly, Laura Davies, and Ernie Els seems to have silenced that theory.

The fact that, more than any other sport, golf can be played at the top level by people as they age suggests that excellence may not depend very much on athletic skills. There must be some minimum physical requirements, but they are probably much less than one thinks. Personality and intelligence don't seem to have much to do with it, either: some top pros are relaxed, others are intense; some are outgoing, others are introverted; some are smart, others are not so smart. "Hard work" in the form of practice doesn't appear to correlate with performance, either. Tom Kite and Vijay Singh today, Ben Hogan and Arnold Palmer in their heydays, and Gary Player to this day are famous for the amount of time they spend on the practice tee. Others either don't (Bruce Lietzke, Carlos Franco) or are physically unable to (Fred Couples, Fuzzy Zoeller) spend much time practicing. Thus, based on casual observation, the general conclusion must be that there is no special individual or behavioral profile for excellence in golf.

Perhaps it is in the swings—maybe top golfers are different as individuals, but perhaps they all swing the golf club in the same way. In the 1960s a team of British researchers sponsored by the Golf Society of Great Britain set out to search for the perfect swing. Their findings were documented in a book of that name (*Search for the Perfect Swing,* by Alastair Cochran and John Stobbs). What they found was a huge variety in most aspects of the swing, ranging from tempo to take-aways. Hogan, for example, had emphasized the importance of swinging the club "on plane," but none of the professional golfers Cochran and Stobbs studied swung the club very close to "on plane," and there was significant variability in the planes they did swing the club on.

High-speed photography reveals the same variety in the swings of today's top golfers on the PGA tour. Paul Azinger, Fred Couples, John Daly, Jim Furyk, and Tiger Woods, to name a few, all have distinctively different swings but can produce similar excellent results (okay, I agree—Tiger's are better!). Commentators often point out that despite their differences, all these golfers reach similar positions at impact with the ball. This is true, but not very helpful. It's a bit like calling it "talent." For as we saw in chapter 4, impact with the ball occurs over two-tenths of a second after the golfer loses conscious control over the swing. And the antecedents, over which he or she has some control, are all slightly but significantly different in top golfers. We end up going in circles—excellence in golf is everywhere in general and nowhere in particular!

The Elements of Excellence

In the absence of any systematic (or systemic) study of excellence in golf, it is helpful to look at another sport that has been studied from a systemic perspective. In the late 1980s, sociologist Daniel Chambliss spent over 1½ years studying top swimmers by living with them and their coaches and conducting a program of interviews with them. The next section is based on his work.

Swimming, like golf, is an individual sport with highly stratified, well-defined levels of performance. At the top are the world- or Olympic-class competitions, the equivalent, perhaps, of the golf majors. Next are the senior nationals, then the junior nationals, the regionals, and so on. These are the rough equivalent of the PGA, Nike (now Buy.com), and other tours. In golf there is a much clearer split between amateurs and professionals, but each sector is stratified in a similar way.

Chambliss was searching for the factors that differentiated swimmers in the upper levels from those in the lower layers of the sport. His conclusions were fascinating:

1. *Excellence is a qualitative phenomenon:* doing more does not equal doing better.
2. *Talent is useless as an explanatory concept:* it masks the concrete actions that create outstanding performance.

3. *Excellence is mundane:* it comes from ordinary actions, performed consistently and habitualized over time.

Excellence Is a Qualitative Phenomenon

Chambliss found that the quantitative differences between one
level of performers and another was not enough to explain performance differences. Improvement as a result of swimming longer
distances during workouts, for example, came only with huge increases, such as doubling the number of hours in the pool. Instead he found a host of qualitative differences:

> Olympic champions don't just do more of the same things that
> summer-league country-club swimmers do . . . they do things differ-
> ently. Their strokes are different, their attitudes are different, their
> groups of friends are different; their parents treat the sport differently,
> the swimmers prepare differently for their races, and they enter dif-
> ferent kinds of meets and events.[*]

He identified three dimensions of difference: techniques, discipline, and attitude. The techniques of top swimmers differed in
myriad different ways from those used by lower-level performers.
These differences were embedded in all the details and nuances of
every stroke and move such as dives and turns. Olympic-class
swimmers, for example, make little splash with their starting
dives. The start is an art of its own. And the combination of all the
arts leaves an overall impression of fluidity that amazes low-level
performers, rather like the impression that top golf professionals
leave with the members of the gallery. Indeed, the phenomenon is
common to all expert performances, ranging from dancing and
ice-skating to reading and writing.

In addition to having better techniques, the best swimmers
were more likely to be highly disciplined than others. They start
workouts on time and follow strict routines. Chambliss observed

[*]*The Mundanity of Excellence,* p. 73.

that Greg Louganis, the Olympic diving champion, "practices only three hours each day—not a long time—divided up into two or three sessions, he tries to do every dive perfectly. Louganis is never sloppy in practice, and so is never sloppy in meets."* One finds the same situation in golf: "I put the ultimate effort into my training," says one top pro. "But it's draining and takes a lot of mental discipline. I give every shot full intention and attention."† We shall see at the end of this chapter how these routines function in the production of superior performance.

Last, Chambliss found at the higher levels of swimming that an "inversion of attitude" takes place—*what lower-level swimmers find boring, top-level performers enjoy: hard practices, challenging goals.* "It is incorrect to believe that top athletes suffer great sacrifices to achieve their goals. Often, they don't see what they do as sacrificial at all. They like it."‡ Similar observations are often made about the "risk-taking" propensities of entrepreneurs. To outsiders, what entrepreneurs do often does look risky, but the entrepreneurs themselves rarely see things that way. They are so obsessed with what they are doing that they don't see it as dangerous at all. This inversion of attitude is a typical condition among top golfers, some of whom are legendary for their obsession with the game and their dedication to the practice range. "I think the happiest moments for a golfer are those that he spends in study and experimentation," wrote Bobby Jones. Tom Watson claims that his theme song was "Home on the Range"!

Chambliss argues that the combination of all these differences makes for different swimming "worlds," rather than different levels. Not everyone wants to get into the next "world," but if they do, it will demand a significant change in their techniques, discipline, and attitude, not just more work. If we transfer this insight to the golfing universe, it would imply that the PGA Tour, the Buy.com Tour, and other levels of competition are qualitatively different in

---

*The Mundanity of Excellence, p. 74.
†Nadeane McCaffrey and Terry Orlick, *International Journal of Sports Psychology* 20 (1989): 256–78.
‡The Mundanity of Excellence, p. 74.

the techniques, disciplines, and attitudes of the players. One certainly seems to see this in the majors. The Masters, the U.S. and British Opens, and the PGA have a way of bringing a small, highly select group of golfers to the fore. In the fourth rounds of these tournaments, it always seems to be that same small group in contention. They are the golfers who, the commentators say, excel on tough courses. Each world of competition, then, has its own patterns of behavior and informal rules of conduct that make it a different context—top performers should be seen as different, not just better.

Talent Is Useless as an Explanatory Concept

Chambliss found that, in swimming, athletes were not described as "talented" until they had turned in some top performances. The concept of talent was used as an after-the-fact reason for superior performance, performance that had already become apparent. In other words, talent is indistinguishable from its supposed effects. This means that talent is a description, not an explanation, and it leads to a circular argument—superior performance leads to a diagnosis of talent, and talent produces superior performance. The existence of talent, then, is a matter of faith. In fact, Chambliss argues, not only does rather little natural ability seem necessary for performance, but many success stories are of athletes whose natural abilities have been damaged in some ways yet have still triumphed over adversity. In the case of Olympic champions, he says, most have overcome some kind of challenge that threatened their ability to perform. Certainly golf is no different, with its stories of Ben Hogan's and Bobby Locke's recoveries from near fatal car accidents, Paul Azinger's fight with cancer, Scott Verplank's injuries and diabetes, back problems for Fred Couples and José Maria Olazabal, John Daly's ongoing struggle with alcoholism, and the saga of Casey Martin and his need to ride a golf cart. The primary argument Chambliss raises against talent as an explanation of success is that other factors give better ones:

We can, with a little effort, see what these factors are in swimming; geographical location, particularly living in southern California where the sun shines year round and everybody swims; fairly high family income, which allows for travel to meets and payments of the fees entailed in the sport, not to mention sheer access to swimming pools when one is young; one's height, weight and proportions; the luck or choice of having a good coach, who can teach the skills required; inherited muscle structure—it certainly helps to be both strong and flexible; parents who are interested in sports. Some swimmers, too, enjoy more the physical pleasures of swimming; some have better coordination; some even have a higher percentage of fast-twitch muscle fiber. Such factors are clearly definable, and their effects can be clearly demonstrated. To subsume all of them willy-nilly, under the rubric of "talent" obscures rather than illuminates the sources of athletic excellence.*

This description, with the substitution of "golf" for "swim" and "course" for "pool," could probably be applied directly to the backgrounds of top golfers. One glaring exception to this, however, is the recent stunning success of Swedish golfers, especially those on the LPGA Tour. I will be discussing the Swedish program later: it will become clear that it too does not depend only upon "talent."

I have spent some time on this section on talent because, when we come to discussing business performance, we will encounter similar problems in our use of language. In management, just as in golf and swimming, the outcomes of performance are continually being confused with the inputs to performance.

From a systems point of view, talent is a property that emerges from the actions of a top performer. The description of a system in terms of its emergent properties tends to mask the concrete actions required for improvement. In management, for example, we say that successful companies are those that have "aligned" their strategies with the needs of their customers. It seems only good advice, then, to tell less successful companies that they too must "align" themselves with their customers. But "alignment" is some-

*The Mundanity of Excellence, pp. 78–79.

thing we notice only in successful companies after they have been successful. It is an emergent property, a description, not an explanation, and thus not a good guide to action. When the webs of cause and effect get really tangled, as they are in complex systems, it is much easier to describe a system by its emergent properties. Thus, when it comes to prescribing action, we default to the use of what have been called "achievement" verbs—verbs like "align," "identify," "monitor," and so on. Because they are verbs, they sound like action, and although we may feel uneasy, we are powerless to argue against them—unless, that is, we realize that they are really the outcomes of effective action. We'll examine this in more detail in chapter 12.

Excellence Is Mundane

Chambliss's most startling deduction from his study is that success in top-class swimming is quite ordinary:

> Superlative performance is really a confluence of dozens of small skills or activities, each one learned or stumbled upon, which have been carefully drilled into a habit and then fitted together into a synthesized whole. There is nothing extraordinary or superhuman in any one of those actions; only the fact that they are done consistently and correctly and all together, produce excellence. When a swimmer learns a proper flip turn in the freestyle races, she will swim the race a bit faster; then a streamlined push off from the wall, with the arms squeezed together over the head, and a little faster; then how to place the hands in the water so no air is cupped in them; then how to lift weights properly to build strength, and how to eat the right foods, and to wear the best suits for racing, and so on and on. Each of those tasks seems small in itself, but each allows the athlete to swim faster.*

Thus the top-level swimmer improves her performance by progressively refining her skills in finer and finer detail, while blend-

---

*The Mundanity of Excellence, p. 82.

ing them into a coherent whole. Excellence, in other words, is systemic, or as Chambliss puts it, "The simple doing of certain small tasks can generate huge results. Excellence is mundane."*

There is certainly a good deal of evidence for the mundanity of excellence in golf. To the casual observer, top golfers work endlessly at drills, which make the most difficult shots routine, and they follow their own routines whatever the circumstances. They will always set up for the same shot in the same way, whether it is on the practice tee or out on the course. And the routines extend to their personal habits—Lee Jantzen always eats a midround snack on the 10th fairway of the course, for example. Sometimes the routines become rituals that shade into superstitions. There is, however, more systematic evidence for this stress on routines. In a 1989 study, Nadeane McCaffrey and Terry Orlick conducted extensive interviews with fourteen top professionals from the PGA and LPGA, as well as with a comparison group of nine club professionals. They compared the results of their study with a similar set of interviews with top athletes from the 1984 Olympics. I will be referring to this study again later in the book, but some of their key findings are as follows:

TOP TOUR PROFESSIONALS	CLUB PROFESSIONALS	OLYMPIC MEDALISTS
	QUALITY PRACTICE	
In addition to devoting many hours a day to perfect their skills, they mentally prepared themselves for high-quality practice.	Both the quality and quantity of practice time was minimal compared to the top pros and top Olympic athletes.	Top Olympic athletes train with the highest degree of quality and prepare themselves on a daily basis for high-quality practice.

*The Mundanity of Excellence, p. 82.

	PRACTICE PLAN	
They had very detailed individualized plans for practice on days without tournaments and practice before and after competing on tournament days.	They lack an individualized practice plan and have little or no structure for warming up or for tournament play.	They mentally prepared themselves for training, had preset individualized training goals, and committed themselves to follow their plans.
	PRETOURNAMENT PLAN	
They have a very structured pretournament plan, for example, for course management and shot making, and a detailed time frame plan for the day.	They recognized the benefits of planning and mentally preparing for tournament but did not have an effective detailed pretournament plan that they executed on a consistent basis.	They had very detailed and refined precompetition plans or procedures that they executed on a consistent basis—for example, for early preparation, warm-up, game preparation, reminders, etc.

Excerpted from Nadeane McCaffrey and Terry Orlick, "Mental Factors Related to Excellence Among Top Professional Golfers," *International Journal of Sports Psychology* 20 (1989): 256–78.

Although the sample numbers are low for the golfers, the findings are certainly suggestive—the top performers seem to be significantly more focused and committed to their chosen skill than the comparison group. The differences also suggest that there may be different "worlds" in golf just as Chambliss found in swimming.

Of course, the learning required to become a top golfer does not take place only on the practice tee using physical skills; golfers have to learn how to handle the distractions and pressures of tournament play and their bodies' reactions to them. When successful professional golfers say that up-and-coming stars have to "learn how to win," they mean that the younger golfers have to learn how to routinely make the big shots in the big tournaments. Winning has to be made mundane.

The difficulty in doing this was graphically illustrated by the unfortunate Len Mattiace during the final round of the 1998 Tournament Players Championship at Sawgrass. Mattiace, who had never won on the PGA Tour, came to the intimidating par-3 island green 17th hole one shot behind the leader and eventual winner, Justin Leonard. Mattiace's adrenaline was flowing so strongly that he hit a nine-iron 155 yards clean over the green into the water. He then hit his third shot into the bunker in front of the green and put his recovery attempt back into the lake. He ended up with a quintuple bogey 8! Mattiace had failed to take into account the systemic effects of a surge of adrenaline on his body and to adjust his mental calibration of club distances. To do that, he would have had to be there before, and of course he hadn't.*

Is Management Excellence "Mundane"?

Technique, discipline, attitude—is that all there is to excellence? And if we include technology in technique, does this apply to management excellence? Does "the simple doing of certain small tasks" generate success? The answer seems to be "yes, but . . ." (the "yes" because that *is* all there is, the "but" because knowledge of these "secrets" is not worth very much). For within a complex system, these characteristics have to be selected from a vast universe of possible tasks, and a huge amount of work is needed to ensure the reliability of their "doing." The choice of priorities, the decision of what to focus on and what to ignore, looms large. And "attitude" and "discipline," desirable as they might be, are really outcomes of processes that are not well understood. How do we build and maintain commitment and develop and focus discipline?

*Len Mattiace finally won his first PGA tournament at the Nissan Open in February 2002.

Summary

This chapter has examined the roots of excellence in sport. The evidence from another individual sport, swimming, is that excellence is mundane. That is, it is a qualitative phenomenon in which top performers have better technique, discipline, and attitude than lesser performers. Their better attitude allows them to pay better attention to detailed actions, to develop better technique, and to integrate the resulting techniques into a seamless performance. There is some evidence that this is the same situation in golf, where top performers prepare for practice in a qualitatively different way from others.

In the next chapter I will start putting some of these ideas together into a coherent framework. This will set the stage for a more detailed discussion of some important systemic aspects of both golf and management.

No. 7

Focus and Feedback

Par-4	478 yards

Keeping track of all critical assignments, following up on them, evaluating them—isn't that kind of . . . boring? We may as well say it: Yes. It's boring. It's a grind.
—R. CHARAN AND G. COLVIN, "WHY CEOS FAIL"

Your average golfer wants to improve, but they don't want to change and they don't want to practice. And I don't blame them, practicing is boring, they don't even know how to practice. *They would rather get out on the golf course.*
—UNIDENTIFIED PLAYER ON THE LPGA TOUR, QUOTED IN TODD W. CROSSET, OUTSIDERS IN THE CLUBHOUSE

It's zero degrees Fahrenheit and the one-piece range balls, which are unresponsive at the best of times, now feel like blocks of ice as I hit them out into the driving snow. And they seem to travel about as far as cubes of ice. It is so cold that their composition probably doesn't matter very much. At thirty-two degrees Fahrenheit a wound Balata ball covers nearly 10 percent less distance than it does at normal summer temperatures, and at this temperature I can't imagine what the loss of performance must be.

I am passionate about golf, but even I felt a little incongruous trudging through the practice range car park carrying my clubs three days after Christmas. The sudden snow squall off Lake Ontario had been unexpected, and it was bitterly cold. I was slightly relieved to see that I wasn't the only one who was crazy. There was one other golfer, dressed up like an Abominable Snowman, hitting balls into the storm. It looked as though he had been given new clubs for Christmas and just couldn't wait to try them out. I didn't have that excuse, as I had come only to try out a slightly different position at the top of the swing in an effort to curb my chronic hooking. But it's sheer lunacy to be out on the practice range in these conditions. After a few shots I start to lose the feeling in my hands. The only plus is that the snow is so white that the ball appears dark gray against it, so I can still see where the shots are going. It's so cold and uncomfortable, however, that soon I find that I can't concentrate on what I'm doing. I've lost my focus, and when one loses either focus or feedback, it's time to stop any kind of practice. After hitting fewer than a dozen balls, I head for home.

Developing Talent in Sport

In this chapter I review briefly the changing concepts of what makes for excellence in sport and the emerging importance of developmental explanations. We saw in chapter 6 how talent is unhelpful as an explanatory concept and expert opinion has moved away from genetic or inborn explanations of excellence to a consideration of the developmental conditions under which high performers train. One of the most significant catalysts for this change in our understanding was the 1976 Olympic Games held in Montreal.

At the 1976 Games in Montreal, the Western world and the United States in particular was shocked by the dominant performance of the athletes from the Communist bloc, particularly East Germany. At these games Russia won forty-four gold medals. East Germany, a tiny nation with seventeen million people, won forty gold against thirty-four for America, a country with twelve times the population. American sports officials were stunned, and their initial impulse, as well as that of the media, was to attribute the East German success to cheating:

The American press began implying that East German athletes (and those of other Communist nations) were being genetically selected, hormonally altered, doped, drugged, brain-washed, enslaved, maybe even surgically redesigned into superhumans. What chance did our playground-produced, free-enterprise mortals have against the laboratory monsters from the Godless Communist enclaves?[*]

In retrospect, as John Jerome has pointed out, the Montreal shock seems to have initiated "a sporting version of the scientific push that followed the launching of the Soviet Sputnik in the late 1950s."[†] Although drugs do seem to have featured in the East German success, the country had also adopted a far more focused approach to sport. Their public schools functioned as a systematically organized farm system—young prospects were identified early, comprehensively tested, and placed in programs run by expert coaches and trainers. Training regimens were controlled using the latest feedback devices to ensure that the athlete was always pushing to the "edge," where the maximum improvements were to be had. This, incidentally, usually involved *less* time spent in training than had previously been the case. Constant monitoring of the levels of lactic acid in muscles, for example, revealed that many athletes regularly overtrained. By pushing themselves "until it hurts," they were going well beyond the point where practice was productive. Sometimes this could lead to burnout—exhaustion, mental fatigue—and often to injury. It's interesting to note that in an organizational context, Frederick Taylor's early studies of work patterns in industry led to similar conclusions—shorter working hours and carefully designed rest periods usually produced better results.

The East German successes and the consequent emphasis on sports science in the West have had a major impact on our thinking about the role of genetics in the acquisition of complex skills. The emerging consensus is that, apart from bone size—the determinant of height and facial features—almost every aspect of the

---

[*]John Jerome, *The Sweet Spot in Time*, p. 220.
[†]Ibid., p. 221.

body is plastic and alterable through focused training. This applies to a wide range of organs and their functions, extending from heart size and lung capacity to the relative quantities of fast-twitch and slow-twitch muscles and the number of capillaries supplying blood to them. The physical corollary to this plasticity of the body is that complex skills are very specific and competencies gained in one skill area may not be easily transferred to another. Perhaps this is why we often find that top athletes in other sports have such trouble when they turn to golf! When Michael Jordan, a good golfer and certified fanatic, retired from the Chicago Bulls in 1999, there was idle speculation that he would soon appear on the PGA Tour. "I'll be playing in the NBA," commented golf pro Peter Jacobsen, "before Jordan gets onto the tour." Nevertheless, the belief in inherited talent dies hard. What may be transmitted in addition to basic physical attributes are attitudes—interest and motivation to train at an early age. Of course, it is likely that these attitudes are learned in early childhood rather than being transmitted genetically. We will be taking a closer look at this in the next chapter.

Deliberate Practice

The set of activities that improves performance is "focused training," or "deliberate practice," as it is sometimes called. Deliberate practice is a distinctive activity that can be contrasted with both work and play. Unlike play, deliberate practice requires effort, and it does not offer the social and financial rewards of work. Its key elements are as follows:*

- Motivation to improve performance.
- Close attention to the task.
- Immediate informative feedback on actions.
- Knowledge of results of performance.
- Multiple repetition of correct actions.

*K. Anders Ericsson, Ralph T. Krampe, and Clemens Tesch-Römer, "The Role of Deliberate Practice in the Acquisition of Expert Performance," *Psychological Review* 100, no. 3 (1993): 363–406.

The purpose of deliberate practice is not to do "more of the same," but to concentrate intensively on activities that result in improvement. The emphasis is on focus and immediate feedback, in addition to knowledge of results. The criteria for effective feedback are stringent, for as soon as feedback either lags action and/or becomes difficult to interpret, learning and improvement stop. *Repetition without effective feedback is useless and may even be counterproductive.* The importance of this last sentence for golfers and managers cannot be overestimated. How often in both activities do we find ourselves repeating actions in which feedback is either delayed or denied to us? As a result, neither learning nor improvement is possible.

The "Ten-Year Rule"

Researchers now see broadly similar patterns in the role of deliberate practice in the success of expert performers across many fields ranging from music, sculpture, and chess to swimming, tennis, and athletics. It seems to take about ten years of focused training under the tutelage of an expert to become a top performer. This finding is so widespread that it has been named by some as the "ten-year rule" and reflects the fact that almost any "overnight success" takes years of hard work.

Candidates are usually identified by their interest in the field and their motivation to improve. By the time they are experts, they will have put in about ten thousand hours of deliberate practice. The ten-year rule implies that this practice takes place at a rate of about one thousand hours a year, or less than four hours a day. Indeed, this is what researchers have found in a wide variety of activities:

- Practice varies from one to four hours per day.
- Sessions are often broken up into one-hour sections.
- Practice beyond four hours is rarely productive.
- Intellectual skills are best practiced in the morning, physical skills in the afternoon.
- Rest is needed after deliberate practice.

It is these clear limits to the rate at which expertise can be acquired that accounts for the success of people who start young. Top violinists, for example, typically start deliberate practice at the age of five or six, with about an hour a week devoted to that activity. By the time they are twenty years old, the best players are putting in four hours a day, seven days a week. By contrast, the average music teacher practices at less than half that rate. And the best violinists also nap regularly in the afternoons to recover from their exertions. They share this habit with top athletes and eminent writers. Indeed, the one-to-four-hour-a-day pattern of deliberate practice seems to be almost universal:

- Elite tennis players at age thirteen practice twenty hours a week, swimmers twenty-four to thirty hours.
- Ice-skaters and gymnasts at age fifteen to sixteen practice sixteen hours a week.
- Top long-distance runners cover 65–140 miles a week, training in twice daily sessions lasting forty-five to ninety minutes each: the afternoon workout is usually harder than the morning session.
- Chess grand masters spend about four hours a day analyzing published chess games of master-level players.
- Top authors write for three to four hours every morning and spend the rest of the day doing less arduous activities.

Dr. Gary Wiren, the well-known PGA teaching professional, suggests that a weekly practice schedule at the professional level might include the following:*

ACTIVITY	HOURS PER WEEK
Short Game (Chip & Pitch)	7¾
Putting	5
Irons	4½

*Adapted from Gary Wiren, *The PGA Manual of Golf,* p. 183.

Woods	3¼
Bunker Play and Other	3
Total on Range	23½

In addition to this deliberate practice, the golfer would play 81 holes (three rounds of 18 and three rounds of 9) and do 4½ hours of aerobics and stretching.

Deliberate Practice in Golf

Although detailed statistics on the use of deliberate practice in golf are not available, there is anecdotal support that the pattern is the same as that for the acquisition of other complex skills, especially in the top ranks. One top tournament pro explains, "Training could be anything from one to three hours of quality focusing. If I'm having a good time, I'll stay there. A lot of guys have the physical and technical ability but have no idea as to the amount of time and effort needed for mental training and waste hours and hours of practice time."

Practice is the bane of most amateur golfers, which is probably why nearly two-thirds of them don't practice and many of those who do don't practice effectively. "Most golfers hit far too many balls on the practice range," says my coach, John Cochrane. "It's just hit and reload, hit and reload, usually with the wrong club and with no clear objectives in mind. Instead of beating balls off at the rate of one hundred or more an hour, they should be taking their time, doing their drills between shots, and developing a very clear goal for every shot. Discipline on the practice range is important if you are going to learn. Unless you're warming up to play a round, there should be no such thing as just hitting a shot."

Top tournament pros say much the same thing: "I see guys go out there and hit eight or nine buckets of balls," says one, "and I wonder how many of those they hit well. I may go out and hit half a bucket. If I applied myself to that half a bucket and I got positive results, I might quit right then."

Not only do most golfers have no clear focus on the practice range, they also have no effective feedback. Of course, it's difficult to get such feedback without every shot being watched by an expert and captured on video. This implies the need for regular visits to a perceptive professional who knows your history and goals. Unfortunately, relatively few golfers take lessons of any kind, let alone regular ones. Nearly 60 percent of men and 40 percent of women have never taken a lesson in their lives, and at any given time, only 14 percent of men (versus 35 percent for women) will tell you that they are currently taking lessons.* "The average golfer," wrote Bobby Jones at a time when most golfers were male, "only goes to his pro for quick corrections. He goes only when his game, instead of remaining bad, has become worse, and he wants something done about it in a half hour or less."† It is not known whether the reluctance of men to take golf lessons is associated with their well-known dislike of asking for directions of any kind, but Derek Hardy, a teaching pro, has taken the logical step to counteract this tendency. He charges $1,000 for a single lesson and $140 each for a series of thirteen. "If you expect a miracle, you should expect to pay for one!" he says.‡

Golfers' aversion to visiting pros and taking regular lessons is an unfortunate one, given the revolution that has taken place in feedback technology. The power of video and computer technology has to be experienced to be believed. Today, in a well-equipped teaching facility one swings in real time with live front and down-the-line shots on a large screen on which the pro can use computer graphics to indicate key positions, planes, and angles. Instant playback of full swings allows the swing to be compared with these markers, for corrective action to be taken and drills to be performed perfectly. Feedback is from multiple sources—vision, touch, hearing, and sensations in the muscles and joints, accompanied by verbal comments from the pro.

The real value of feedback in all these modes is that it allows the player to move from a *conceptual* understanding of what he or she

*Source: National Golf Foundation.
†Bobby Jones, 1920s syndicated column.
‡Source: *Golfers on Golf.*

has to do to an *embodied feeling* of what is required. In my own case, for example, I had known (in a conceptual sense) for many years that my chronic hook was due to my taking the club back "under" the plane. This resulted in a flat swing, requiring a lot of manipulation with my hands to get the clubface square at impact. I would make attempts from time to time to "raise" the plane of my swing, but it never seemed to stick, especially during a game. When I first saw my swing on home videotape, I was horrified, for I could see that my swing was still far too much to the inside. But try as I might, I still could not fix it. I kept relapsing into a swing that felt comfortable but was deeply flawed technically. Then, for the first time, I saw and felt my swing at the same time on a real-time video setup with graphics on the screen marking the desired positions and a pro to comment on what I was doing. What had felt so natural looked terrible and, conversely, what looked right felt awful. And changes that looked minor felt huge, reflecting the much greater sensitivity to movement of the muscles and joints. But now I could see and feel the moves I had to make—I could duplicate those "awful" feelings and also know when I had not done so. In the process, I had begun to develop my own internal real-time feedback on my swing and on the position of the club head on the backswing. And the same method can be applied to all the other parts of the swing, even the ballistic downswing, which, although it cannot be changed in real time, can be reprogrammed at short notice.

Professionals have feedback systems that allow them to make such adjustments, consciously or unconsciously. One famous instance of this is Jack Nicklaus's one-iron against the wind to the par-3 17th hole at Pebble Beach during the 1972 U.S. Open. Here's how he described it:

> Swinging back, I felt myself closing the clubface and working the club too much to the inside. But my tempo and timing had been outstanding all week, and now it produced one of the most memorable shots of my career.
>
> Frequently when you get closed and too much to the inside going

back, the clubface will remain closed through impact and you will hook the ball badly. Now, thanks to my fine sense of pace, coming down I was able to block or delay the release just sufficiently to catch the ball with the face square. The result was a low, boring flight dead on the stick. . . . When I got there I found the ball two inches from the hole. It had struck the flagstick and almost dropped in for an ace.*

And that's the key message about change in golf and management: *Intellectual knowledge of what has to be changed is not enough—we have to be able to feel in real time that what we are doing is wrong so that we can make changes on the fly—exercise dynamic control.* As Timothy Gallwey put it, "What the body needs to control the path of the club head is not a lot of instructions, but accurate, moment-by-moment feedback about the position of the club head."† In golf this takes the kinesthetic skills that are developed by real-time feedback in multiple modes. In management this requires sensitivity to real-time feedback from people: an ability to assess in real time their responses to one's words and actions.

The Importance of Feedback

Further technological developments, which are not yet widely available, involve wiring the golfer so that even subtler faults can be detected and immediate feedback given. As Cochran and Stobbs have suggested: "If . . . a machine could be devised which would give the golfer an electric shock as soon as it detected an error in the back swing, the rate of progress of beginners, and others, would be enormously increased."‡

There are, however, many basic, do-it-yourself feedback techniques that are rarely used on the range. After all, the great benefit of the practice tee is that you can use feedback devices that are

---

*Jack Nicklaus: My Story, written with Ken Bowden (New York: Simon & Schuster, Fireside ed., 1998), p. 289.
†*The Inner Game of Golf*, p. 23.
‡*Search for the Perfect Swing*, p. 107.

not allowed on the course. Take the simple act of laying down a club pointing toward the target. This allows you to check your alignment and sets up a simple feedback situation that eliminates what can be a major problem early in the swing cycle. Yet how many golfers on the practice tee does one see doing this? Very few. Timothy Gallwey even suggests that golfers can set up their own subtle feedback system by humming a steady tone to themselves during their swings. Tensions can be recognized immediately as glitches in the tone! Indeed, many practice drills are aimed precisely at setting up feedback conditions for parts of the swing that are not usually checked. But how often does one see amateur golfers doing drills of any kind outside of a lesson?

The pros go much further, often setting up a practice "box" with objects such as shafts, tees, and balls laid out to indicate "marks" they want to hit at various stages of the swing. They can then see immediately when and where they go wrong and can drill the correct move. As was mentioned earlier, one of the findings by Cochran and Stobbs (*Search for the Perfect Swing*) was that professional golfers set themselves up much more consistently at address than do amateurs. This consistency is the product of deliberate practice and the core of the truth behind the saying "Practice doesn't make perfect, only perfect practice makes perfect." The need for feedback often extends to the choice of equipment. Tiger Woods prefers a steel shaft in his driver because he says it gives him a better feel for where the club head is. Nick Price describes how, at the age of sixteen, he started playing with the larger American ball, even though the smaller English ball was still legal in what was then Rhodesia (now Zimbabwe). He felt the ball was harder to use and, because it accentuated hooks and slices, required better ball striking. For similar reasons, many top golfers prefer playing with forged irons, even though they have a smaller sweet spot and less "forgiveness" than perimeter-weighted cast irons. The forged blades allow finer control because they give more sensitive feedback—professional golfers don't want to be "forgiven" for bad shots; they want to learn. And learning in complex systems is most effective at the edge, just this side of chaos.

Rules for Deliberate Practice

Given the desire to improve, the first challenge is the identification of the priorities in a multitude of improvement opportunities. Invariably, with all but the most skilled golfers, these will lie deep within the hierarchical activities that make up the swing. If the golfer is to improve, he or she, together with a coach, will have to reach down to the deepest, earliest level in the swing and fix the faults there, one level at a time, before moving on. The golfer will have to think about the many levels at which changes can be made and how the effects of those changes might cascade through the system.

Once the priorities have been identified, the golfer will then need a set of drills to work on to improve those elements as well as to cope with the compensations he or she has been making to offset the basic faults. "You always have to fix things in pairs," says David Leadbetter. "First the basic fault, and then the compensating moves that the golfer has been making to offset it." This is the reason why, when making changes to one's golf swing, final outcomes (results) often get worse before they get better. Until the faults and their offsetting moves have been changed, overall performance may not improve.

This quirk of complex systems puts a considerable burden on the golfer that can be sustained only by trust in the coach and the methods being used. For during deliberate practice, he or she must focus on the *execution* of the elements of the swing, not on the *outcomes* produced by the swing. This does not mean that one should ignore outcomes, only recognize that they are very coarse, possibly misleading guides to the systemic causes of poor shots. What is needed is finer-grained feedback that relates to each component of the swing, so that the execution of these intermediate stages can be examined and corrected.

One can now see why in complex systems priorities are not only difficult to set but become tangled immediately when one starts to act on them. For every variable is connected to several others in complex ways. The tangling of priorities can make them difficult to keep track of from session to session. Many golfers keep a practice journal to maintain the major threads on what they are working on and thinking about. Keeping a practice journal is also helpful for people who practice infrequently and don't want to start their deliberate practice from scratch every time.

The setting and maintenance of priorities and the focus it allows the golfer merely create a platform on which, in the right context, effective feedback can take place. *And the crux of deliberate practice is that it cannot be performed without timely, effective feedback.* For without effective feedback on the execution of the components of the swing, the golfer is forced to rely on final outcomes—learning stops. In addition, when we want results, we tend to default to actions that are old and familiar: this is why, without effective feedback, golfers end up "grooving" their faults.

The Purpose of Practice

In golf the term *practice* covers both deliberate as well as other forms of practice. One of the more surprising statements from Cochran and Stobbs is that the purpose of practice in golf is not to "groove" a swing, but to build up a series of alternative methods of producing acceptable outcomes. Given the variety of conditions and circumstances encountered on a golf course and the physical and psychological changes in the human body, no two swings are ever quite the same. But Cochran and Stobbs's recommendation is an interesting one:

> Once a golfer has reached a stage of having . . . a "swing," he should deliberately introduce variations and extra difficulty into practice sessions. By doing so he broadens his experience (increases the variety of memory traces) and develops alternative nerve and muscle routes for producing acceptable shots.[*]

Their advice is best interpreted from a systems perspective. At one level of analysis, deliberate practice is clearly about repetition

---

[*]*Search for the Perfect Swing,* pp. 108–9.

of individual movements. For a particular shot under particular circumstances—a fifty-yard lob wedge from a flat fairway lie with no wind—consistency and repeatability are essential. But at the systems level "above" that there are multiple ways of moving the ball fifty yards closer to the hole. Indeed, as one approaches the green, the variety of shots playable increases dramatically. One can hit a high flop shot, a hard spin, a bump-and-run, and a variety of other shots using a variety of clubs. Each shot has its own risk/reward trade-off, depending upon the skills of the golfer, the physical conditions, and the game being played—in match play one will often select very different shots from those used in medal play. Working on all these different kinds of shots on the practice tee clearly increases one's "arsenal" of weapons. This variety is critical to increasing resiliency under adversity—the ability of a golfer to scramble and produce acceptable outcomes even when he or she may not be hitting the ball very well.

What, then, should be the uses of practice in golf? There seem to be only a few that make systemic sense, which implies that everything else is not a good use of one's time:

1. *Warming up* to get the muscles loose and circulation going. If you have limited time, the pros suggest hitting a few chip shots as the best minirehearsal of the full swing.
2. *Ensuring deliberate practice with effective feedback* on aspects of the swing (including putting), usually from a skilled observer with technical (real-time video) support with a view to identifying the most suitable drills.
3. *Performing prescribed drills* to improve components of the swing that need attention: backswing drills, impact drills, extension drills, and so on.
4. *Hitting a variety of shots,* as suggested by Cochran and Stobbs. For example, pick the hundred-yard marker and hit to it using pitching wedge through five-iron. When using the longer irons, try both fading and drawing the ball into the marker.
5. *Playing a simulated game* by picking a course you know well and playing it in your imagination, using the appropriate

clubs on each hole and living with the consequences of each shot. This keeps you changing clubs and hitting the variety of shots that you might play on a real course.

What all of these practice activities have in common is discipline and a clearly defined purpose. Trying to hit drivers over the back fence does not have either of these qualities!

The Problem with Putting

The essence of deliberate practice is focus and timely, specific feedback. These demands allow us to understand immediately why putting represents such a challenge to golfers. The dramatically smaller scale of activities required by putting (when compared with the rest of the game), together with the context in which it takes place, makes deliberate practice problematical:

- In full shots, the distance the ball travels is controlled primarily by club selection; in putting, it's an additional variable (and perhaps the most important one) to be controlled by the golfer. This immediately divides our attention between aim and distance control.
- The fine control and sensitivity required by putting tends to engage the "small, fast" systems of the body and the minimal physical effort required allows the conscious mind to intrude more readily into the shot.
- The smaller scale of the shot means that mistakes and variations in the swing are harder for outsiders to spot and for golfers to feel.
- Feedback is confounded by the relatively large influence of the contour and grain of the green, as well as spike marks, the "volcano effect" round the hole toward the end of the day, and other environmental factors that make it difficult to tell whether a putt was misread or mishit.
- Many golfers find practicing putting even more boring than practicing their full shots.

The bottom line is that whenever we set out to practice our putting under normal conditions, we place ourselves in an impoverished feedback environment, where deliberate practice is virtually impossible. We cannot connect action and results because we are not sure exactly what we did, and the results themselves may be due to myriad other factors. No learning can take place. Short-game guru David Pelz contends that as a result of this, most putting practice is counterproductive: bad habits are reinforced. Perhaps most golfers' reluctance to practice their putting makes systemic sense!

From a system's perspective, there are three approaches to the problem:

1. *Practice the putting stroke only in controlled environments,* where results are not confounded by "externalities" such as surface texture, contour, and grass grain. Paul Stankowski says that he prepares for the Masters by putting on the smooth concrete floor of his garage. Swedish golfers are convinced that they are good putters because they are forced to practice indoors by the short Swedish golf season.
2. *Crank up the feedback so that you are more sensitive to what it is you are doing during the stroke.* This implies, of course, that you have a solid theory of cause and effect so that you know what you are doing in the intermediate stages will produce acceptable results.
3. *Keep the practice sessions short so that attention remains focused.* Set yourself up for each putt so that you focus on aim first and then forget about it to concentrate on distance control.

Many golfers already do some of these things, although they may not understand the systemic sense that they make. They take off their golf glove to enhance feel, close their eyes during their practice strokes to cut out distractions, and so on. Pelz and other pros sell a variety of devices to supplement those that some players make for themselves. All of these are geared toward enhancing feedback from the intermediate stages of the putting stroke rather than using the final results—final outcomes are only a secondary guide to correct actions.

Deliberate Practice in Management

This is a good time to point out that in organizations, the systemic counterpart to putting is meetings. Indeed, everything that can be said about putting applies in spades to meetings. Putting constitutes roughly 50 percent of the strokes played on the course; meetings typically consume two-thirds or more of an executive's time. Outcomes of meetings are difficult to judge even if the desired objectives are specified in advance, which they often aren't. Even when clear objectives are set, people are likely to find it hard to pay attention unless determined efforts are made to keep them focused. For meetings often demand small-scale activities that we find acutely boring. In short, as soon as people enter a typical business meeting, they are placing themselves in an impoverished feedback environment where learning is difficult, if not impossible.

The remedies for this situation would seem to be the same as those for putting: control the environment, boost the feedback, especially during the process phase of the meeting, and keep the sessions short so that attention remains focused. Workplace design, for example, by controlling the environment can go a long way toward mitigating the need for meetings and ensuring that they are more productive when they are held. It's important that the purpose of the meeting be identified—is it to generate ideas? narrow options? make decisions or take action? Does the meeting context match the purpose? Round tables and comfortable chairs are essential for creative meetings, as they encourage participation from all. Decision-taking meetings, on the other hand, will benefit from a hierarchical table layout, with the position of the decision maker clearly identified. What are people's expectations of the rules that govern interaction at the meeting? Should the sessions start and end on time? Should speakers stand while listeners sit? And so on. There are several varieties of process-support software that can be used in conjunction with live meetings to enhance feedback and help keep events on track. And at the end of a meeting it often helps to take five minutes to poll people on what worked and what didn't. "All you are trying to do is to make the invisible visible and to make the automatic deliberate," says Mike Begeman of the 3M Meeting Network, developer of many of the ideas mentioned above. He even suggests polling people at the beginning of a meeting, asking them to voice any current concerns and issues, so that they can clear their minds and be truly "present." This practice applies as directly to golf as it does to management.

Now to some readers this emphasis on improving the quality of meetings might sound trivial. But time is as precious to managers as strokes are to golfers! Can you, as a manager, imagine what it would be like if every meeting that was called had a clear purpose, with all the correct participants present? How much time would become available in the organization if such meetings never ran longer than ninety minutes? And what would happen if similar discipline were applied to other time-consuming activities like writing and reading reports? What would happen if all capital expenditure requests were in a standard format that fitted on one page? It would be like the average golfer being guaranteed that he would never have more than thirty putts a round! Performance would soar.

Of course, such improvements in business meetings and other managerial activities cannot be achieved by issuing top-down instructions. As the boss, you can arbitrarily chop meetings off at ninety minutes—once, twice, a few times—just to get people's attention. But there is no guarantee that they will have achieved their purpose. You are trying not to *impose* discipline *on* people, but to *instill* discipline *in* them. They have to be committed to practicing the meeting drills day by day until they get the process right. For in the final analysis there is no substitute for these disciplines being embedded in the organizational culture and continually reinforced by those who practice them. Some firms like Intel and Toyota are well-known for the focused discipline with which they meet. Principles for effective meetings abound, just as they do for effective putting. We just can't implement them without the discipline—the focus and feedback—generated by deliberate practice.

Summary

This chapter has shown how talent is developed in many skilled activities through the regular application over long periods of time of focused training or deliberate practice. This type of practice is characterized by a powerful motivation to improve, close attention to the task, immediate, specific feedback, knowledge of results, and multiple repetitions of correct moves. We saw how effective practice demands both focus and feedback. It's the absence of suitable conditions for deliberate practice that makes putting and meetings a systemic challenge to golfers and managers, respectively. The systemic solution to this challenge requires a controlled environment, cranked-up feedback, and short sessions to keep attention focused.

No. 8

Doing and Thinking

| Par-5 | 608 yards |

A growing body of data points to the conclusion that people act their way into a way of believing as readily as they believe themselves into a way of acting.
—JEROME BRUNER, ON KNOWING

Telling our bodies how to do something is not the most effective way to improve performance. Our muscles don't understand English, and our thinking minds really don't understand hand-eye coordination.
—TIMOTHY GALLWEY, THE INNER GAME OF GOLF

The lead article in *Fortune* magazine on June 21, 1999, was entitled "Why CEOs Fail," and it examined the causes for the downfalls of a number of once prominent chief executives of large organizations. It concluded that they failed not for lack of intelligence or vision, but for their inability to execute, to get things done. This failure was attributed in turn to their inability to get the right people into the right jobs and to fix people problems as the situation required them to. Many of the CEOs had espoused plausible strategies for their businesses, but in the absence of their ability to execute, these had come to naught. The article went on to describe the motto of the successful CEO as "People first, strategy second." The writers acknowledged that strategy was a "sexier obsession" and that while a good, clear strategy was necessary for success, it was not sufficient for survival; only solid execution could ensure that.

What the *Fortune* article did not do was connect the CEOs' inability to execute with their (and our) relentless exposure to a head-down theory of knowledge. In North America, the head-down, brain-centered theory of knowledge, with its assumption that conscious thinking and logic either does or ought to precede intelligent action, has dominated our concepts of teaching in many fields, including those of both golf and management.

In the case of golf, it is at least recognized that practice is an essential component of competence. No one would dream of standing up and lecturing golfers for hours on end, without allowing them either to touch a club or to get out on a course. In the case of management, however, we have no compunction in putting aspirant managers through months of lectures, seminars, and assigned readings and cases. At the end of a prescribed period, they are examined on the explicit knowledge that they have accumulated, and then, too often with little or no practical experience, they receive certificates describing them as "masters" of the activity! Of course, one can perhaps argue that management demands more intellectual capacity than golf, but even if this were true, the practical application of ideas, the ability to implement strategy, is critical to effectiveness. It is here that our bias toward a head-down theory of knowledge allows us to gloss over the process of implementation and the relationship between our brain-based ideas of intelligence and our body-based effectiveness on the ground.

In this chapter I explore the view of knowledge as *embodied,* rather than *embrained.* I develop a model that has very different implications for learning, teaching, and the meaning of competence and mastery of a skill. It implies that consciousness, and the use of logic that sometimes accompanies it, is merely the visible tip of a vast iceberg, the bulk of which is hidden from our awareness. Just as the tip of an iceberg is supported by the vast, invisible mass of ice beneath it, so consciousness emerges from the complex dynamics of the processes within our bodies. It is these processes, all of which have been selected for and laid down over evolutionary time scales, that are the roots of intelligent behavior. These primary processes form the lower layers of the tangled hierarchies that constitute the complex systems we know as our body. Consciousness is secondary, an emergent phenomenon. This does not mean, of course, that conscious processes are not important, only that they have to be seen within the context of the total system, not as somehow standing apart from it. Intelligence in this model is *the capacity to take effective action in a given environment.* In short, in an embodied theory of knowledge, intelligence is synonymous with competence.

Becoming Competent

Researchers on the development of expert performers have identified three broad phases in the learning process. The phases are present to some extent in all cases, but the duration of each phase varies across both activities and individuals. In addition, the transitions between phases are neither neat nor orderly. There may be sudden breakthroughs, as well as plateaus and regressions: sometimes progress inches along, at other times it proceeds in leaps and bounds. Nevertheless, the phases make a useful classification system for thinking about the process of development and marking the distinctively different moods of each. What follows is based on the work of well-known University of Chicago educationist Benjamin Bloom, who together with his colleagues has studied the development of high-performing individuals in a wide variety of activities.

Phase One: The Early Years—Building Commitment

These are the playful years, full of fun and immediate rewards. The learning process begins in the home with encouragement from the parents, especially the mother, who in most of the cases studied played a 1950s-era role, staying at home with the children. The age at which the activity began depended on the skill involved and the equipment used. Violins such as those used in the Suzuki method can be scaled down for three-year-olds to play, but pianos cannot. Sports like golf and tennis are usually not taken up until the age of six or older, although the home movies of a very young Tiger Woods swinging a club show that this is not a hard-and-fast rule. Typically, the parents have no long-term goals for their child—the activities are just extensions of their own interests and passions. They involve their children in them and are warm in their praise and enthusiasm for the child's efforts. The child's first teachers, who are often described as "kindly" and "nice," sustain this warmth and help create an incubator for early development. Thus, instruction in phase one is informal and personal, and there is not much concern for achievement by either student or teacher. The child is enticed into an enjoyable activity of which mother and teacher both approve, and the child's urge to win that approval plays a key role in his or her motivation.

Phase Two: The Middle Years—Drilling Technique

After a few years, typically past the age of ten, the child begins to show a real desire to work at developing the skill. Virtuoso violinist Isaac Stern put it this way:

> Somewhere along the line, the child must become possessed by music, by the sudden desire to play, to excel. It can happen at any time between the ages of 10 or so or 14. Suddenly the child begins to work, and in retrospect the first five or six years seem like kinderspiel, fooling around.*

The word *possession* is apt, for at one time or another nearly all of us have had that visceral feeling of fierce conviction that *this* is what we want to do. The depth of this feeling goes well beyond anything associated with rational decision making. We are con-

*Isaac Stern, *The New York Times Magazine*, December 23, 1979, quoted in Benjamin S. Bloom (ed.), *Developing Talent in Young People* (New York: Ballantine Books, 1985), p. 415.

sumed by the activity, possessed by the pictures and feelings, spend much of our waking time thinking about it, and arrange our affairs so that the activity has the highest priority. In short, it is a feeling familiar to every serious golfer! Butch Harmon, Tiger Woods's coach, makes and sells videos entitled *Conquering Golf.* It's a pleasant fantasy, but the idea is a fiction. The true spirit of golf is never one of ownership on the part of the golfer, only that of possession by the game. We can never own golf. It owns us— even Tiger!

In the life of an expert in the making, this is the time when the parents realize the child has "real talent." They start to search for a new teacher, usually someone with a reputation in the field who will take the child to the next level. In phase one, the child's first teachers are usually chosen because of their availability and the convenience of their location. Their contribution is to supply a warm, nurturing "incubator" environment for the young child and stimulate interest and excitement; they are usually not technically expert in the field. The new teachers will be renowned for their technical skills and ability to impart discipline. They will generally be located farther away from the family, charge more for lessons, and want to screen the students through audition or try-out before they choose to accept them. By signing up with such a teacher, the student will be joining a peer group that will supply emotional support as well as competition.

The emphasis in phase two is on discipline, precision, and accuracy. The new teachers are often hard taskmasters and perfectionists, expecting and demanding much. Every student talks about the repetitions in this phase, repetitions of the basics with immediate feedback from the teacher. Moves are made over and over again until they get them right. And they will often go back to revisit earlier, more basic drills to ensure that they are being done correctly. The deliberate practice required between lessons now increases to two to three hours a day. The relationship between student and teacher changes from love to respect. High levels of individual motivation are a condition of entry into the class, and if students are not prepared to work, teachers in this phase of the development process can't help them. The students' motivation will be sustained less by the warm feelings of their families, although a peer group will help, and more by hard results—progress assessments from the teacher and success in competitions.

In this phase the pupil is introduced to formal competition. The teacher will make students aware of contests taking place and suggest that they take part in them. Teachers and students may now work long hours together preparing for the contests. There will be special summer camps that require teacher recommendations for the student to gain entry. The competitions pit pupils against their peers and in many activities supply objective standards against which students can both set their goals and measure their progress. At the same time, they will be exposed to increasing psychological pressure and learn to cope with their emotions under competitive stress. The excitement of performing before growing audiences at higher and higher levels of expertise is both a reward and a relief from the long hours of monotonous, grinding practice. After a period of four to six years, some students may be ready to go beyond the disciplines and start the search for master teachers to take them into the third phase of development—personal mastery.

Phase Three: The Later Years—Acquiring Mastery

By now the student is a competent performer with sound techniques and disciplined habits. In the third phase of development, he or she will have to transcend the mechanical qualities of the disciplines to reach the freedom that makes each performance personal and unique. To this end, the student will need another teacher, typically described as a master teacher, whose understanding of the skill goes well beyond technique—details are less important now, it's the larger conception that counts. In this third phase, the belief seems to be that someone who has not personally had the experience of performance at the top level cannot impart what is to be learned. Indeed, the search for a master teacher is even more arduous than that in the previous phase. Master teachers are scarce, almost by definition, and the competition to work with them is intense. Their demands on their students are legendary, and their relationship with a student may be the equivalent of that between taskmaster and slave:

> He was an impossible taskmaster. It was incredible. He would just intimidate you out of your mind. He would sit there. . . . You played a concert, you didn't play a lesson. You walked in prepared to play a performance. . . . You would get torn apart for an hour.[*]

These demands are not technical, for effective technique is taken as a given. Rather, the demands are to go beyond mere technique, and this requires a new sensitivity, a new kind of feedback. A highly competent pianist described the feeling as follows:

> All of a sudden my ear is telling me something is not quite right about the way I am playing. There are certain kinds of technical things that are sounding very harsh. And the more I am listening to the recordings of great masters, I think, "Gee, their tone is so wonderful, what's wrong with mine?"[†]

The role of the master teacher is to cultivate this new sensibility, opening up to the student possibilities for interpretation that he or she cannot yet imagine. To the basic techniques, the master teacher brings an encyclopedic knowledge of the history of the activity. The teacher supplies the context against which the student can use his or her skills to make a unique contribution. In the physical activities, the student is developing strategies and the ability to analyze his or her own performance and those of competitors. Students learn to coach themselves by being able to get real-time feedback from their own activities.

---

[*]Quoted in Benjamin S. Bloom (ed.), *Developing Talent in Young People* (New York: Ballantine Books, 1985), p. 421.
[†]Ibid., p. 420.

A Helpful Model

The three phases of learning—building commitment, drilling technique, and acquiring mastery—have a broad application to all kinds of activities. The following diagram introduces some dimensions into the process and outlines the implications for learning competence in a bottom-up, embodied theory of knowledge:

Developing Professional Competence

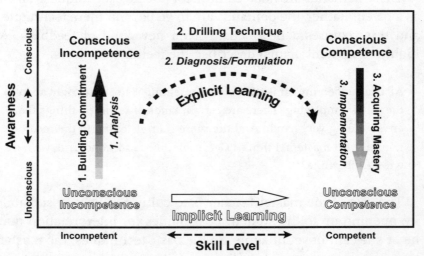

Source: Adapted from I. Nonaka and H. Takeuchi, *The Knowledge-Creating Company* (New York: Oxford University Press, 1995).

The two dimensions in the diagram are awareness (unconscious/conscious) and skill level (incompetent/competent). The interaction of these two dimensions generates four quadrants showing the different combinations of awareness and skill level.

The diagram shows two learning pathways from the initial state of unconscious incompetence to the final goal of unconscious competence. The first and most direct route is that of implicit learning, through which the learner acquires skills and becomes competent without being aware either of the learning process or of what is being learned. The second, more circuitous route is that of explicit learning. In this process, the learner is aware of the learning process and the content being acquired. In this model, explicit learning consists of three phased processes that parallel those identified by Bloom and his colleagues. Their three processes have been placed on the outside of the arrows in the diagram to show where they fit. I'll explain the processes on the inside of the arrows shortly.

Of course, it may take a number of "trips" through both learning processes for a high level of unconscious competence to be achieved. Each of these learning processes needs to be discussed in more detail.

Implicit Learning

This is the root learning process whereby every one of us has acquired our basic behavioral and social repertoire. Babies typically develop these skills, including their use of language, unconsciously as the environment and their actions in it evoke their innate dispositions, "hardwired" over evolutionary history. Action—movement—is critical to implicit learning. Experiment after experiment has shown that it is not enough for animals or people to be exposed passively to the environment; they have to move about in the environment for learning to take place. Anyone who has been a passenger in a car knows that it's much easier to learn a route if you drive it. Acting demands that you focus your attention; only through acting can feedback loops be constructed and causes connected with effects. This learning is accompanied by little, if any, conscious awareness of the process. And the skills are performed without any conscious effort—they become "habits."

As such, implicitly acquired skills are typically smooth, fast, automatic, and efficient, requiring little, if any, conscious intervention other than to start or stop them. They are usually situation-specific, evolved to deal with problems encountered over and over again. Given the long evolutionary history of the dispositions on which they are based, skills learned during early development are extremely robust and resistant to change. Work with brain-damaged people, for example, finds that these implicit skills are much less likely to disappear after the injury than those learned explicitly. As we shall see, this robustness of implicit skills is both a strength and a weakness in the achievement of competence in golf and management.

Another characteristic of implicit learning is that it takes place in "real time"—that is, the skills are learned as they are practiced in their totality. In the development of a child, implicit learning often requires the right environments at the right times to evoke the various behaviors. If a developmental window is missed and certain skills are not learned, it may be very difficult to pick them up later. Witness our struggle as adults to learn a foreign language, compared with the facility with which young children pick it up! Indeed, there is now evidence that language acquisition in later life takes place in a different part of the brain from that which we use when we are young.

It seems likely that implicit learning is possible only if the skills make use of processes already "wired" in by evolution. So while babies learn to speak and understand language implicitly, as they grow older they will have to be taught explicitly to read and write. Reading and writing are not embedded in our biological inheritance, although they make use of myriad basic, "hardwired" processes. Indeed, all learning makes use of a mixture of implicit and explicit processes.

Golfing skills, like the reading and writing of language, are also skills that have to be taught explicitly, although they clearly rely heavily on physical processes that are hardwired. So, like reading and writing, they too are a tangle of implicit and explicit skills.

Explicit Learning

Explicit learning is the process with which everyone who has attended school is familiar—it is "formal" education: indeed, we often call it "teaching" and make a distinction between it and "learning." For explicit learning, in contrast with implicit learning, is halting, slow, deliberate, and inefficient. Much explicit learning is based on language or the use of symbols and, as such, is a heavy user of conscious capacities. The three subprocesses identified on the inside of the arrows in the diagram can be explored further. I have given them their "management" names:

1. *Analysis:* a complex process is broken down into its components, and the most important of these are identified and named so that they can be measured.
2. *Diagnosis/Formulation:* performance within each of the components of the process is compared with high-performance models generated either from theory or from the practices of others. The components are then redesigned to optimize performance. These new designs are then transmitted to the learner via formal means—books, lectures, and so on— all of which are heavily based on reading and writing.
3. *Implementation:* the learner takes the concepts and, working slowly and deliberately, transforms their implications for action back into a seamless performance. This means that myriad subtasks must be allotted to different components within the system, and each of them must be drilled and rehearsed until performance is automatic. These performances must then be blended into a seamless whole.

It's helpful to contrast Bloom's phases of learning with their management counterparts:

THE PHASES OF EXPLICIT LEARNING

Phase	Bloom's Phase	Management Concept
1	Building Commitment	Analysis
2	Drilling Technique	Diagnosis/Formulation
3	Acquiring Mastery	Implementation

The management concepts seem rather abstract, whereas Bloom's are more action oriented—visceral, one might say. I would argue that the difference between these two perspectives is their unstated assumptions about the nature of knowledge and the mind. The management concepts come from a traditional top-down "embrained" view of knowledge. Bloom's concepts are based on a bottom-up "embodied" perspective. Nevertheless, from the model's point of view both perspectives are dealing with the same phases of the process of learning a skill explicitly. And both perspectives can help us understand the nature of deliberate practice, the process at the heart of the explicit learning process.

The most important difference between explicit and implicit learning is clearly the presence or absence of awareness and the demands made on our conscious mental capacity. But it is important to note that, unlike implicit learning, explicit learning does not take place in the "real time" in which the skill is performed in its totality. Indeed, during the first analytical phase the object of analysis is paralysis! Action is frozen so that the analyst can break a flowing process into its component parts. This allows the second phase, diagnosis/formulation, to take place out of real time—that is, in the formulator's own time. Typically each of the component activities is then compared with "world class" processes used by experts in each identified function. New, improved processes are then designed to replace the old incompetent activities.

Making changes in this phase is relatively easy, often consisting in the substitution of one set of concepts or procedures for another. This means that the central challenge in the third, implementation phase of the explicit learning process is to take all the newly designed functions, train the actors within the systems to perform them, and then put the entire process back into "real time." Only then can the new competence become unconscious and not require any outside intervention to run successfully. This need for integration in real time will become the central issue when I deal later in the book with the challenges of rhythm, tempo, and timing in golf and management.

Explicit Learning in Golf

As the following diagram shows, the consciousness/competence model can be applied directly to golf, and this allows us to explore in more detail the learning process that it maps out:

The Golf Learning Cycle

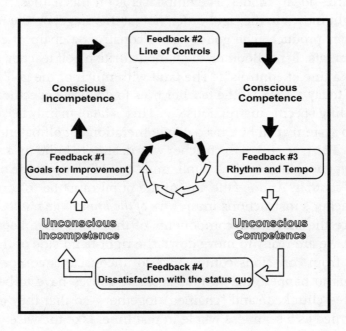

As golfing beginners, we start in the bottom left-hand quadrant as "unconscious incompetents." If we are to move from this quadrant to the one above, we have to develop personal improvement goals for the game and measure our performance against them. The comparison between our performance and our goals generates an internal feedback situation (feedback #1) that focuses our feelings of discontent with the status quo and our excitement at the prospect of making changes to improve—we become committed to change. In the next chapter we will find that the most important components of these goals for improvement are images—pictures and feelings of both the outcomes and the activities required to attain them. As we measure our progress against our goals, we become conscious of our incompetence and move up to the top left-hand quadrant.

Now that we are consciously incompetent, the next challenge is to become consciously competent. To do this, we must receive a second kind of feedback (feedback #2). This feedback allows us to compare the different elements of our swing with those of some standard, "ideal" model. The emphasis is on mechanics, making the right moves in the right order, not (at this stage) on the results that they produce. The golfer has to construct a chain of correct movements. Percy Boomer, the famous British golf teacher, called them "a line of controls": "The fault with much of the golf teaching of today . . . is that the teacher tries to eradicate specific faults by issuing specific instructions. . . . This is fatal, mainly because it has no system at all but just a conglomeration of golf patent medicines. The true aim of the teacher who desires to build up a sound and dependable game in a pupil, must be to link up in the pupil *a line of controls*. And . . . the aim of the pupil must be to carry out the teacher's instructions *irrespective of the immediate results*."*

Once the individual components of the swing have been perfected, we are ready to move down the right-hand side of the diagram, from conscious competence to unconscious competence. For this to happen, the various separate moves have to be integrated—"chunked" and "chained" together—so that they can be performed as a seamless whole in real time. Like the wise watchmaker in chapter 3, the effective golfer "chunks" the elements into larger wholes and then combines these modules to form the totality of the swing. This is accomplished by using graduated drills, which steadily entail more and more of the movements of the total swing.

The final drills are those designed to build tempo and rhythm, ideal qualities of the total swing. Yet another type of feedback (feedback #3) is needed in this phase of the learning process. It is

---

*On Learning Golf, p. 15, original emphasis.

feedback that goes beyond the critique of technique to assess the totality of the performance and the degree of integration of the parts. In ice-skating, performers are scored separately for "technical merit" and "artistic impression." Feedback required at this stage is closer to "artistic impression." For it is recognized that performers may be extremely competent without being able to go beyond technique to make a unique contribution. Their performance may be technically perfect, but it comes across as mechanical and artistically dead. Conversely, some individuals may be able to make a unique integration without achieving anything near technical perfection. Many of our greatest performers in all fields come from the latter category—golfers Bobby Locke, Arnold Palmer, Gary Player, Lee Trevino, and a host of successful players have used idiosyncratic swings that one would have hesitated to recommend to others. Yet their ability to hold their swings together under pressure has been the hallmark of their careers.

Of course, the trip round the explicit learning cycle is not a one-shot deal, but a continual iteration, as the circle of arrows in the center of the diagram suggests. At the bottom of the diagram on the boundary between unconscious competence and unconscious incompetence I have shown a fourth kind of feedback (feedback #4) that is generated internally within individuals. It leads to a pervasive restlessness, a continual state of discontent with the status quo. Such individuals are never satisfied—they always want to improve. Recent research suggests, unfortunately, that this is not characteristic of everyone. Many people who are incompetent at certain skills also lack the competence to recognize their ineptness. It is as if they are incompetent on two levels, first to perform the task and second to assess the merit of the result. When asked to rank their own skills, they will systematically overestimate their ability. This is particularly true of skills where accurate, timely feedback is not available. Interpersonal skills are a good example of such activities. In business situations people rarely tell managers exactly how they feel about them. As a result, managers often get an exaggerated impression of their own effectiveness. As we will see later in the book, this is one of the real benefits of 360-

degree feedback. On the golf course, in contrast, golfers are almost always aware of their competence or lack of it. "Golf is a square shooter," writes John Updike. "In the sound of the hit and the flight of the ball it tells us unflinchingly how we are doing, and we are rarely doing well."

Implicit Learning in Golf

Implicit learning is the oldest, most pervasive form of learning, so it is not surprising that it takes place in golf. Many youngsters acquire their first swings by imitating the moves made by another person. Although they sometimes go on to take formal lessons, the rhythm and tempo acquired in their early years often stays with them. It seems unlikely one could move directly from unconscious incompetence to unconscious competence without going through a program of formal instruction and practice. Golfers may, of course, be self-taught, but they would have found their own source of instruction and set up their own feedback systems. Larry Nelson, who now plays on the Senior PGA Tour, claims to have learned to play by reading Hogan's *Modern Fundamentals of Golf,* shooting 70 nine months after he started! But his story is exceptional; most successful players have had one or more teachers. Some mature golfers claim that they find their tempo improved if they spend time watching the pros with good tempo. Often the women professionals offer the best examples, as they usually swing the club more slowly than the men do. Indeed, rhythm and tempo, because of their holistic quality—they disappear under analysis—may be best acquired through imitation. The more technical aspects of the swing are probably not—watching golf is not a substitute for formal instruction and timely, specific feedback.

Putting may offer the greatest opportunity for implicit learning, and skills acquired in that way may be robust under pressure. In an intriguing experiment, a psychologist allowed one group of novice golfers to learn putting through a combination of instruction and practice (explicit learning), while another group learned only implicitly.* The fastest improvement in performance came from the explicit learning group: the instructions seemed to help them focus on the key variables in putting. This finding, that explicit instructions accelerate the acquisition of motor skills by helping learners focus their attention on the key variables, is a fairly typical finding in psychology. After several sessions, however, both the explicit and implicit learners performed at roughly the same levels. As one might expect, however, the explicit learners knew a great deal more about the theory of *what* they ought to be doing.

Choking

Each group was then placed under stress by being told that a professional golfer was evaluating their performances and that an incentive would be tied to the results. Under these conditions, the performance of the implicit learners continued to improve, while the explicit learners (including the control group) "choked" and experienced a significant drop in performance. So the conclusion from this experiment is that when it comes to putting, a fairly simple motor activity, implicit learning is possible, and although it may be slow, it does result in the development of robust skills. Explicit instruction can accelerate the process, but the skills acquired are not as robust under pressure.

The experimenters concluded that choking resulted when, under pressure, what should have been automatic processes became conscious. This is probably what happened to Greg Norman at the 1996 Masters, and it seems to plague many players who get too mechanical with their games. From a systems perspective, what they are trying to do is run the system using "small, fast" variables (their conscious minds) instead of trusting their bodies, the "big, slow" factors. It seems that under stress, players try to use the conscious mode because of the greater accuracy it appears to allow

*R. S. W. Masters, "Knowledge, Knerves and Know-how: The Role of Explicit Versus Implicit Knowledge in the Breakdown . . . ," *British Journal of Psychology* 83 (Aug. 1992): 343.

them, but this interferes with the more basic unconscious moves required to sustain the whole dynamic.

I believe that a very similar dynamic exists in many managerial activities. The explicit techniques taught to young managers in the business schools, with their emphasis on logic and rationality, emphasize intellectual smarts and the importance of being "right." Strategies presented in abstract words and symbols are often difficult to disagree with under the best of circumstances, but when raising questions challenges the presenter's intelligence, the chances of having a good dialogue are low. In addition, a lockstep adherence to analytical routines can often interfere with the ability of a manager to behave authentically. And, as will become clear in the chapters that follow, authenticity is the central requirement for effective leadership.

Learning in Management

In the workplace, on-the-job learning, preferably under the tutelage of an expert, has been the predominant form of development ever since the origin of cooperative action. We see the process at work in the medieval craftsmen guilds and the various apprenticeship schemes that followed them. But the method goes back much further in time. Indeed, its evolutionary roots probably go back to our primate ancestors and those of the handful of other mammals that have learned the use of tools through the imitation of the behavior of others. In business organizations, prior to the emergence of internal company programs and business schools, it was the primary method of transmitting knowledge. The result of this process, however, is that a great deal of know-how remains tacit and locked up in the minds of workers. Traditions can be transmitted reliably, but behavior and performance may be difficult to change. It was to tackle this problem that Frederick Taylor formulated his principles of scientific management. In his view, the task of making workers' tacit knowledge explicit was one of the duties that had to be assumed by management.

Although Taylor described "intimate cooperation" as the hallmark of scientific management, he never specified how this integration was to be achieved in the workplace. His emphasis was always on analysis, never on synthesis. He was insistent that, with few exceptions, no worker at any level could understand the scientific complexities that underpinned his own work activities—only a scientific manager could do that. His engineer colleague, Henry Towne, in the foreword to *Shop Management* put the nub of scientific management bluntly:

> [T]he best manager is he who organizes the forces under his control that each individual shall work at his best efficiency and shall be compensated accordingly. Dr. Taylor has demonstrated conclusively that, to accomplish this, it is essential to segregate the *planning* of work from its *execution;* to employ for the former trained experts possessing the right mental equipment, and for the latter men having the right physical equipment for their respective tasks and being receptive of expert guidance in their performance.*

As we shall see in chapter 15, in modern contexts, only when planning is *not* separated from doing can we get true cooperation on the shop floor.

Once one moves away from the shop floor, however—as the variables being managed become more abstract and the processes get fuzzier—the whole approach gets into trouble. Taylor's separation of thinking from doing was gradually extended all the way up the corporation, culminating in the strategic planning mania of the 1970s, when the formulation of corporate strategy became almost completely separated from its implementation. Concepts were everything—knowledge of the operational details was considered to be inessential. Young, bright planners, who had never met a payroll, made grizzled veterans jump through hoops in the preparation of paper plans that could never be implemented. It was the head-down theory of knowledge gone berserk—nothing the "body" of the corporation knew or did was accepted as valid—everything was examined, reduced to numbers, and redesigned

---

Shop Management, p. 10, original emphasis.

for conscious implementation one step at a time. Little effort was made by academics to understand how strategy making and implementation really worked in practice, and the planners did not have any relevant experience they could turn to as a guide. The assumption was that the rational, analytical approach, the head-down model, was inherently superior. As Henry Mintzberg has pointed out, however, we now know better:

> [S]trategy making is an immensely complex process involving the most sophisticated, subtle, and at times subconscious of human cognitive and social processes. We know it must draw on all kinds of informational inputs, many of them nonquantifiable and accessible to strategists who are connected to the details rather than detached from them. We know that the dynamics of the context have repeatedly defied any efforts to force the process into a predetermined schedule or onto a predetermined track . . . the process requires insight, creativity, and synthesis, the very things that formalization discourages.*

Successful strategy making, like successful golf, is a complex mix of thinking and doing, explicit and implicit learning, and improvement in each activity has to be understood via a cycle that combines both processes. To paraphrase Henry Mintzberg, doing follows thinking, implementation follows formulation, as the left foot follows the right: we can step off on either foot, but we will have to make repeated use of each if we are to progress effectively.

The Gulf Between Consciousness and Unconsciousness

There is a great gulf between the upper and lower pair of quadrants of the cycle, the conscious and the unconscious regions. It is the golfer's (and manager's) counterpart to the Cartesian split between brain and body and, I think, the principal source of the most serious problems in the teaching and practice of both golf

---

*The Rise and Fall of Strategic Planning, p. 227.

and management. For both golf and management, particularly management, are usually taught using the words and symbols of the explicit learning process. This creates a conscious competence, where practitioners have an excellent idea of *what* they ought to be doing but little idea of *how* to do it.

Effective performance demands an unconscious competence, and the implementation modules of the explicit learning process used in the teaching of both golf and management have not been able to address this challenge effectively. In management in particular, implementation has far too often been relegated to a box or an arrow on a chart, symbols that ignore the quantum jump required across the conscious/unconscious dimension. In golf, unconscious competence requires that the verbal and symbolic analysis and instruction of the upper two quadrants be forgotten completely. The golfer must rely on the automated moves repetitively drilled into the body, and the role of the thinking mind is only to start and stop these processes.

Timothy Gallwey has written one of the best descriptions of this gulf between the conscious and unconscious regions and the sometimes schizophrenic dynamic that is played out in the mind of every golfer. In his well-known book, *The Inner Game of Golf,* Gallwey set out to counter the bias that institutional education has toward conceptual (that is, head-down) learning at the expense of what he calls "natural learning." He named the explicit and implicit aspects of our minds Self 1 and Self 2, respectively:

A major breakthrough in my understanding of the problem of control of mind and body came when, as a tennis instructor, I became aware of a constant commentary going on inside my head as I played. . . . I was surprised to discover that there seemed to be two identities within me. . . . I observed that the one doing the talking, whom I named Self 1, thought he knew all about how to play and was supervising Self 2, the one who had to hit the ball. In fact, Self 1 not only gave Self 2 instructions, but criticized him for past errors, warned him of probable future ones, and harangued him whenever he made a mistake. . . . I noticed that when I had more confidence in my ability to hit a shot, there was a corresponding decrease in instructions from Self 1, and that Self 2 would perform amazingly well without him. . . . In short, I found that Self 1—the verbalizing, thought-producing self—is a lousy boss when it comes to control of the body's muscle system. When Self 2—the body itself—is allowed control, the quality of performance, the level of enjoyment and rate of learning are all improved.*

One could make the same systemic point to expound the virtues of an empowered workforce over one controlled by instructions from top management. This topic will be addressed directly in chapter 15.

Summary

This chapter started with Benjamin Bloom's three phases of learning and then outlined an idealized learning matrix through which a learner moves from unconscious incompetence to unconscious competence. Implicit and explicit learning describe two routes a learner may follow. Implicit learning—learning without awareness of what is being learned—is the way in which we acquire our most basic behaviors and habits. Behavior developed in this way is robust and resistant to change. Explicit learning as exemplified in formal education makes extensive use of words and symbols. Feedback loops of different kinds play an important role in the transitions from quadrant to quadrant of the model. The power of the model is that it emphasizes the difference between conscious and unconscious modes of operation. Conceptual change can be made relatively easily during the conscious phases of the explicit learning cycle, but this does not necessarily result in changed behaviors that are robust under stress. The challenge faced by explicit learners is that of implementation. They may learn *what* to do fairly quickly, but *how* to do it remains a problem—how are

---

*Gallwey, pp. 18–19.

complex moves integrated in space and time? For unless competences are made unconscious, they tend to break down when under pressure. In golf, this results in the phenomenon of choking, which, I believe, can be found in many other activities, including management.

No. 9

Remembering the Future

Par-4	325 yards

You can't do it unless you've imagined it first.
—PETER JACOBSEN, QUOTED IN DOWNS MACRURY,
GOLFERS ON GOLF

Images are not pictures in the head, but plans for obtaining information from potential environments.
—ULRIC NEISSER, COGNITION AND REALITY

"I never hit a shot, even in practice," wrote Jack Nicklaus, ". . . without having a very sharp, in-focus picture of it in my head. It's like a color movie. First I 'see' the ball where I want it to finish, nice and white and sitting high up on the bright green grass. Then the scene quickly changes and I 'see' the ball going there: its path, trajectory, and shape, even its behavior on landing. Then there's a sort of fade-out, and the next scene shows me making the kind of swing that will turn the previous images into reality. Only at the end of this short, private, Hollywood spectacular do I select a club and step up to the ball.*

Jack Nicklaus's description of the pervasive role of imagery in his game is probably the best-known endorsement of the role of imagination in golf. And his use of comprehensive imagery even

*Golf My Way, p. 79.

in practice is reminiscent of Greg Louganis's emphasis on perfection during diving practice described in chapter 6. Nicklaus starts with an image of the desired outcome of the shot and then runs the film backward to cover intermediate goals, ending up with images of the chains of cause and effect needed to produce the desired results. There is solid evidence that such imagery can improve performance in many fields, including that of management. Indeed, the past decade has been marked by a sharp rise in the use of imagery by elite performers, and the presence of a sports psychologist seems to be essential in many sporting activities.

Images and Action

In the last chapter I outlined a framework for *thinking* about learning that stressed the importance of feedback as we move around the cycle of learning. But the learning cycle framework still did not really touch the issue of implementation. The problem was described, but not grasped. How do we *do* anything intentionally? How do we move physically? How, for example, do we use our hands to reach out and grasp something? The evidence from behavioral science is that *all action is accomplished through acts of imagination—imagination is embodied.*

All voluntary acts are learned. Our capacity for intentional physical movements develops from the host of involuntary motions we make when we are babies. Under conditions of immediate and specific feedback, we rapidly link cause and effect, moving swiftly from groping to grasping. The feedback we get from our actions consists of images, pictures, and feelings, and individual actions quickly become associated with specific images. As we mature we learn to use this remembered feedback, the pictures and feelings, to create the actions that then re-create those images.

So if I want to pick up a coffee cup with my hand, all I need to do is form an image of how my hand will look and feel grasping the cup and then "release" the hand to perform that action. My brain does not tell my hand what to do. It just releases a repertoire of well-rehearsed moves. If successful, I will be rewarded with the actual experience of the pictures and feelings that I had previously imagined. The identical process is used during the mental re-hearsal of athletic movements, and it has been well established by sports physiologists that the imagination of a physical act actually produces low levels of firing in the relevant muscles.

Thus, although it operates beneath the conscious, verbal level at which goals and intentional actions are discussed, imagery appears to be central to our ability to act. The following diagram captures some of these aspects of implementation. I call it a "do loop."

The Do Loop

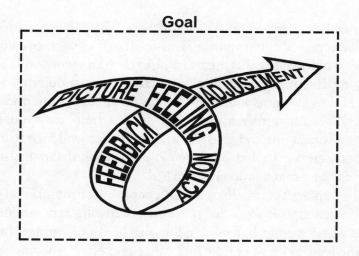

To keep things simple, the diagram shows an isolated goal. In practice goals are always part of a hierarchy of objectives, ranging from slow-changing lifetime ambitions to simple physical move-ments. They may also be part of a sequence of goals. The do loop with its curling trajectory reminds us that acts are never isolated: all action is part of a feedback loop. In this stylized representation, action begins with images, pictures, and feelings derived from a goal. These images evoke the complex actions, the results of which are fed back to the actor for adjustment, if necessary. The ability to articulate in words, to say what one has done, is a process that takes place higher up in the system and usually *after* the action.

Imagery in Golf

The do loop lies at the core of deliberate practice, and it can be applied directly to golf. My golf coach, for example, divides the swing into a sequence of many different positions. Each position is a goal: it has to be held correctly statically and checked by feedback either from the coach or by me looking in a mirror. Then each correct position and move has to be felt and the feeling stored in memory, from whence it can be recalled as a desirable image of the future. Each move is rehearsed, adjusted if necessary, felt, stored, and recalled for performance. Then the positions are chunked into units and chained together into the sequences. One looks for a "handle," a feeling that can set in motion multiple actions. The images of the swing slowly develop into a series of complex feelings, otherwise known as "swing thoughts," with each one being triggered by the feeling before it. Of course, swing thoughts aren't concepts; they are images—pictures and feelings. Gradually the stop-action positions are linked together into a smooth flow, and their practice becomes habitual; if we have gone through the process correctly, we become unconsciously competent.

The picture-feeling-action sequence can also be applied to a practice swing, which is a minirehearsal, a simulation, of the images and action required to produce a given outcome. Of course, the feedback during a practice swing is not quite as rich as that from the actual swing, but its proximity to the actual swing helps to update the images required for that swing. In addition, of course, if the practice swing doesn't feel right, the player can still make adjustments.

Among the top tour professionals, whether it was in practice or in competition, in prospect or in recall, performance is intimately associated with the capacity for imagination. Consider these quotes from the study by sports psychologists McCaffrey and Orlick mentioned in chapter 6:*

> When things are going well, my imagery is crystal clear and I do visualization everywhere. I feel the execution of the shot, see the target area, visualize the entire sequence, go through it, and expect it to go into the hole.

> My best all-time round, I visualized it and then played it. I visualized the night before, the morning, and then let it happen. Feel it happen and then do it. When I am playing well the feel stays with me. I can practice less and the mental part and the visualizing maintains the feel. The importance is to feel each shot and visualize it.

> My best ever eighteen holes was eight birdies in a row and that game helps my visualization for recalling that feeling, particularly when I'm down and not making a lot of birdies, I'll bring that feeling back up.

> I remember shots that were played at critical times during certain events. I can recall them with extreme clarity and bring back the emotions and the situation. The recall helps in other situations, and you can certainly draw upon that. That is why good players who have achieved success go on and have more successes, because they do in fact feed upon those.

While Jack Nicklaus's quote at the beginning of this chapter stressed the visual element of imagery, these quotes emphasize the feeling aspect of golf imagery. Effective images can be both pictures and feelings and include all the senses. Indeed, Percy Boomer, in a happy phrase, once described golf as a game that depended upon "remembered feelings." The quotes from the professionals conjure up the image of positive, self-reinforcing cycles where good images lead to good outcomes that then supply fur-

---

*Top tour professionals quoted in McCaffrey and Orlick, pp. 261–62.

ther good images for the future. In a virtuous cycle, a good integrated image (picture and feeling) is followed by a good shot that
sustains and reinforces the image, making it easier to produce a
similar outcome the next time. As a result, performance improves. Our shorthand description of the pleasant feelings that accompany such a virtuous cycle is "confidence."

Confidence-destroying, vicious cycles run in the opposite direction: fuzzy images are followed by poor shots. This further blurs
the imagination and interferes with our ability to produce good
pictures and feelings. A player's capacity to recall positive images
from better times would seem to be an important component in
preventing a vicious circle from perpetuating itself. The process is
one of selecting the best images from the past and, by using them
as goals, taking effective action in the present. As we shall see in
chapter 14, good players (and their coaches) are always on the
lookout for triggers that might start virtuous circles, while avoiding those that might initiate vicious ones.

The interviews by McCaffrey and Orlick covered the topics of
goal setting and imagery with touring and club pros and compared their responses with those of Olympic medalists:

TOP TOUR PROFESSIONALS	CLUB PROFESSIONALS	OLYMPIC MEDALISTS
Goal Setting		
Goals were very clearly defined, for example, daily goals, practice goals, tournament goals, yearly goals, and long-term goals.	Goals were not clearly defined, nor were they set on a daily basis. For example, they do not have predetermined long-term goals or clearly defined practice goals.	Goals were very clearly defined and applied on a consistent basis: e.g., daily goals for training, for compe-tition, and for long-term goals.

	IMAGERY	
Mental imagery was used on a daily basis for a variety of purposes, for example, to prepare for practice, for shot making, for making corrections, for tournament preparation, for tournament play, and for building confidence.	The club pros recognized the value of imagery but did not practice or utilize it on a daily basis, nor did they have the quality or control of imagery as did the other groups.	Mental imagery was used on a daily basis for a variety of purposes: for example, preparation for training, skill improvement, corrections, imagining success, competition preparation, etc.
	TOURNAMENT FOCUS PLAN	
They approached each tournament with a focus plan for best play. The ideal mental state was described as being "in the zone," which reflected a depth of concentration and total connection to their task.	They recognized where their focus should be and can describe detailed focusing procedures, but they rarely enter a tournament with that focus plan, practice it, or execute it in the tournament.	They have discovered what focus works best for them, have a focus plan for implementing it in competition, and practice holding that focus in training. The best focus was viewed as one that allowed an absolute connection to the task.

Excerpted from Nadeane McCaffrey and Terry Orlick, "Mental Factors Related to Excellence Among Top Professional Golfers," *International Journal of Sports Psychology* 20 (1989): 256–78.

Imagery in the Corporate World

There is solid evidence from the corporate world that supports the findings of McCaffrey and Orlick that the success of top golfers and athletes depends heavily on their capacity to visualize—picture and feel—both their goals and the means for attaining them. It seems that cultures of top-performing corporations help their people focus, commit, and persist in their work. In their popular book *Built to Last,* James Collins and Jerry Porras report on a study in which they examined matched pairs of companies drawn from the same industry. One member of each pair was selected because of its premier position in its industry and its capacity for sustained performance over time. This did not mean that their stories were of seamless success. All companies, like all golfers, stumble, sometimes badly, but these companies seemed to have an unusual resiliency, an ability to bounce back from adversity. These special, elite institutions were designated as visionary companies. The comparison companies were each in the same industry as their visionary counterparts but had less stellar histories. They were good, but not outstanding—players, but not champions.

Thus, in a sample of eighteen pairs of firms, Hewlett-Packard was contrasted with Texas Instruments, Marriott with Howard Johnson, Procter & Gamble with Colgate, Walt Disney with Columbia, and so on. Collins and Porras found that the key differences between the companies were in the "softer" qualitative aspects of management, a difference they tried to capture in their descriptor "visionary."

When it came to goals, the visionary companies went well beyond verbal and numeric objectives to embrace visceral goals that engaged the passions of their people. In a memorable phrase, Collins and Porras named these "big hairy audacious goals":

Visionary companies may appear straitlaced and conservative to outsiders, but they're not afraid to make bold commitments to "Big Hairy Audacious Goals" (BHAGs). Like climbing a big mountain or going to the moon, a BHAG may be daunting and perhaps risky, but the adventure, excitement, and challenge of it grabs people in the gut, gets their juices flowing, and creates immense forward momentum. Visionary companies have judiciously used BHAGs to stimulate progress and blast past the comparison companies at crucial points in history.[*]

There are, of course, numbers and words that may be associated with BHAGs, but the important ingredient seems to be their power to evoke compelling images, pictures, and feelings in the minds of those who share them.

The conclusions of Collins and Porras echo the results of Chambliss's study of swimmers covered in chapter 6—excellent performers in both business and sports would seem to be *qualitatively* different from their less successful colleagues.

Embodied Imagination

Jack Nicklaus's description of his experience of "going to the movies" is supported by what is currently known about human perception. The evidence is that when we use visual imagery, our brains recruit the same processes and structures used for perception and memory. In our brains, one of the early destinations of input from our eyes is the so-called visual buffer, a variety of structures where the spatial relationships between the stimuli are preserved. Although the analogy is extremely superficial, the buffer functions a bit like a movie screen, where "pictures" can be held and inspected while their content is processed further. The analogy is superficial because our eyes do not function like cameras and there is no one "inside" to look at the screen, but it does reflect our feeling that using our imagination is "as if" we were going to the movies. The pictures on the "screen" of the visual buffer need not come from outside—they can be retrieved at will from memory and projected there. Images can also be used in combinations to project totally imaginary scenes that may never have ex-

[*]*Built to Last*, p. 9.

isted in reality. This means that we can run the images either forward from the past or backward from the future. And by running the images backward from desirable futures, we can actually make those futures more likely to occur. David Ingvar, a Swedish neurologist, describes this capacity of the brain as our ability to create "memories of the future."

Like memories of the past, these images can be summoned at will and reviewed in great detail. We can rehearse our plans and change them as required. If one route to a desirable future is blocked, we can switch our attention to another. Our memories of the future seem capable of "pulling" us toward them by acting as filters. The images determine what we pay attention to in the ongoing flux of everyday existence, allowing us to extract some information and ignore other data. Without these filters our attention would become hopelessly divided among many competing stimuli. On the screen of our imagination we gather past, present, and future, allowing us to take concrete action in the present to use the best from the past in service of creating a desirable future.

Implications for Goal Setting

While the importance of goal setting has been confirmed across a wide range of human activities, the central importance of imagery—pictures and feelings—has not always been emphasized sufficiently. Typically, researchers in the behavioral sciences emphasize the need for clear, challenging goals but pay little attention to the *form* in which they are held. The implication is that verbal and numerical goals function just as well as goals that can be pictured and felt. Indeed, this is what one often finds in many businesses—multiple verbal and numeric goals, buttressed by monetary incentives. But without imagery that engages embodied minds, individually and collectively, how can such goals focus activities, gain commitment, and enhance competence?

Imagination—our ability to retain and recall pictures and feelings of action—is the medium of memory and the vehicle for our visions of the future. It is the primary catalyst for our taking of effective intentional action; it is at the core of what we mean by will. The implications for the managers and golfers are clear:

- *Goal setting may start out as an intellectual task, but to be effective, it has to result in visceral change.*
- *Goals set using only words and numbers are unlikely to be effective* as catalysts for changing behavior because they do not engage the embodied mind.
- *Goals have to be felt*—tasted, touched, sensed—if they are to act as compelling targets for action.
- *Goals have to be broken down into their elements, the means for their achievement,* and each of these must be associated with compelling images before they are chunked and chained together.
- *The process seems to work across all the scales* of human systems—from individuals to companies and societies.
- *The richest source of compelling images is from the past,* in the experience of individuals and groups and the stories they use to convey that experience.
- When used as goals, *compelling images in combination with timely, specific feedback can be used to improve performance.*

Summary

This chapter has focused on the primary role of images—pictures and feelings—in initiating action. The idea that imagination is embodied within every one of us is a radical departure from the head-down theory of knowledge with its romantic, "head in the clouds" notion of the role of imagination. In the head-down view, imagination is a process that takes place outside and removed from the hard box of logic. From this perspective, imagery is the special province of artists, poets, and other creative people, who are not concerned with practical affairs. Occasionally it can help others break "out of the box," but it is seen as a separate process. In an embodied theory of knowledge, imagination is woven through every level of our entire existence, both mental and physical. It is the mediator of perception, underpinning our notions of rationalism and reality. Indeed, it is through using imagery that we focus our attention on the aspects of reality that are meaningful to us. Goals set using words and numbers have to be turned into images—pictures and feelings—if they are to be made compelling.

No. 10

Practice and Performance

| Par-4 | 325 yards |

Good golfers train *by analyzing and thinking. They* play *by feeling and seeing.*

— JIM FLICK, ON GOLF

Analysis and abstraction we must and do make in the most everyday conduct of our affairs; but when we mistake the elements for the concrete we destroy the usefulness of the analysis. Executive decisions are preceded by analysis . . . but the decision itself is synthetic.

— CHESTER BARNARD, FUNCTIONS OF THE EXECUTIVE

It was still dark when I arrived at the downtown corporate office of Hugh Russel Inc. early one Monday morning in February, with the city held fast in the depths of a Canadian winter. I recognized by sight the bulky figure sitting in the lobby. He was the managing partner of a prominent investment banking house, and as I approached him he rose to greet me. Unaware that I was a humble financial planner at that time, he handed me a sheet of white paper. "I am here as a courtesy to management," he told me. "My clients have authorized a bid for the entire common equity of this company. When the market opens this morning we will be offering eighteen dollars a share. Good morning to you."

The investment banker's clients were the Belzberg family from Vancouver, a well-known group of "greenmailers" at that time. Greenmailers were short-term financial speculators who bought shares in vulnerable public companies, trying to put them "in play." They would then turn around and sell their stakes at a profit either to management or to any higher bidder. Many intimidated management teams paid off the greenmailers, hence the derivation of the term. In our case the Belzberg bid put our management-controlled public company on the auction block, and management found itself outgunned by a number of apparently well-heeled bidders. Within a month we were acquired in a highly leveraged buyout on the eve of what was to prove one of the sharper recessions of the era. Our acquirer, the eldest son of a family of legendary wealth and business acumen, turned out to have little access to his personal wealth and no support from his family. Indeed, in making the deal, he had further alienated both his father and siblings, and in its aftermath they all fought ferociously with one another. Fortunately for our survival as a team, our acquirer had no management resources of his own—we were "it." Within a year the corporation would be insolvent, but owing our bankers so much money that it was their problem, not just ours. We went into the deal with four thousand people and $700 million in revenues and emerged three years later with new ownership, eight hundred people, and $220 million in revenues. These three years were also to provide one of the finest learning opportunities for an entire team of managers.

Learning Under Fire

Military people contend that a week on the battlefield is worth a year on the parade ground. Although the two experiences are not direct substitutes for each other, there is no doubt that learning "under fire" is greatly accelerated.

This chapter looks at why this is so in both management and golf. I suggest that the primary reason must be the great clarity of goals and priorities, their ease of measurement, and the speed and specificity of feedback on one's actions. Not to mention, of course, especially on the battlefield, the threat of negative outcomes! Certainly this was our experience during the tumult of the next three years. Almost overnight (actually it took about six weeks) we went from a classic finance-driven, management-controlled conglomerate to a cash-starved wreck. Our shareholders and bankers, who had previously been invisible, now became harsh taskmasters and vocal critics. The media played up our problems and those of our owners with a series of sensational reports that alerted the unions and governments in all jurisdictions to our plight. Our predicament became a talking point throughout the industry, a conversational staple for our customers, suppliers, and competitors. Job offers flowed into our best employees, who were understandably concerned about our apparently imminent demise. Nervous suppliers threatened to cut off our access to credit. We used to not hear from all these audiences from year to year, but now our performance was being scrutinized on a weekly basis in multiple dimensions.

The old hierarchical structure faded into the background as nineteen task forces addressed a host of unfamiliar problems. Our acquirer's moribund steel fabrication businesses had been thrown into the deal, and the management team suddenly found itself engaged in the construction industry with troubled projects all over North America. Comprising people drawn from throughout the old organization, these task forces cut across all the old functional silos and operating divisions. Information that had been previously held "in confidence" at corporate headquarters was now given to these task forces, and they were instructed to come back with recommendations for urgent action. There were no committees and few forms. Our mantra became "Cash is king" as we single-mindedly did what we had to do to dig the corporation out of the deep hole into which it had fallen. A quick triage divided operations into three categories: keepers, sellers, and junk. We would keep and protect the keepers at all costs, for they would become the kernels of the new business. The sellers were good businesses that were either off strategy (what's "on" and "off" strategy changes radically in troubled times) or capable of generating large chunks of cash on disposal. The "junk" consisted of everything else, a polyglot of assets and operations that could not generate positive operational cash flows and would be difficult to sell. Much of the junk would have to be "warehoused" and disposed of over time, using a variety of inducements for buyers and renters.

Under these conditions of sharp focus and fast cycle time, learning takes place at impressive speeds. Feedback is fast and specific; you take action and very quickly know whether you have been successful or not. And if it hasn't worked, you try something else. Topics that had previously been trivial now became critical. The management of cash flow was elevated to a science as we zoomed in on the nuances of receivables and payables. We had to hit daily cash targets at the bank and, honing our skills daily, became experts in the forecasting and control of "float," that magical gap in time between the cutting of a check and its presentation to one's bank. Our skill became a tiny "edge" that was worth a lot of money. At the same time, we revamped the entire corporate reporting system to address multiple audiences, each of whom wanted its information presented in very different ways. Sophisticated spreadsheet models allowed us to produce rapidly any projections based on any assumptions. These management techniques were enormously important, but while they could help us travel in a given direction more efficiently, they could not help us decide which directions we should be going in. This demanded the use of many skills that we had previously been only dimly aware of.

In the old finance-driven conglomerate, the organization's stakeholders, at least on the surface, appeared to have common interests—shareholders wanted more profit and growth, bankers wanted to earn interest on their loans and fees from financing deals, customers wanted lower prices, employees wanted more money, and so on. As long as we produced more of everything, the stakeholders would be happy. Now the stakeholders were hopelessly split. The bankers wanted their money back—now—although there was much disagreement within the bank over how best to do this. Some wanted to call the loans immediately, others were prepared to work with us for a while. The patriarch of the acquiring family wanted to teach his wayward son a lesson and made his life as difficult as possible. The siblings wanted to avoid financial losses while pursuing their personal vendettas. Clouds of accountants, attorneys, consultants, and advisers of many stripes, all of whom had personal agendas of one kind or another, swarmed around these players. If all of them were to pursue their own interests separately, the entire financial structure of the corporation would collapse. We spent our lives in meetings and found out fast that there was a critical need to be able to "read" an audience—that is, to be able to penetrate behind the words, the positions, and the postures to understand the real issues. This required not only a great sensitivity to body language and the nuances of communication, but also the development and use of a broad network of contacts to yield multiple perspectives on an issue and the positions of the various players. We found ourselves having long, open conversations with many "trusted advisers" who would be able to "move" their clients in various directions. Premeeting meetings became essential if we were to navigate successfully through the treacherous waters of the actual meetings.

Gradually we began to build a ragtag coalition of disparate interests. We could use our key contacts to disseminate the real facts about the situation, and as the various players came to realize what their options were, we could develop a consensus for joint action. Slowly a vision emerged of an outcome that might be in everybody's long-run best interest. At first it was vague, no more than a hope that all the players would get out with their skins intact. Players continually threatened to bolt the young coalition, grandstanding either to improve their own positions or to weaken those of others. We had to work hard behind the scenes to get people back onside through a combination of appeals to the greater good and apocalyptic speculation on what the bankers might do if the consensus fell apart. In an erratic, wandering way, a strategy began to emerge that would get everyone out of the mess. As we pulled in more expert advisers, it seemed that a sophisticated, tax-effective scheme would see the bank get their money back (well, more or less), the family not have their personal guarantees called upon, and individuals be able to go their separate ways. Under new corporate ownership, suppliers would be paid, customers would be served, competitors would be thwarted, and the business would be saved!

Over a period of three years, we eventually produced order out of chaos. And in the confused, jumbled process we discovered that we had learned the essence of leadership.

The Essence of Leadership

Until the 1950s, the term *management* was used to cover all the organizational activities that a senior person might engage in. Typical management principles at that time were summarized in management writer Lyndall Urwick's ugly but memorable acronym POSDCORB—planning, organizing, staffing, directing, coordinating, reporting, and budgeting. With the rise in prestige and influence of the business schools, however, the meaning of the word began to change. Catalyzed by the burgeoning consultant industry, "management" became identified with a rational, analytical activity that relied on calculation and technique to enhance the performance of organizations.

In the 1970s, in the aftermath of multiple failures of these techniques in both business and government, many people began to question whether management and leadership were the same activity. Harvard Business School professor Abraham Zaleznik wrote a seminal article in 1977 entitled "Managers and Leaders: Are They Different?" Zaleznik's conclusion was that they differed fundamentally in their worldviews, arguing that managerial goals are passive and impersonal, arising out of the necessities of the existing business rather than desires of people. Managers work to limit choices and reduce risk in pursuit of these goals. Their relationships with people are cool and are dominated by the roles that people play in the overall process. Managers see themselves as conservators and regulators of the existing state of affairs.

In contrast, leaders are active and personal in their goals, shaping ideas, changing the way people think about what is desirable, possible, and necessary. They see their role as opening up options and encouraging risk taking. Their relationships with people are intense and personal, often evoking feelings of love and hate. Far from being conservators of the system, leaders see themselves as creating something new and different.

Zaleznik's intellectual heir at Harvard is John Kotter, who through long, careful study of managers and leaders in a number of organizations has amplified on the differences between the two:

MANAGEMENT	LEADERSHIP
Planning and Budgeting—establishing detailed steps and timetables for achieving needed results, and then allocating resources necessary to make that happen.	Establishing Direction—developing a vision of the future, often the distant future, and strategies for producing the changes needed to achieve the vision.
Organizing and Staffing—establishing some structure for accomplishing plan requirements, staffing that structure with individuals, delegating responsibility and authority for carrying out the plan, providing policies and procedures to help guide people, and creating methods or systems to monitor implementation.	Aligning People—communicating the direction by words and deeds to all those whose cooperation may be needed so as to influence the creation of teams and coalitions that understand the vision and strategies and accept their validity.
Controlling and Problem Solving—monitoring results vs. plan in some detail, identifying deviations, and then planning and organizing to solve these problems.	Motivating and Inspiring—energizing people to overcome major political, bureaucratic, and resource barriers to change by satisfying very basic but often unfulfilled human needs.

Produces a degree of predictability and order and has the potential to consistently produce key results expected by various stakeholders.	Produces change, often to a dramatic degree, and has the potential to produce extremely useful change (e.g., new products that customers want).148

John Kotter, *A Force for Change* (New York: The Free Press, 1990), p. 6 (shortened slightly).

From Kotter's distinction between the two activities, it is quite clear that what our management team learned during those tumultuous years was mostly about leadership rather than management. The lessons in leadership did not invalidate or replace what we knew about management so much as they allowed us to go beyond management—to handle situations that could not be approached using only conventional analysis and rationality. Indeed, we needed those management techniques more than ever; we could not have survived without plans and budgets, organization and problem solving. The disciplines of management were still there, but they seemed to be operating on a "lower" level than in the pretakeover times. In the earlier days, as an independent public company, the paraphernalia of modern finance, return on equity and cost of capital, seemed to hang over us—we were servants and they were master. Now, in these turbulent times the relationship had turned through 180 degrees—we were masters and the tools of management were our servants.

Despite our dire predicament, the task forces and all who came into contact with them experienced a strange sense of elation. In our weakness we found strength, in the madness logic could prevail: if we had owed the bank less money, we would have been in more trouble; if the shareholders had been more rational, we would have had less control. Adrift on a corporate wreck in a deep recession, we paradoxically felt that we could take charge of our own destiny. And a group of leaders emerged who would do just that.

How Leaders Learn

The role of talent in the development of leaders has been disputed as fiercely as that in sports, and the debate has evolved in broadly similar ways. Just as was the case in sports, "natural talent" ruled as an explanation for a long time: the view was that leaders were born, that their skills were innate or largely the result of very early experiences. The more recent view is that leaders are largely made—that early experiences do matter, but that the development of leadership skills can be greatly enhanced by later experiences. Indeed, the brief story I have told of how, in turbulent times, we as a group of managers learned to lead is quite typical. The findings of researchers at the Center for Creative Leadership on how leaders are developed are unequivocal:

> The essence of development is that diversity and adversity beat repetition any time. The more dramatic the change in skill demands, the more severe the personnel problems, the more the bottom line pressure, and the more sinuous and unexpected the turns in the road, the more opportunity there is for learning. Unappealing as they may seem, being shocked and pressured and having problems with other people teach most. For future executives, comfortable circumstances are hardly the road to the top.*

McCall, Lombardo, and Morrison identified three overlapping types of experience that seem to be most important to the development of effective executives:

1. Challenging assignments
2. Significant bosses
3. Hardships

*Morgan W. McCall Jr., Michael M. Lombardo, and Ann M. Morrison, *The Lessons of Experience* (Lexington, Mass.: Lexington Books, 1988) p. 58.

Challenging assignments covered a variety of challenges, each of which offered slightly different lessons. Project and task force assignments taught young managers to go beyond their technical specialties and to see situations from other people's points of view. They learned how to negotiate and deal with conflict. Switching from line to staff responsibilities often demanded that they take a strategic view of the business. Greenfield start-ups—operations started from scratch—placed an emphasis on getting priorities right and working with people over whom one had no authority. Business turnarounds were frequently cited in the development of executives as teaching the necessary toughness and the need to make difficult decisions. Big promotions to large jobs forced managers to learn how to delegate effectively and to motivate their subordinates.

Significant bosses could be either good or bad. The majority of the bosses cited—about two-thirds—were seen as good ones, who acted as role models for the executives. The other third were bad bosses who taught executives what not to do. Some of the most compelling teachers were flawed bosses, those with great strengths in combination with great weaknesses. Executives learned that strengths and weaknesses often go together in pairs, with the one being the other side of the coin from the other. A tough decisiveness, for example, may make one deaf to the views of others; self-confidence can lead to arrogance. Strength in one context may turn out to be weakness in another. Talented managers can derail precisely because they are so talented. We are all blends of strengths and weaknesses, but flawed bosses with their more extreme, volatile combinations seem to be the best teachers of the relationship between the two.

The last category of experience identified as important in the development of executives was hardships: crises and reversals of fortune. These included personal trauma (divorces and family breakups) career setbacks, changing jobs, business mistakes, and problems with subordinates. At the time of their occurrence, these events, like the physical setbacks experienced by sportsmen and -women, usually looked like unmitigated disasters. Often an executive's first response to hardship was to distance him- or herself from the situation. Given the complexity of cause and effect, this was relatively easy to do. Nevertheless, if the executive could accept responsibility, these events usually taught valuable lessons, often about the need for the learner to rebalance his or her activities in some way or another. Executives whose personal lives had collapsed realized that they had to readjust their priorities. Career setbacks often precipitated a much-needed pause for reflection on where they were going and what they had achieved and so on.

Why do all these events teach so powerfully? The short answer is their compelling focus and the timely, multidimensional feedback they offer to the actors involved. Managers found themselves in situations fraught with risk, where the consequences of success or failure were significant. Often the priorities were very clear, which allowed feedback to be specific, and the feedback on action taken was usually fast. When cause and effect can be identified, learning is rapid.

Practice and Performance in Golf

It's been a dreadful day on the course. My postgame analysis shows me that I pushed nearly every drive into the rough on the right. How did that happen? I *never* (well almost never) push drives on the practice tee. Why would I suddenly push them on the course? Then there was that bunker shot. It was a perfect lie, slightly uphill about twenty feet from the pin, and I blew it over the green. I can play that shot in my sleep. What happened? Come to think of it, why are conditions so much different on the course? How is it that we can strike the ball perfectly on the practice range and then mess things up so comprehensively on the course?

The consciousness-competence model developed in chapter 8 gives us some clues as to why this is so. During deliberate practice there is little pressure on us to perform in real time. We can be detached and analytical and take our time. We can break the swing down into its elements and rehearse them separately; we can chunk them together into various combinations. No one's counting our strokes, and we can play a shot over and over again until we get it right. It's rather like doing another iteration on a spreadsheet! But on the course it's quite different—we have to perform in real time. We can take as many practice swings as we like but are not allowed a practice shot. And it's our stepping up to the ball that makes the difference—that act takes us into real time: the shot counts. We can no longer be detached and analytical: the requirement is for integration, a synthesis of all our skills, a seamless integration of myriad moves. The club can no longer be a tool or instrument: it must be an extension of our bodies—of our minds. Thus, as we shift from practice to performance, the logic changes from an *instrumental* logic, where the rational intellect plans and dominates, to an *embodied* logic, where feelings and habits rule. In golf these two logics echo those of management and leadership found in organizations. The logics and the relationship between them can be seen most clearly in Jim Flick's contrast between the training ground and the playing ground:*

TRAINING GROUND	PLAYING GROUND
1. Conscious mind in control.	1. Subconscious mind, habits in control.
2. Respond like a mechanic, find out what's wrong, fix it.	2. Respond like an athlete, create positive image, do it.
3. Focus on individual parts of the swing.	3. Focus on the whole swing.
4. Swing mechanics oriented.	4. Target oriented.
5. Analyze.	5. Visualize.
6. Verbalize.	6. Feel.
7. Construct, develop.	7. Execute, play.

*Jim Flick, *On Golf* (New York: Villard Books, 1997), pp. 21–22.

The contents of this table are thought-provoking in their own right, as one ponders the relationship between these two dynamics and what is involved in switching between them on one's path to competence in the game. The concepts can be separated in columns and distinguished verbally, but clearly the relationship between them is dynamic and complex. Ideally it should be complementary, with the freedom of performance founded upon the discipline of practice. But there is plenty of scope for conflict: the analytical, mechanical features of practice may intrude upon performance, changing the tempo and breaking the rhythm. Conversely, serious mechanical faults may be offset for a while by a good "natural" swing, only to surface abruptly as the swing collapses.

Laid on top of the similarities developed between golf and management during the first nine chapters of this book, the implications are stunning. Does this mean that superior performance in a wide range of human skills, including golf and management, depends upon the interplay of similar dynamics? We have many names for their myriad different aspects at the generic level—detachment and commitment, thought and action, discipline and freedom. Can one generalize about their roles and transfer insights from the learning of one set of competencies to another? And what are the implications of this for managers and golfers? These questions will be answered in the chapters that follow, but in order to do that it's helpful to understand the dynamics common to all such activities—the dynamics of the ballistic mind.

Summary

In this chapter I contrasted practice and performance, first in management and then in golf. The narrower definition of management as a rational, technical activity seems to correspond to the equivalent of practice in golf. It is an analytical, deliberate procedure that focuses on the parts of the system, usually in a controlled environment. Its role is to build solid habits and sound disciplines that can then be employed in producing effective performance. Practice is not the same as performance. Effective performance in both golf and management depends upon another dynamic and takes place in a variety of environments. This mode of action integrates the basic routines and allows them to be selectively employed in creative improvisations. These creative improvisations permit the system flexibility in the face of stress and the production of acceptable results in a variety of circumstances.

No. 11

Concentrating the Ballistic Mind

Par-3	229 yards

Ninety percent of this game is half mental.
— JIM WOHLFORD, QUOTED IN GOLFERS ON GOLF

Saying that the "mind" commands the hand to move really doesn't buy you much of an explanation. It has taken us a while to realize, however, that such a statement is little better than saying, "God did it," when there is an earthquake.
— WILLIAM CALVIN, THE CEREBRAL SYMPHONY

The first half of this book outlined the nature of complex systems and used their characteristics as a lens through which to study golf and management. As we "played" the 10th "hole," the reader may have noticed that the stress was a little more on management and a little less on golf. As we head for home, this emphasis will be continued for the next few chapters. In their position (but not their layouts) Chapters 11, 12, and 13 can be usefully thought of as this book's counterpart to Augusta National's "Amen Corner," the same three challenging holes where fortunes are often made or lost on Sunday afternoon at the Masters. The chapters are challenging because as the emphasis shifts to management, we have to acknowledge that a large component of management behavior is verbal. So we need to take a closer look at the development of language and its roots in our evolutionary past, perspectives that will challenge the conventional wisdom of the nature of the human mind. This short chapter looks at some of the latest thinking about the structure and evolution of the brain and its origins in the movements of the body, the results of which I have called the ballistic mind.

The Ballistic Mind

It is well-known that our brains are physically separated into two halves, the left and the right, connected by a thick band of fibers. The brain functions of all individuals, however, even those who are ambidextrous, are divided unevenly between these two halves of the brain, with the left half dominating in over 90 percent of individuals. For the sake of unity of command, it would make sense for one hemisphere of the brain to dominate, but why is the left brain (which controls the right side of the body) predominant?

Neurobiologist William Calvin has developed an intriguing hypothesis about the origins of left-brain dominance. In his book, *The Throwing Madonna,* he proposes that right-handedness might have been selected for during the process of evolution because it allowed women to hunt while holding their babies in the left arms. Although our hearts are positioned centrally in our bodies, the beating portion is felt most strongly on the left. Babies are soothed by the regular sound of a heartbeat and are more placid if held on the left. Calvin goes on to suggest that the requirements for hunting by throwing objects at animals may also have led to particular kinds of neurological specialization in the left brain. A stone thrown at an animal is a ballistic object. That is, once it is thrown, no further changes in its trajectory can be made; everything has to be programmed in advance. Conceptually the situation is identical to that of a golf club at the top of the backswing—its path on the downswing is ballistic—feedback can no longer be used to make corrections in real time. As a result, Calvin contends, *the left brain became adept at sequencing movements in advance, and this ability was fine-tuned by feedback from every stone thrown.*

The part of the brain that performs this function is the premotor cortex, which specializes in setting up sequences of actions like putting a key into a lock, turning the doorknob, and pushing open the door. People with damage to this part of their brains can perform the movements individually but have trouble chaining them together into a fluent motion to create a "kinetic melody." When we take a practice swing, we are tuning up our premotor cortex, particularly the left one (in right-handers).

This tuning up of the premotor cortex takes place even if we don't actually move physically. Neurons in the premotor cortex fire when we just imagine swinging a golf club. Thus, purely mental rehearsals of the "kinetic melody" of the golf swing can strengthen our ability to perform it physically. Johnny Miller insists on the beneficial effects of playing entire tournament rounds in his head before stepping onto the course. In his book, *Flow*, Mihaly Csikszentmihalyi reports the case of a U.S. Air Force pilot who was imprisoned in North Vietnam for many years. He lost much of his health in a jungle camp, but on his release one of the first things he asked to do was play a round of golf. To the amazement of his fellow officers, he played a superb game, shooting 75, despite his emaciated condition. He explained to them that every day of his imprisonment he had imagined playing eighteen holes, selecting clubs shot by shot and systematically varying courses. This practice had preserved not only his sanity, but also his golfing skills!

Ballistic Moves

The key aspect of ballistic moves is that they have to be programmed in advance. Calvin suggests that once our brains had the neural machinery that allowed us to master one ballistic move (throwing stones at animals), then over evolutionary time that machinery could be adapted for use with other such moves:

> The planning process probably requires a holding queue, what in business we would call a serial buffer. Telephones that remember your 10 most-used numbers have 10 serial buffers, each more than a dozen

digits long. Each is like a sidetrack, whose train sits poised, waiting to be selected and let loose on the main line. . . . Our planning queue for a ballistic movement has to provide for dozens of muscles and activate them at just the right times, just so hard, and for just so long. We carefully plan during the "get set" period to act without feedback. And the action itself is a carefully orchestrated spatiotemporal sequence, like a fireworks finale launched from a half dozen platforms. . . . So, though playing a Beethoven sonata seems quite unlike baseball, the pianist may well be using neural machinery that was shaped up for hammering or throwing. . . .*

One important question is how we achieve fine motor control, especially with rapid movements like the golf swing or piano playing, using neurons that are always somewhat erratic in their firing. Motor neurons, as Calvin explains, are inherently jittery even at their most constant firing rate—the interval between impulses always varies a little. We are faced with the problem of making a clock with a precise beat using unstable components. Nature, as Calvin explains, solves this problem in a distinctive way:

Nature does one thing extremely well: *making duplicate cells,* as when a cell divides. Solving the jitter problem by making a hundredfold extra cells may be far easier than redesigning the cell to reduce jitter. A hundred imperfect cells rather than one perfect cell, as it were. Besides, nature seems to *like* variability (its way of keeping options open)—and apparently doesn't mind some inefficiency or waste. Indeed, waste seems to be its key to making things better: that's what natural selection is all about, wasting the less fit.†

Thus, precision in ballistic movements emerges through the law of large numbers, as the efforts of many small, erratic components are combined to form a regular beat. The rhythms of the nerve cells, like those of pendulum clocks in a clock seller's store,

---

*William Calvin, *The Cerebral Symphony*, pp. 239–40.
†*The Cerebral Symphony*, p. 246, original emphasis.

become entrained, swinging in unison. Of course, when we train a specific ballistic movement our brains do not manufacture more neurons; rather, we borrow them from other, higher areas of the system, where the neurons are less specialized. This recruitment of more general-purpose nerve cells to "sing along" in choral mode may be the reason golf is such a mental game and why purely mental rehearsals help. The high level of precision required by golf demands the recruitment of many neurons arranged in serial buffers. Any activity or thought that distracts us from this recruitment task leads inevitably to deterioration in performance. The essence of "concentration" and "paying attention" is the loading of all available serial buffers with the same sequence of movements so that the message is reinforced.

We can now see the neurological foundation to the recommendation that before playing a shot, golfers should recall the last time they played a similar shot well. As was suggested by the reports of successful players (in chapter 9), memories of past successes do help. The effect of a vivid image—picture and feeling—is to recruit some of the serial buffers that were engaged in the last successful effort, concentrating attention and creating the neural equivalent of an all-star team! In contrast, negative thoughts that dwell on past disasters are likely to recruit a disastrous collection of inept misfits who will perpetuate disaster. At the same time, before putting the brain into "choral" mode, it is helpful to have a number of variants to choose from. In golf, this variations-on-theme mode is where the multiple-shot types, practiced on the range, can be brought into consideration. Given the situation, we can select the shot that promises the best range of payoffs and recall how we played the last successful version of it, loading the sequence into as many serial buffers as are available. In choral mode we can then execute the shot with some confidence in the outcome.

The Emergence of Language

William Calvin goes on to suggest that during the course of evolution, the serial buffers developed for storing sequences of movements were also used for storing sequences of sounds and (later) symbols. These sounds and symbols would then be chunked to form more abstract concepts and chained to form more complex sequences. *Thus language emerged, based on the same neural mechanisms that had been used to handle movement.* We can detect our use of serial buffers in the way we speak. It is estimated that our serial buffers can hold somewhere between five and nine elements, although each element may, of course, itself be a chunk composed of multiple elements. Words are examples of particularly useful chunks. Therefore when we deliver a speech, we tend to proceed in ballistic bursts of about seven words, "reloading" the buffers between bursts. In between bursts, of course, if we can "read" the audience, we can modify the contents of the next chain based upon our audience's responses to earlier ones—we can exercise dynamic control over a series of ballistic moves.

With the development of our ability to manipulate sequences of sounds and symbols, we could test the viability of different courses of action against our memories and those of others. Trials could be conducted without physical risk; without having to execute them in practice, our risky ideas could die instead of us. Obviously this skill would be of huge survival advantage, and in it, it has been argued, we have the origins of rationality and planning—our ability to formulate courses of action that can be tested in abstract before they are applied in practice.

Who Is in Charge Here?

If the brain is a complex system and our bodies play such a significant role in our behavior, where does that leave consciousness and our sense of self? Who is in charge here? High-level order, such as consciousness, emerges from the interaction of myriad lower-level components, but how does it influence them to take coherent action?

The latest thinking is that the brain and the body function as a complex ecology in which Darwinian mutation and selection processes operate just as they do in nature. Any coherence in our actions is the outcome of these:

> In our brains there is a cobbled-together collection of specialist brain circuits, which, thanks to a family of habits, inculcated partly by culture and partly by individual self-exploration, conspire together to produce a more or less orderly, more or less effective, more or less well-designed virtual machine.... By yoking these independently evolved specialist organs together in common cause, and thereby giving their union vastly enhanced powers, this virtual machine, this software of the brain, performs a sort of internal political miracle: It creates a *virtual captain* of the crew, without elevating any one of them to long term dictatorial powers. Who's in charge? First one coalition and then another, shifting in ways that are not chaotic thanks to good meta-habits that tend to entrain coherent, purposeful sequences rather than an interminable helter-skelter power grab.... We are not like drifting ships with brawling crews; we do quite well not just staying clear of the shoals and other dangers, but planning campaigns, correcting tactical errors, recognizing subtle harbingers of opportunity, and controlling huge projects that unfold over months or years.[*]

This Darwinian process and its outcomes is accompanied by a continual stream of verbal rationalizations from the interpreter of our experience that seems to reside in the left brain. Sometimes the interpreter gets the logic right, but often, when the webs of cause and effect are complex, the left brain has to make it up; it has to tell a story:

> We ... are almost constantly engaged in presenting ourselves to others, and to ourselves, and hence *representing* ourselves—in language

---

[*]Daniel Dennett, *Consciousness Explained*, p. 228, original emphasis.

and gesture, external and internal. . . . Our fundamental tactic of self-protection, self-control and self-definition is . . . telling stories, and more particularly concocting and controlling the story we tell others—and ourselves—about who we are. . . . Our tales are spun, but for the most part we don't spin them; they spin us. Our human consciousness . . . is their product, not their source.*

In short, as Daniel Dennett suggests, through the telling of stories to ourselves and to others we create a narrative "center of gravity." A physical center of gravity allows complex physical objects to be represented as points. A narrative center of gravity allows complex storytelling organisms to be represented as individuals. It creates the unity that we experience as a sense of "self," as well as the continuity and individuality that we see in others. The same process takes place within organizations for the same purposes.

Stories accomplish this task by allowing us to weave together our experiences in space and time. For we live simultaneously in several worlds, where the natures of cause and effect are quite different from each other. In the physical world of objects and matter, cause and effect operates on Newtonian principles of force and mass governed by the laws. In the living, biological world, cause and effect are based on the unfolding of inner processes of growth and development and the effects of environment. In the psychological world, cause and effect depend on our perceptions and intentions, memories and feelings. In this latter world, we are not cold agents, objects waiting to be "motivated," but warm, vital actors with our own needs and wants.

It is the tangle of physical inevitabilities, biological necessities, and psychological choices that leads to the complex webs of cause and effect that characterize complex human systems. As we shall see, it is the metaphorical nature of language that permits it to operate at several levels simultaneously. This allows us to weave together in our stories all three of these dimensions, the physical, the biological, and the psychological, and to place our experience

---

*Daniel Dennett, *Consciousness Explained*, p. 418, original emphasis.

in time. Stories, like music, are about memory and feeling, continually reminding us of the role played by the past in the present. They allow us to reconnect events, to reconstruct meaning, and to understand what has happened.

By telling stories, leaders nurture and sustain an organization's narrative center of gravity. Through the use of stories, effective leaders create between vision and history a present where there is a sense of evolution and progress. Here there is a space in time that can become full of meaning for the people in the organization—a sense of permanence in a pattern of change. Indeed, every time leaders tell their organization's story, they help others make sense of who they are. For it is precisely this sense of permanence and rootedness in the past that *is* the organization's identity, and with its articulation, events and activities take on a new significance for people within it. The organization's identity acts as the touchstone for determining its priorities, a catalyst for self-organization that allows workers to manage their own priorities to benefit the system as a whole. And, just as is the case in the golf swing, the lower the center of gravity in the organization, the better: when everyone can tell the story—can articulate the organization's identity—people can organize themselves.

Summary

This chapter has outlined the fundamentally ballistic nature of the mind. Although the theory is speculative, it seems reasonable to suppose that our ability to use language and to plan ahead could have evolved from our ability to execute ballistic moves physically. Our capacity to focus and pay attention to an activity is thought to be due to our ability to entrain general-purpose neurons to "sing along with the choir," to work together in the same cause. The combination of good habits and our use of language to tell stories leads to the development of "narrative centers of gravity" in both individuals and organizations. Stories allow us to both explain and understand the complex webs of cause and effect that weave their way through the physical, biological, and psychological worlds in which we live. The lower the narrative center of gravity is in the organization, the better.

This chapter has tracked the emergence of language from behavior. In the next chapter I will tackle the challenge of going in the opposite direction, of turning language into behavior.

No. 12

Building Commitment— Body Language

Par-5	562 yards

Electromyographic analysis of the follow-through reveals that the subscapularis, pectoralis major and latissimus dorsi muscles in both sides continue to be active.
—PAUL GEISLER, "KINESIOLOGY OF THE FULL GOLF SWING"

When I was hitting the ball well, there were always one or two things which I made certain of doing, and the doing of them would assure success for a while. But they were not always the same things. One conception was good for only a limited time, and when the charm wore off, I would begin looking for something else.

—BOBBY JONES

The throb of the *djembe* drums fills the large room and must be echoing throughout the hallways and stairways of the building. I am sitting in a circle of drums with a dozen managers, our facilitators, and an instructor. We're beating out a rhythm—*ba-di-di, ba-di-di, boom-di-di,* go our drums. The leader points to each of us in turn, inviting us to play a solo. Around the circle he goes: some participate, others decline. I accept and thump out what I fondly imagine to be an improvisation on the theme; the invitation moves on. Once around the circle the lead drummer raises his hand to signal "faster!" (there is no signal for "slower" in *djembe* drumming), and the tempo accelerates: *ba-di-di, ba-di-di, boom-di-di,* go our drums. Now, on another signal from the leader, the tempo splits into two. Half of our group is playing on the off-beat—*ba-ba-di-di-di-di, ba-ba-di-di-di-di, boom-boom-di-di-di-di,* we go. Faster! The pace accelerates, the drums go wild. For some time it has been impossible for me to think about what I am doing, but now I've lost it completely: only the experts can keep up. Most of the other participants have lost it, too, and we have been reduced to playing only the bass notes: *boom . . . boom . . . boom,* go our drums.

The finale is a brilliant riff from the leader, followed by his clenched-fist signal for "stop!" The stillness is tangible. . . . Merciful silence! My body feels jellified, as though it has been restructured at the molecular level. Every organ is trembling, vibrating at a high frequency, but there's also a sense of peace, of reduced stress, as if the knots of tension within my body have been shaken loose and smoothed away, annealed by the drumming.

Djembe drums are found in most parts of West Africa. They are goblet-shaped drums that come in many sizes, although the most popular size is about twenty-four inches high and fifteen inches in diameter. There are three sounds that can be played on the drum: an open "tone," which is played with the heel of the hand on the edge of the drum; a "slap," which involves the fingers of the hand; and a "bass," which requires the palm of the hand to impact the center of the drum. The hands are used alternately, left-right, left-right and that's it—two hands, three sounds—what could be simpler or easier? Well, it turns out not to be simple or easy at all. Rhythm is to African music as melody is to Western music, and the limited note range of the drum allows rhythm to be explored in all its rich dynamic complexity. Between every note there is a universe to be explored.

The challenge for the beginner in learning the *djembe* is to build a set of basic routines that can later be assembled into repertoires. The task for the teacher is to build a bridge between the formal verbal instructions—"play an open tone, then a slap, then a bass"—and the muscular movements required. The successful bridges are always metaphors, images that evoke familiar feelings that accompany the movements required. Thus, instead of using the descriptors "tone," "slap," and "bass," teachers substitute the word-sounds *di, ba,* and *boom,* which mimic more closely the sounds required. "If you can say it, you can play it," is the mantra of the teachers.

Mind into Muscle

Observers of symphony conductors during rehearsals have noted the same hunt for so-called motor-affective metaphors to evoke the right sound from the activities of musicians:

> Anyone who has been to a concert knows that a conductor can convey the desired expression of a piece with his body and facial expression. Some conductors are flamboyant in their expression, while others convey their meaning in the raising of an eyebrow. And in rehearsal, while preparing and instructing the orchestra, the conductor often communicates desired rhythm, dynamics, and tone quality through mimetic singing and vocalization, for example, "It shouldn't be BOOM, BOOM"; "It's ra-ta-ta-TUM."[*]

The function of such motor-affective metaphors, then, together with the movements and postures that accompany them, is to get ideas into action, to put mind into muscle. It would be surprising if a similar process did not work in golf, and there is a good deal of evidence that it does. When John Daly won the PGA tournament at Crooked Stick in 1991, his caddy said the same single word to him before every shot. The word was "kill," a metaphor that seems to have evoked all the right moves and fitted Daly's aggressive style and raw power. Other caddies will say to their players, "give me a smooth one," or some other soft phrase in an attempt to convey their expectation of a good shot and create the right attitude in their player. As we will see in chapter 15, different

[*]Sybil S. Barten, "Speaking of Music," *Journal of Aesthetic Education* 32, no. 2 (Summer 1998): 91–92.

folks require different strokes. In some cases it is the power of certain words to produce the wrong actions that makes us wary of them. This is surely the reason many golfers refuse to use the word *sh——k*—because of its uncanny power to produce that shot.

Ideas into Action

The key message of this chapter is that words matter. They matter both to golfers and to managers, because of their potential power to convey attitudes and generate action—effective and ineffective, right and wrong. For managers in particular, words, images, and the body language that accompanies them, are action. Used in meetings, speeches, presentations, and conversations, they are the primary catalysts for shaping the behaviors of people within the organization by building commitment and focusing attention. In their fine book, *Beyond the Hype*, Harvard Business School academics Robert Eccles and Nitin Nohria draw a powerful contrast between the rhetorical skills of Roger Smith, CEO of GM, and Jack Welch, CEO of GE. Both these highly visible CEOs took over their respective organizations in 1981 and tried to promote their vision of the future. Here are some samples of the language they used to describe it:

> GM today is the leading car manufacturer in the world by a wide margin. We build and sell nearly one out of five cars purchased in the entire free world. Precisely because of our great organizational and financial strengths, we have been able over the recent years to transform GM into a 21st Century corporation, so that we can be expected to grow even stronger in the years ahead.[*]

Roger Smith never did explain exactly what being a "21st Century corporation" entailed, and anyway it sounds as though the battle has been already won. You would never know that in this year GM lost market share and underperformed the market financially.

---

[*]General Motors Annual Report 1987, quoted in *Beyond the Hype*, pp. 32–33.

Now consider this extract from one of Jack Welch's annual reports:

> We want GE to become a company where people come to work every day in a rush to try something they woke up thinking about the night before. We want them to go home from work wanting to talk about what they did that day, rather than try and forget about it. We want factories where the whistle blows and everyone wonders where the time went, and someone wonders aloud why we need a whistle.[*]

Even though we are looking at tiny vignettes, the contrast between the styles of the two men is clear, and if management were judged as a performing art, Welch would get a Tony Award and Smith would not. There is no challenge to GM—the transformation has been accomplished already. Welch's statement is masterful. Told as a ministory, it conveys personal obsession and excitement. People who would behave like that are not detached, rational beings; they are committed, passionately involved in the enterprise. The resulting intensity has a visceral appeal—Welch is speaking the language of the body. *And by doing that, he is turning ideas into action.*

Modes of Consciousness

The *djembe* drumming session with which I began this chapter is part of the Leading Creatively program (LCP) at the Center for Creative Leadership (CCL) in Greensboro, North Carolina. The course breaks new ground in leadership development, for its objective is, quite literally, to restore managers to their senses. That is, the course is designed to deliver experiences that reopen channels of perception and expression that have often become closed, both by formal management education and from many years of working in large bureaucratic organizations. During the week-long program, managers will draw, build collages, make music,

[*]General Electric Annual Report 1989, quoted in *Beyond the Hype*, p. 33.

write and tell stories, and receive a variety of feedback on their leadership practices, their creative styles, and the climate within their organizations.

The philosophy of the course is that in its essence, leadership is a creative activity that requires aesthetic competencies. Now the word *aesthetic,* with its highbrow and perhaps effete connotations, may be intimidating to golfers and managers alike, but think of its opposite, *anesthetic.* To be anesthetized is to be senseless and unconscious, unable to feel or to respond. All golfers have experienced mild anesthesia on the course, during those bad spells when one feels numb and powerless, bereft of any kind of feeling. Managers too can lose the feeling of how an effective organization should function; indeed, the cultures in many organizations are hostile to imagination, intuition, and feelings. The purpose of the Leading Creatively program is to bring them back to full consciousness.

Central to the LCP is the work of Betty Edwards, an artist whose book, *Drawing on the Right Side of the Brain,* was first published in 1979 and has revolutionized the teaching of art. Her writing was inspired by neurosurgeon Roger Sperry's research on patients with split brains—people who have had the connection between the two halves of their brains cut, usually to alleviate debilitating attacks of epilepsy. Edwards's simple but profound conclusion is that some people draw better than others not because they have better drawing skills, but because they can generate effective feedback between what they do and what they see.

Edwards contends that when it comes to perception, artists use a more right-brained mode of looking than other, less artistic people. This helps them see the unique aspects of what is there. If people allow the left-brained mode of seeing to dominate, this interferes with that ability. For the left brain is adept at classifying objects into categories. If the left brain is too dominant, we as artists lose the real-time feedback between what we do and what is. Instead we end up drawing internally generated generic objects that do not have the unique qualities of *this* object: we draw what we *know* rather than what we *see.*

Edwards dubbed these two ways of grasping the visual world

the "L-mode" and the "R-mode," respectively. In healthy individuals different functions are not clearly localized in the brain, so these descriptions must be seen as metaphorical rather than anatomical. Nevertheless the two modes do seem to be distinct states of consciousness that can be switched between, although neither can ever be suppressed completely. Edwards describes the characteristics of the two modes as follows:[*]

L-MODE	R-MODE
Verbal: Using words to name, describe, and define.	*Nonverbal:* Awareness of things but minimal connection with words.
Analytic: Figuring things out step by step and part by part.	*Synthetic:* Putting things together to form wholes.
Symbolic: Using a symbol to *stand for* something; e.g., + for plus	*Analogic:* Seeing likenesses between things; understanding metaphoric relationships.
Temporal: Keeping track of time, sequencing one thing after another.	*Nontemporal:* Without a sense of time.
Rational: Drawing conclusions based on *reason* and *facts*.	*Nonrational:* Not requiring a basis of reason or facts; willingness to suspend judgments.
Digital: Using numbers, as in counting.	*Spatial:* Seeing where things are in relation to other things and how parts go together to form a whole.
Logical: Drawing conclusions based on logic; one thing following another in logical order.	*Intuitive:* Making leaps of insight, often based on incomplete patterns, hunches, feelings, or visual images.
Linear: Thinking in terms of linked ideas, one thought directly following another, often leading to a convergent conclusion.	*Holistic:* Seeing whole things all at once, perceiving the overall patterns and structures, often leading to divergent conclusions.

[*]Adapted from B. Edwards, *Drawing on the Right Side of the Brain* (New York: Tarcher/Putnam, 1989), p. 40.

Clearly the two modes ought to be complementary—the relationship should be "both . . . and," rather than "either . . . or." Nevertheless, the modes can clearly be in opposition to each other, especially if a culture and an education system favor the development of one mode over another. Of course, this is exactly what the head-down theory of knowledge does, promoting the L-mode at the expense of the R-mode.

Edwards's views received dramatic support from a recent traumatic incident in the life of Katherine Sherwood, an art professor at UC Berkeley. In 1997, at the age of forty-four, she experienced a massive stroke in the left half of her brain that paralyzed her right side and temporarily left her speechless. After months of therapy she recovered some of these functions, but without fine motor control on the right side, she was unable to use her right hand for painting. She began painting with her left hand, and to her amazement she found that she could produce much better work. Leading art critics describe her work as "radically transformed," "raw," and "intuitive," "more visceral and less intellectual."

Prior to the stroke, Katherine Sherwood had employed a highly cerebral approach to her art and had labored to produce technically well-executed but rather uninspired pictures. Brain specialists say that the part of her brain damaged by the stroke was the so-called interpreter, which seeks order and reason to our activities. With her internal critic out of action, Sherwood now finds that the artistic process just seems to flow from perception to execution without any intermediate conscious thought. "Sometimes I look at my work now and ask, 'Did I paint that?'" she says. "There's a sense of disconnect that was never there before. It's almost as if the ideas just pass through me, instead of originating in my head."* Neuroscientists say that suppression of the interpreter in the left brain allows her to stay in the "thin moment" of the present. Rather than worrying about past and future, she can pay complete attention to the present. This is the same place that golfers call "the zone."

Edwards contends that if students are to improve their *drawing*

Wall Street Journal, May 12, 2000.

skills, they must first improve their *perceptual* skills. Accordingly, her teaching program consists of a number of exercises that are specifically designed to do this. And it is for this purpose that her exercises, as well as others, such as *djembe* drumming, are used in the LCP. Drawing provides a context in which managers can easily *feel* the shift from the one mode to the other. Once they can feel it, they can learn to make the shift consciously. For example, one exercise consists of copying a complex line drawing held upside down and revealed progressively, one step at a time. This procedure prevents the beginner artist from recognizing the objects or their components and invoking the categories to which they belong. It forces her to copy *exactly* what she sees—to *pay attention* to *this* line, *here* and *now,* not some generic line from "there" and "then." In that process she experiences the shift to R-mode as the L-mode gives up on the task and becomes the subordinate state.

Modes in Golf

Edwards's L-mode and R-mode look very much like Jim Flick's description of golfing habits on the training ground compared with those on the playing ground (see chapter 10). Golf, like management, is usually *taught* in L-mode but must be *played* in R-mode. The two modes also sound like Gallwey's Self 1 and Self 2 and are clearly closely related to the concepts of explicit and implicit learning discussed earlier. A radical thought is that some golfers may play better than others not so much because of their superior motor skills, but because of their superior perceptual skills. Good golfers may play better because they sense and feel differently from others. They know where their club head is at all times on the backswing and can pay better attention to the task in hand. This implies that they would be more effective at suppressing the critical Self 1 and engaging Self 2, the golfing equivalent of the R-mode, which depends upon nonverbal cues, pictures, and feelings to function. This may be the primary benefit of having lessons with real-time video feedback—when I go through the process, I get to associate pictures and feelings with my swing *right now,* rather than having to translate the verbal descriptions of generic moves from generic swings contained in books.

In good golfers, of course, all this assumes that the fundamentals are in place. Poor fundamentals can put your body into positions from which it is impossible to make a smooth ballistic move. But once the basics are in place, the rest is integration, and integration would seem to require the golfing equivalent of the R-mode. In right-handed players, this would require that during play (as opposed to practice) the L-mode become subordinated: that pictures and feelings replace the instructions and words. As Percy Boomer put it, "You must be mindful, but not thoughtful as you swing. You must not think or reflect; you must feel what you have to do."* Again, in right-handers this implies that, to the extent we have any thoughts during the swing, we should be aware of the big muscles and left sides of our bodies, areas of responsibility controlled by the right brain. This may be the reason so many teaching pros emphasize the importance of the left side in golf. There is no doubt that *physically* golf is a bilateral game, with muscles on both sides of the body contributing significantly to the swing. But *mentally* it may be that golf (once again in right-handers) has to be a left-side game if the R-mode is to be invoked and the L-mode suppressed.

Modes in Management

Edwards's two modes also map directly onto the distinctions made in chapter 10 between management and leadership. Is it conceivable that superior managers, like their golfing and artistic counterparts, are effective not because of their technical skills, but because of their superior perceptive skills? Are they just able to read and respond to situations faster and more effectively (exercise better dynamic control) than their less competent colleagues?

---

*On Learning Golf, p. 59.

Certainly our own experience during the hectic times of the take-over (related in chapter 10) was that our effectiveness often depended on our ability to "read" people and anticipate their needs. At meetings it was often essential to be able to distinguish between the real issues and the positions being taken, without the benefit of verbal explanations. Recently, skills such as these have received a good deal of publicity under the banner of emotional intelligence. Emotional intelligence can be thought of as a manager's capacity to function in R-mode just as the more familiar concept of intellectual intelligence (IQ) can be used to measure aspects of their facility in the L-mode.

The Role of Emotion in Decision Making

In his fascinating book, *Descartes' Error: Emotion, Reason, and the Human Brain,* neurologist Antonio Damasio tells the story of Phineas Gage, a physically fit, capable, intelligent man who is horrifically injured in an accident while working on one of the early railroads. While tamping down an explosive charge in a drill hole with an iron rod, Gage accidentally sets off the gunpowder. The rod, which is 43 inches long, $1^{1/4}$ inches in diameter, and pointed at one end, is fired out of the drill hole like a bullet from a rifle. The point enters Gage's left cheek and penetrates the base of his skull, and the entire rod exits at high speed through the top of his head to land more than a hundred feet away. Gage has a huge hole through his head, but amazingly he is alive, conscious, and able to walk and talk shortly after the accident. After two months of careful medical treatment he is physically healed, apart from the loss of sight in his left eye, but mentally he is a changed man.

The changes were strange: prior to the accident Gage had been a shrewd, smart businessman, able to plan, make decisions, and execute them through persistent action. Now he seemed unable to stick at anything. He would make many plans but abandon them as soon as they were made. This behavior was accompanied by a complete change in his social behavior. His language became foul and so profane that women were advised not to go near him lest he offend their sensibilities. After drifting from job to job and a spell of exhibiting his grotesque injuries at freak shows, Gage died in San Francisco in 1861 of an epileptic seizure. His skull was preserved, and a century and a half later Damasio and his associates were able to reconstruct the injuries that he must have sustained to his brain. Gage had given himself a crude prefrontal lobotomy, an invasive operation that in the middle of the twentieth century became almost commonplace in severely disturbed psychiatric patients. The purpose of the operation was to reduce the emotional highs and lows experienced by patients, but too often it reduced them to zombies. Thanks to modern pharmacology the operation is no longer performed, but the horror of its outcome is etched in the minds of all who recall the end of the movie *One Flew Over the Cuckoo's Nest.*

It is now well recognized, at least by neurologists, that Phineas Gage and people with injuries like his are unable to make decisions and stick to a course of action because of a *lack of emotion.* Damasio tells of patients who can lay out courses of action, examine their implications, and consider alternatives, but they cannot act on a particular option: they cannot decide. They just keep on calculating, gathering information, and weighing odds, and there is always more data to gather, more options to be considered, and more complex interactions to be disentangled. It seems that a significant emotional component is essential to decision making if options are to be eliminated and a halt called to further calculation. Indeed, our selection and interpretation of facts depends entirely upon our needs and desires—our "attention." We need our emotions to value outcomes and decide which options are worth pursuing and which are not. In short, we need a context to prune the tree of possibility—real managers have to use their feelings— their intuition, instincts, and "guts"—to make decisions. And in this process they rarely behave as logical machines.

In 1976 Henry Mintzberg wrote an article in the *Harvard Business Review* entitled "Planning on the Left Side and Managing on the Right." It too was inspired by Sperry's research, as well as

Mintzberg's own observation of working managers. A year earlier, also in the same journal, in an article entitled "The Manager's Job: Folklore and Fact," Mintzberg had fired the first shot in a war on the conventional wisdom of what managers should do and thus how they should be trained. Indeed, the war continues today.

The managers Mintzberg observed did not behave as hyper-rationalists; instead they relied heavily on face-to-face communication and snippets of information that could hardly be described as data. Instead of staying in their offices, they would prowl the passages and shop floors, searching for opinions, immersing themselves in problem situations. Rather than detaching themselves from day-to-day affairs, they seemed to have a hunger for reports from the field and authentic face-to-face contact with customers and frontline employees. Explicit analysis was not always used, even where it was appropriate and possible. Decisions were made by judgment, intuition, and "'gut feel" rather than rational calculation. Of course, it had been known for some time that this was the way most managers behaved, but it had usually been interpreted as a deviation from the ideal rational model.

Mintzberg's contribution was to argue that what the managers were doing made good sense under the conditions they faced. It was the rational model that was inappropriate—managers were being trained in the use of a "think, then act" model that could be described but not applied in the turbulent environments in which they had to operate. Here effective performance demanded a much more complex interweaving of action and reflection.

This is shocking news to the head-down theory of knowledge and the rational school of decision making that accompanies it. Most of us have been taught to think with a cool head and to not allow emotion to affect our decisions. But that does not mean we can eliminate emotion entirely. An excess of emotion may well distort perception and decisions, but the message from Damasio's research is that too little emotion is just as dysfunctional as too much. Why should this be? I contend that it is because of the embodied nature of our minds: there is no such thing as "undistorted perception." The body is not a general-purpose instrument being

used by an independent, rational scientist. It is an integrated system of organs that has evolved over time to ensure the survival of
the organism. And, as was suggested in the last chapter, the high-
level processes such as planning, decision making, and the use of
language are based on low-level motor skills.

Language and the Real World

In the head-down theory of knowledge there is a clear, literal, one-
to-one relationship between words and objects. This allows words
and concepts to be manipulated according to the laws of logic in
an abstract way. An embodied theory of knowledge sees all language, including formal languages like mathematics, as depen-
dent on our bodily experience of the world. In other words, *all
language is metaphorical—it works by referring to and reminding us of
our bodily encounters with reality.* The head-down theory of knowledge has been dismissive of metaphor, regarding it as suitable for
decorative flourishes by poets and playwrights but irrelevant to
logic and rationality. But from an embodied perspective, metaphor
underpins them both. Indeed, as we shall see, it is the profoundly
metaphorical nature of language that allows the L-mode to cheat
in its use!

Metaphors

Calvin's work (discussed in chapter 11) suggests strongly that our
higher-level brain processes make use of the same mechanisms
and processes as do the lower-level sensory and motor processes.
It is not surprising, then, that our bodily experiences make up the
primary metaphors in language, although we are rarely aware of
them. Thus, at a very basic level, things that are "up" are usually
good, and things that are "down" are usually bad. Health and life
are up, as in "I am at the peak of health," while sickness and death
are down—we "fall" ill. Consciousness and rationality are also

up—we "wake up," have "high level" intellectual discussions, and so on. Unconsciousness and emotionality are down—we "slump" into comas and conversations and "descend" into mud slinging. In religious metaphors heaven is, of course, up and hell is down.

These expressions sound so natural that it is surprising to realize they are metaphors that use familiar body experiences to grasp (there I go again) more abstract ideas. Metaphors help us communicate images—pictures and feelings—of the most complex concepts, but that great power is also their greatest weakness. In particular, metaphors and other related figures of speech often muddy our understanding of cause and effect. It is the L-mode's unintentional cheating with language that creates the "verbal wands" that so unnerved Fritz Roethlisberger.

Cheating with Language

Take, for example, the advice often given to corporations that they should "align" their organizational structure with their strategy. In its most basic interpretation, this metaphor treats structure and strategy as if they were physical objects that have to be placed in a linear relationship with each other. Now we all can, at least to some extent, align our putters with the golf ball and the hole, and we can check our alignment with setsquares and lasers on the practice green. But these methods cannot be transferred to the alignment of structure and strategy in business organizations.

So while "align" looks like an action verb in the management advice, it's really what philosopher Gilbert Ryle calls an "achievement verb." Consultants can point to successful organizations that have their strategies and structures aligned, but that gives me no clue as to what action to take in my situation. It's a bit like being told that despite their very different swings, all good golfers have similar positions at impact. Even if that's true (and it probably is), it just tells me that they have solved the problem with which I am struggling. It gives me no clue as to how to reach a good impact position with my swing!

Ryle pointed out that there are a number of verbs in English that confuse the achievement of successful outcomes with the taking of action. He described the difference between the two as a contrast between "know-that" and "know-how." In the example just given, most managers *know-that* strategy and structure should be aligned, rather fewer *know-how* to achieve that alignment. This may sound to some readers like an abstruse philosophical point, but it is directly relevant to our ability to take effective action in both golf and management. When we use verbs describing outcomes, the *how* of achievement gets lost and becomes taken for granted. Thus the copious use of achievement verbs in management (and golf) advice makes the advice sound useful, when all it counsels is desirable outcomes. These outcomes are impossible to disagree with, but in the absence of actionable processes, such advice is not very helpful.

Identifying Customer Needs

This problem bedevils much of management advice, including injunctions like "Identify the customer's needs." I can identify my golf ball in the rough because it has prominent physical markings that I have seen before, but a customer's needs are rarely displayed. Indeed, their needs are often latent—unknown to the customers themselves. The success of products like 3M's ubiquitous Post-it Notes and Sony's Walkman is a testament to the emergent quality of customer needs. Asking people what their needs were would not have led to the development of either of these products.

So how does one identify customer needs? It seems that the most effective way is to immerse oneself in their activities, to take action in their world. In short, *to understand their problems and develop solutions, we first need to share in their experience.* This is perhaps the central message from management guru Tom Peters, who tells story after story of people going out to live in their customers' worlds and experience exactly what they experience—see what they see and feel what they feel.

Hallmark Cards uses this approach to keep the creative juices flowing in the organization and to develop ideas for new products.

Their program comprises two kinds of "sabbatical" on which employees are sent. Both types of sabbatical are aimed at renewal rather than relaxation. The first focuses on artistic development by sending teams of roughly ten people to work at a hands-on craft of some kind—ceramics, glassblowing, engraving, and so on. The objective is to get people away from the abstractions on their computer screens and back into the sensual world of making something real. Their people come back revitalized after six months in such rich environments, with new insights in how to express themselves in the old medium of the greeting card.

The second type of sabbatical aims at researching a particular issue or problem. A smaller team of four to six volunteers is sent off to immerse themselves in a community that exemplifies the issue. To research the emerging role of ethnicity in society, Hallmark people went to live in Seattle, the city that seemed to epitomize the new trend. They attended folk festivals, went to playgrounds, looking, listening, and feeling the multidimensional nature of the issue. This perspective on ethnicity could not be gained easily in Chicago or New York, and certainly not in Kansas City, where Hallmark is headquartered. It could be gained only on the ground in a community that was undergoing the change. To get a handle on the resurgence of jazz music, however, Hallmark researchers might well spend time living on Chicago's West Side. If they wanted to develop a new series of cards for those suffering from AIDS, the team might work in a hospice in New York City. After these immersions, the Hallmark team would be much better equipped to capture and express the feelings experienced by those who live in those situations every day.

Muddling Cause and Effect

In management writings, the unintentional cheating with language is often compounded by the widespread attribution of action to corporate entities, as in "Motorola installed a companywide quality system" or "Dell pioneered the direct selling of computers." Our ability to track the web of cause and effect, to understand exactly *how* a desirable outcome was achieved, is blocked by these figures of speech. Action is also glossed over, however, when the successful results of what must have been collective action are attributed to a single individual, usually a senior person. For example, one reads statements like "Lee Iacocca launched the Ford Mustang" and "Bill Clinton reduced unemployment." Neither of these two people, capable though he might be, could have achieved these results single-handedly. Although both men were happy to claim credit for the outcomes, they were the results of enormously complex processes operating over long periods of time. There may have been key points in the processes when individuals played critical roles, but the description ignores these. Once again, a figure of speech makes for convenient shorthand, but it is not helpful in understanding cause and effect in complex systems.

Swearing

Perhaps it's our frustration with language and its inability to convey action that leads some of us to curse so much in both golf and management! Profanity pervades both golf and management, although its presence on the golf course is rather better known than it is in the executive suite. Management organizations present a polite face to the public, but internally the situation is often very different. When the Nixon tapes were released, the American public was shocked to hear the frequency and pungency of the expletives used by both Nixon and the members of his administration. The situation is not very different inside organizations, from shop floor to boardroom. *The Wall Street Journal,* for example, describes the typical manager at General Electric, a cradle of American management, as "casually profane." In this company, profanity may indeed be an integral part of the corporate "body," a culture that emphasizes directness and a single-minded focus on action.

In management, profanity can perform a similar function to that in golf after poor business outcomes—it reduces tension. But used in a social context prior to action, the visceral authenticity of swearing can also be used to create tension. Sometimes it can be used to build commitment toward action by demonstrating the bodily commitment of those in favor of the course of action. At other times it can be used as part of a power game, to manipulate people, to intimidate, and to compel compliance.

The Modes in English

English is the only major language that is based on a system of double derivation, from both Germanic and Romance roots. Although England is an island, it was invaded repeatedly. The Roman invaders in the first century seem to have had relatively little impact on the spoken language, only on the place names. The waves of Angle, Saxon, and Jute invaders during the first millennium, however, seem to have wiped out the language of the indigenous Celts and laid a strong Germanic base, which was built upon during the various Danish incursions. From 1066 to the 1340s, however, the Normans, who retained strong links with their native France, ruled Britain.

French became the language of the upper class and was used in all the institutions of power with which they were involved. The English of the legal world is dominated by words with French derivations: *judge, jury, court, sue, plaintiff, defendant, attorney, felony,* and *property* are examples. The same is true of religion and the military. French also dominated the pleasures of the upper class—sports, dress, and food.

During this period, English became a language with two distinct tiers: a lower, "guttural" Germanic base with monosyllabic vigor (R-mode); and a "cerebral" Romantic upper level with a (usually) polysyllabic elegance (L-mode). Thus we call farm animals cows, calves, and sheep (from the Germanic *Kuh, Kalb,* and *Schaf*) because their herders were Anglo-Saxon. But we eat beef, veal, and mutton (akin to the French *bœuf, veau,* and *mouton*) because the people who got to eat them originally were Normans. The nuclear family—*mother, father, sister, brother, son, daughter*—are all Germanic, as are the words expressing relationships—*before, after, under, on, in, to, of, for, and.* All our swear words are Germanic in origin, and their popularity would seem to stem from their unique ability to express activities of the body! Some key contrasts between the two layers of language are as follows:

ROMANCE	GERMANIC
cerebral	visceral
sacred	profane
polysyllabic	monosyllabic
high caste	low caste
abstract	concrete
thought	action

As a result, many things can be said in English using either the Germanic or the Romance vocabulary. The plainness and directness of words of Germanic origin is also obvious in these examples from business English. When corporations are trying to finesse their actions, they often use the Romance versions:

ROMANCE	GERMANIC
Execute	Do
Terminate	Fire
Employ	Hire
Initiate	Start
Exercise	Drill
Competency	Skill

Skilled professionals, particularly lawyers and doctors, have typically used Romance-based language to separate themselves from the common folk. Surgeons refer to the parts of the body by their Latin anatomical names; this makes for precision in description and also helps distance the surgeon from the person who owns the body part. Legal language has the same effect, enhancing the dispassionate rationality of the judicial process. It can also be used to distance actors from their actions: President Clinton's lawyer in the Lewinsky affair told the Senate impeachment proceedings that his client was prepared to "accept the obloquy" (from the Latin word *obloquium*, meaning "talk against") due him because of his behavior. It sounded almost like an award of some kind!

We can now understand why the terms *pronation* and *supination*, which writer Herbert Warren Wind used in Hogan's book, *The Modern Fundamentals of Golf*, are so unsatisfactory. They are polysyllabic Romance-based words and sound like descriptions from an anatomy class rather than actionable words with real physical connotations. They are technically correct but extremely hard for the reader to grasp—to internalize and translate back into competent action. But Wind, like every writer on golf and management, was faced with a dilemma—how does one describe physical moves in language? It would have been no use to ask Hogan—he could do it, but he couldn't describe it—which was why his book, like those of so many other golfers, was a cooperative effort with a professional writer. Presumably, Hogan hoped that his tacit knowledge, the feelings and images that he used when playing golf, would be made explicit in Wind's words.

The bottom line for managers is that as speakers, writers, and teachers, through their choice of vocabulary, they can create very different attitudes toward action. To gain legitimacy for management action from both outsiders (that is, shareholders) and their superiors, managers usually use English's elegant Romantic lexicon without any accompanying body movement or inflection of voice. This is the language one typically finds in corporations' annual reports, where managers want to give the impression of rational thought and flawless execution. This abstract language, however, tends to distance managers from action. So if you want to get things done, to compel people to take action, and to show your own commitment to it, use the plain-talking Germanic word hoard with strong body language and marked changes in the pitch and timbre of your voice.

It follows from this that those elegant, "bulletproof" presentations designed for external stakeholders should *never* be used for internal audiences, other than to show them "what we are telling the analysts." For such presentations are too impenetrable, too smooth, too "finished." They don't invite viewers to participate, only to admire. What is needed is a much rougher, flip chart report on "work in progress" that asks questions and invites contributions. It is this invitation to participate that lies behind the compelling power of stories to coordinate experience and drive action.

Summary

In this chapter I looked at the challenge of turning language into action. The contrast between the rhetorics of GE's Jack Welch and GM's Roger Smith reveals the enormous power of words both to motivate and to turn off listeners. The work done on programs like the LCP at CCL suggests that there are two distinct but complementary modes of consciousness, exemplified by Betty Edwards's concepts of L-mode and R-mode. The former deals with the generic features of situations and depends on reason and facts. The latter, R-mode, focuses on the unique features of situations and relies on metaphors and patterns. We find these modes in both golf and management. In golf they seem to capture the difference between practicing and playing. In management they map onto the contrast between management and leadership. The competencies that support the two modes in management have been described respectively as intellectual intelligence and emotional intelligence. There is evidence that superior artists, golfers, and managers perform well because of their ability to use feedback to adjust their performances in real time.

The metaphorical nature of language allows people to cheat with it. The confusing role of language was underlined by Ryle's distinction between "know-that" and "know-how," and it was shown why sensible-sounding advice is often worth very little. We saw how customers' needs can be effectively identified by total bodily immersion in the customer's experience. The power of metaphor is that it allows us to create a conceptual world based upon our shared bodily experience of the physical world. It is this power that makes stories such a compelling medium for coordinating our experience and generating action.

No. 13

Beyond the Quick Fix

Par-5	652 yards

One who has had long experience, therefore, hesitates to lay down any rules to induce anyone to think that, beyond the fundamentals, anything very definite can be prescribed.
—BOBBY JONES

[Professional g]olf is probably capitalism at its barest form. If you do well, if you do your best, you get paid the best. If you don't, you may make thousands or you may make nothing. You don't get paid for showing up. You don't get paid for sitting on the bench. You get paid for your performance. That's what makes it interesting. It can make it very rewarding.
—UNIDENTIFIED PLAYER ON THE LPGA TOUR, QUOTED IN TODD W. CROSSET, OUTSIDERS IN THE CLUBHOUSE

The strategic planning and budgeting process at Federal Industries was a harrowing ordeal that everybody hated but no one seemed able to stop. It would begin every year about a week after Labor Day, with the receipt from corporate headquarters by each division of a voluminous set of forms in spreadsheet format. The instructions said they were to be filled out and returned, together with their supporting documents, by the middle of October. The forms were a standardized set of five-year financials; profit-and-loss statements and balance sheets, together with key ratios and numbers such as inventories; receivable and payables days; planned capital expenditure; and so on. The key economic assumptions to be used, such as interest rates and GNP growth, were attached to the package.

Usually the president of each division delegated the responsibility for the package's submission to a staff person, who then sent out the division's own set of forms to the business units that constituted it. These forms too were almost exclusively financial in nature; the instructions called for their submission back to the division by the end of September. Thus the planning and budgeting process cascaded down to the smallest branch operation and spread itself throughout the entire conglomerate. After a few weeks of frantic number crunching, the process reversed itself as a wall of paper and spreadsheets roared back upstream, gathering speed and height as it was forced into the narrowing channels of divisional headquarters. Stack after stack of paper began to accumulate on the boardroom tables, swamping the credenzas and spilling onto the floors. The accountants worked in shifts, their computer monitors glowing around the clock, to aggregate the forecasts and put them into divisional and corporate formats. These inch-thick summaries were then distributed to the senior divisional managers, who pored over them at marathon meetings that lasted from dawn until well into the night.

Everything at these meetings was geared toward presenting numbers that were thought to be acceptable to the corporate office. The conglomerate guidelines called for a 15 percent per year growth rate in revenues and a 25 percent return on net assets before interest and taxes, and woe betide the manager who could not meet them—at least on paper. Often much hacking and cutting was called for. The communication lines between the divisions and their operations worked overtime as negotiations over the numbers raged to and fro. Head counts were cut; pay raises were either reduced or deferred, and the training budget was slashed; items were leased instead of being bought, and maintenance was postponed or items were repaired instead of being replaced; inventory turns were jiggled, payables lengthened, and accruals reduced, as the business units turned out their "bottom drawers." Estimates were refined, rationalized, justified, and supported. Then a few final "tweaks" and the plan was on its way to corporate headquarters. Here the same ritual took place—mammoth meetings, while behind the scenes haggard accountants manipulated myriad pixels on a thousand screens.

The summit meetings between the corporate office and the various divisions took place in late November in a single three-day session; some at corporate called it "hell week." After well-rehearsed, bulleted list (we called them "bulletproof") presentations from each of the divisions, the corporate staff, who had already fed the CEO in advance with some of their very best ammunition, sang treble to their master's bass and did their damnedest to shoot holes in the plan. Wrapping themselves in the mantle of shareholder value, they argued that their contribution to the budget process was to run a contention system that challenged the operators. During its heyday, IBM made the contention dynamic famous as a method for surfacing the best ideas and the best people, and it does work well when there is a level of trust and confidence among participants that they are all dedicated to the same goals. In a less trusting climate (which IBM eventually became), however, the contention process can be counterproductive, promoting endless bickering in multiple bureaucratic games, where scores are built by making debating points at high levels of abstraction. Most of the divisions had anticipated the tougher questions in advance; some had actually left trivial errors in their statements for the corporate staff to find, reasoning that they too had to justify their pay and that a flawless plan would only make them mad. So the ritual questions got the ritual answers, minor adjustments were made to satisfy all parties, and with all those involved complaining about the difficulty of the process, the plan and budget were finally "put to bed." Among the participants there was a feeling of relief that the process was over for another year and that they had survived the ordeal.

Then reality took over. Often even before the end of the first month of the new accounting year, many of the actuals were already starting to diverge from forecast. The direction of the variances would depend in part on how good the previous year had been. If it had been a good one, all would be well—the "bottom drawers" would be stuffed with accounting "goodies" for use on a rainy day. If, on the other hand, the prior year had been a tough one, and managers had been under the gun to make their numbers, then some of January's deliveries might have ended up being booked as sales in December and the first month of the new year would be a struggle. Positive variances required little comment, other than for management to take the credit! But if no deals had disturbed the "apples with apples" comparisons, then negative variances needed to be explained. Because the forecasts dealt only in financial outcomes, however, there were many, many possible reasons for these—just as there are for bad golf shots. Most of these reasons were plausible, especially to executives situated a long way from the action and unfamiliar with the nuances of each business. If head office executives proved impatient, however, or the negative variances continued, corrective action might be proposed. It was usually thoroughly unsystemic—a general reduction in costs, the decision not to hire or replace a person here, the postponement of some expenditure there, anything to let the year run a little further and get to the stage where actual events had made comparisons meaningless. If results really started to deviate from budget, the division's accounting legerdemain would be summoned to smooth the picture. Revenues and expenses could be recognized or deferred, assets could be written up or down, and myriad other adjustments could be made. Even in an indifferent year, most good operators could make it to Labor Day, when the whole process would begin again.

Adding Value

Some readers may feel that I am offering a cynical caricature of the corporate budget and planning process, but discussions with many managers suggest that such annual processes are quite typical in most large organizations. The apparent precision of numerical targets and the speed with which numbers can be manipulated on a spreadsheet can exert a mesmerizing hold on managers. In addition, the technology has enabled the practical use of a number of sophisticated financial concepts whose mathematical elegance appeals to executives and academics alike. Nowhere is this reflected more than in the hype surrounding the use of cost of capital (CoC) as a criterion for corporate performance.

The rigorous concept of how firms should price their sources of capital was developed in the business schools during the 1960s and 1970s. It was a time of revolution in the thinking about corporate finance, and it swept away the fuzzy rules of thumb that had existed before then. It has now been popularized and made operational under the banner of names like economic value added (EVA). In 1993 *Fortune* magazine went so far as to hail EVA as "the Real Key to Creating Wealth" and described the close link between EVA and stock prices. Now CoC *is* a neat concept: it allows a measure of financial performance that is portable from company to company and for comparisons to be made despite variations in industry risk and financial structure. Conceptually it is not dissimilar to par, course rating, and slope in golf. Par is an abstract target score that does not reflect the relative difficulty of different courses. Course rating and, more recently, slope allow players to adjust their handicaps so that performances on different courses can be compared more fairly. But the correlations of superior performances on CoC-type measures with firms' market values are no more surprising than the correlations between scores below par and money winnings on the PGA Tour. The knowledge of this relationship is useless to an aspirant golfer. For being told that the secret to success is to "shoot under par" is the equivalent of "buy low, sell high" advice for making money on the stock market.

For this reason, EVA cannot be a key to wealth creation in any helpful sense. Like par, course rating, and slope, cost of capital just allows us to describe more precisely the performance challenge, the "lock" we have to unlock. EVA-type measures can certainly be used as the numerical components of performance goals, but they will still be subject to all the problems that accompany the use of such outcome measures. Indeed, I have seen them used by corporate offices either as a way of raising the hurdles their divisions have to jump or as just another set of bludgeons with which to intimidate and beat up on hapless operators!

In any organization, the wrangling over budget numbers can easily create an interpersonal tension and animosity that can destroy what little cooperation may exist within the organization. Instead of the different parts of the organization working together harmoniously, they end up at loggerheads, united only by their antipathy toward head office. For the conventional budgeting process is bottom-up only in theory—the exclusive use of financials ensures that in practice it is top-down. As a result, everyone concerned in the budgeting and planning process ends up working with abstractions, "black marks on white paper," which can be changed, however, at the tap of a key to generate tangible benefits. These benefits accrued not to the businesses, but to the players of the game in the form of incentives, promotions, and the like. As we shall see, it's inevitable that almost everyone gets sucked into the earnings game.

It is for this reason that the budgeting process in most organizations bears an uncanny resemblance to David Leadbetter's description of a typical golfer's practice session mentioned in chapter 4. Instead of being used to develop coordination among the functions and to rehearse and test the skills that will be demanded in the real world, the budget becomes a contest to produce satisfying outcomes under highly artificial conditions. The process ends up as the financial equivalent of trying to hit monster drives over the back fence of the range. The damage it does to the players, however, lasts much longer—it's the organization's tempo that can be shot for the year!

From Budgeting to Practice: Translating the Model

The problem with the traditional budgeting process is that it focuses exclusively on outcome goals and not on the performance and process goals, which lie earlier in the web of cause and effect in every complex system. This can be seen quite graphically if we translate the standard budget dialogue between corporate office and the operating divisions into a hypothetical discussion between a golfing coach and a player. The standard annual "discussion" might go something like this:

COACH: It's time to set some goals for improvement and make plans for next year. What do you plan to shoot in an average round on your home course?
PLAYER: Well, okay, based on past performance and allowing for some improvement, it looks like an 85.
COACH: That's totally unacceptable! Par is 72, and we won't accept anything worse than that. Take a look at it hole by hole. What have you got on the 1st—it's a par-4, isn't it?"
PLAYER: Well, I don't have the card filled in hole by hole . . . 85 was an overall score. But I'll break it down now. . . .

Later

PLAYER: I've got a 5 on the 1st; it's a tough opening hole, and sometimes it takes a while to get going.
COACH: That's no good at all—you can't start that way and hope to shoot par or better. What's the best score you've ever made on the 1st?
PLAYER: Well, I once made a birdie playing off the white tees. . . .
COACH: See, you can do it! Write in 3.
PLAYER: Well, okay . . . if you say so.
COACH: Now look at the 2nd. It's a par-5, and you should birdie that, too.
PLAYER: But I have never reached that green in two shots; it's just too far for me.
COACH: With the new titanium driver you're getting, that will be no problem; you're just too negative in your thinking. Write in 4.
PLAYER: But I haven't seen the driver yet, and it will take time to get used to it.
COACH: Nonsense! The manufacturers say that it will take strokes off your game right away!

A little later

COACH: What's that triple-bogey 7 on the 10th? It looks like an easy par-4 hole to me.

PLAYER: Well, it looks short, but it's a really tough dogleg left, and I slice the ball. I usually have a blowup somewhere on the course, and I have put it there. . . . (Miserably) I suppose it's sort of a balancing item.

COACH: That's ridiculous! We can't stand surprises like that. No triples or doubles are allowed under any circumstances. Take them off the card!

Later still

COACH: That par on the 18th should be a birdie, but we'll let it go at that for now. What's your total?

PLAYER: (Doubtfully) Well . . . if I can play like that, I'll shoot 69.

COACH: Well done! Excellent! I like your positive attitude. Submit that number and we'll watch you do it . . . hole by hole.

PLAYER: Maybe I need some lessons. . . .

COACH: It's too late for that now—anyway, we've slashed the training budget—you're on the tee . . . and don't forget the incentive plan!

Clearly there are few golfers who would find value in being harangued by a coach in this way. The discussion dealt only with outcomes from the system, not with the behaviors that produce them. Zooming in on the detailed results on every hole doesn't get the discussion any closer to dealing with causes and effects. The only changes that were made were superficial ones; the dysfunctional dynamics of the system remained intact. The problem is not one of motivation and incentives, but how to learn from experience. Such a process would not improve golfers' games, and if they did find themselves browbeaten into "shooting a number," they would almost inevitably be forced to cheat to make the score, especially if there were a monetary incentive and little chance of being caught.

The Numbers Game

This is, of course, exactly what we see in the corporate world, as managers "adjust" their firms' reported earnings to give share-holders and analysts the best impression of their performance (and perhaps trigger their own incentive systems). This "exploitation" of the accounting rules or "cheating" (depending on your point of view) has become widespread. We have now come to expect the continual use of the accounting "foot wedge" to improve rough lies, the taking of occasional below-the-line "mulligans" to erase rank bad shots, and the perennial use of "winter rules"—the infamous "pro forma" accounting—to smooth performance.

This practice is followed by the most respected of public corporations, including many (if not most) of the Fortune 500 companies. Indeed, as suggested by a recent *Fortune* article (March 31, 1997), the problem is built into the system: every public company that wants to succeed has to learn to play the earnings game. We experienced these pressures firsthand as our corporate office tried to establish the firm's brand in the financial marketplace. With their executive bonuses riding on results, the conglomerate head office cultivated and pampered an inner circle of investment analysts who acted as the corporation's cheering section. Earnings were managed to smooth over the roughness of reality and present a picture of a well-oiled "money machine" with "no surprises." Every quarter the expectations of favorite investment analysts were "shaped" and earnings were then crafted to fit the profile. Given reasonable financial results and lots of deals, the complexities of the financial transactions handled at that level, together with the intricacies of foreign currencies and tax systems, ensured that the only possible limit to the entries was imposed by the imagination of the personnel involved. One senior financial executive became so adept at producing financial rabbits out of his hat that one year his colleagues presented him with an elaborate certificate awarding him a CIDA accounting designation. There is no official accounting body of that name—the acronym stood for "credit income, debit anything!"

A Saner Process

What would a sensible corporate budget dialogue look like? It would have to get into depth, going well beyond the final numerical outcomes to unearth the practices responsible for producing such results. In a golfing context, the discussion might go something like this:

COACH: It's time to set some goals for improvement and make plans for next year. What do you plan to shoot in an average round on your home course?

PLAYER: Well, okay, based on past performance and allowing for some improvement, it looks like an 85.

COACH: Hmm . . . that's not going to be acceptable even on a bad day. Tell me something about your history and how you see your game, and then I'll take a look at you swinging a club. . . .

Later

COACH: Par is 72 and we are going to have to get there as soon as we can. What do you personally want to achieve, and are you prepared to put in the time and effort required?

PLAYER: Well, I want to be able to shoot par, and I am prepared to work really hard at it!

COACH: I hope that you really understand how much work that entails—hours and days of practice and drills . . . Okay. Can you tell me, on average, how many fairways you hit, how many greens you reach in regulation and how many putts you take?

PLAYER: Well, I've never kept those kinds of numbers before. Let me see if I can reconstruct them for a few recent rounds. . . .

Later

PLAYER: From my last three scorecards I estimate that I hit 7 out of 14 fairways (50 percent), hit 7 out of 18 greens in regulation, and took thirty-nine putts a round.

COACH: Well, that's helpful, because it shows us immediately that you are probably hitting the ball fairly straight and far, but your putting is dreadful. Take a look at these statistics based on the average scores from a range of amateur players:

AVERAGE SCORE

Category	71	75	79	81	85	89	91	95	99
Greens in Reg.	12	10	8	7	5	3	2	0	0
% Fairways	81	71	61	56	46	36	31	21	11
Putts/Round	29.0	30.3	31.7	32.3	33.7	35.0	35.7	37.0	38.3
Birdies	3.2	2.4	1.8	1.5	.8	.1	0	0	0
Pars	11.8	10.3	8.8	8.1	6.6	5.1	4.3	2.8	1.3

Adapted from L. J. Riccio, "Statistical Analysis of the Average Golfer," in Alastair J. Cochran (ed.), *Science and Golf* (London: E & F.N. Spon, 1990), pp. 153–57.

The way you strike the ball at the moment, you should be scoring in the low 80s. How much time do you spend on your putting? Have you had lessons?

PLAYER: Well, no—I just hate practicing putting and chipping—it's no fun.

COACH: Let's get you together right away with someone who can give you a detailed critique of your short game, help you set some specific targets, and give you some drills to do. In the meantime, keep capturing those new statistics.

PLAYER: I was hoping to get a new titanium driver . . . what do you think of that?

COACH: Well, they are a lot of fun to hit, and if you can afford it, by all means get one. But from what you have told me, it won't take any strokes off your average score!

Now this discussion is illustrative only. Most students of putting, for example, know that putts per round is too gross a measurement to be of much use because it ignores both the number of greens hit in regulation and the distances of the putts. Nevertheless, the difference between this hypothetical discussion and its predecessor is striking: instead of a superficial discussion, this dialogue immediately gets into depth, focusing on the areas that need attention by identifying the constraints on performance. Technological solutions are seen not as panaceas, but as responses to specific constraints. If a specific technology does not release a specific constraint, there is not much point in going to the trouble and expense of getting and installing it. Key constraints can be identified only by chasing problems back to their root causes.

From a systemic perspective, then, budgeting should be the organization's opportunity to practice, to "warm up" for the year ahead. It is an opportunity for management to both give and get feedback on the skills needed to improve the business; to identify the drills to be practiced; to develop alternative ways of producing desirable outcomes; and to simulate what the year ahead might look like. A number of questions must be answered before the budgeting and planning processes in most firms can be made more effective:

- *What is the purpose of the process*—is it to practice or is it to perform? Too often the traditional process encourages theatrical performances from all the parties involved when what is desperately needed is serious practice.
- *What is the role of the managers at all levels*—are they coaches or are they critics? Theatrical performance allows both these roles to be performed, but effective practice demands a coach.
- *How can the performance emphasis be moved from final outcomes to execution?* Interestingly, the words *financial* and *final* have the same linguistic root.
- *What are the skills and resources required to produce effective results other than financial resources?*
- *What drills—training, simulations, and exercises—are needed to develop skills identified?*
- *How can timely, relevant feedback be given to people in the lower levels of the organization?*

In the absence of coherent answers to such questions, the inevitable outcome of most budgeting and planning exercises is that, like ineffective golf practice, they result in organizational faults being grooved. No improvement takes place. The exclusive emphasis on financial results is particularly pernicious. For, just as is the case in golf, the human mind, under pressure for good outcomes, defaults to familiar habits. Unlike golfers, however, managers deal with abstractions of results, black marks on white paper, instead of actual outcomes. Projected financial outcomes are even easier to fix than accounting results! All it takes is a few changes in the spreadsheet assumptions. Of course, this leaves the basic value-creating processes untouched and the skills required for superior performance unexamined.

Deliberate Practice in Management

Discipline, commitment, focus, effective feedback—it sounds so easy, but it can be so difficult. At least in golf, it is usually possible for an expert, using real-time video equipment, to diagnose the condition of the system and identify the priorities. If you focus on the problems in their proper systemic sequence and remember to deal with the offsetting moves as each problem is fixed, you can be sure that, at least conceptually, the approach is correct. In management, just as is the case in golf, there is always scope for doing things better, and the improvement process never ends. But a few key improvements may make a huge difference, with beneficial effects that cascade throughout the system. One of the benefits of looking at both golf swings and organizations as complex systems is that when one thinks about change, one has to think about the scale and timing of the possibilities. In both activities there are myriad variables that *can* be changed; the problem is choosing the key items that *should* be changed.

In an organization, however, in contrast with golf, finding the key items is more difficult:

- There are *multiple stakeholders with different interests*, and rarely is there any consensus on their priorities.

- *Sudden events*—business recessions, takeovers, technological breakthroughs, and the like—can change the priorities overnight.
- The *webs of cause and effect are extremely tangled,* and there are myriad possibilities for improvement—problems that present themselves are usually effects rather than causes. We'll see a classic example in chapter 15, where apparent inefficiency in a credit department was actually an effect of management's misguided marketing strategy.
- *Focus is difficult to achieve among multiple, conscious agents performing many specialized functions* that are difficult to "drill" in the same way muscles are.
- *Effective feedback is rare* except under very specific circumstances, such as tightly connected production and distribution flow lines.
- *The role of and place for deliberate practice in organizations is not well understood.*

Advice for Improvement

In many organizations, the traditional budgeting process and the management practices it promotes violate all the rules for deliberate practice:

- Quick fixes are everywhere.
- Feedback on behavior is absent.
- The focus is on outcomes, not on execution.
- Drills to develop skills are rarely considered.
- Priorities are unclear.

There Are No Quick Fixes

Managing an organization, like playing golf, demands constant adjustments—adjustments to meet external situations as well as to regulate the internal state of the organism. These adjustments can be effective only if they are layered on top of sound fundamentals—in organizations there are no quick fixes to systemic problems. *Quick fixes don't work well in organizations for the same reason that they are ineffective in golf: they are usually aimed at too superficial a level and deal with symptoms rather than fundamental causes.* For, as we have seen, all organizations are built hierarchically over time, and as they grow more complex, routine activities are buried in systems and procedures beneath the awareness of individual actors. Yet these buried routines, or habits, may be the root of the problem, and they can be difficult to change.

In general management situations, corporate America's favorite candidate for the quick fix is the incentive scheme. No matter what the desired change in behavior, it seems to be an article of American management faith that all one has to do is attach rewards to the appropriate performance index and the behavior will emerge. As a result, corporations seem to spend their lives tinkering with incentive plans. The evidence that incentives can be used effectively in this way, however, is slender. It seems that too often one can get only temporary compliance, rather than long-term commitment to a desired course of action. Financial incentives can produce a superficial, external assent to the "letter" of results, but not a deep, internal dedication to the spirit of the vision. They encourage gaming of the system and if individually focused can damage relationships between people, undermining their interest in their work. We found in our steel distribution business, for example, that an incentive based on return-on-investment criteria discouraged managers from investing in new equipment. As the existing machinery was run into the ground and production tolerances became harder to hold, the operators took less care and pride in what they were doing.

From a systems perspective, the challenge in using incentives is to create relevant, timely feedback that can help people understand the cause-and-effect relationships between their efforts and financial results. At the same time, it should be helpful in the improvement of skills. The very best kind of feedback for rapid learning is "natural" feedback, generated in real time directly by the work itself. The problem is that financial outcomes don't provide this kind of feedback—the feedback they do provide is too late and too aggregate to be helpful. In short, both in theory and in practice, incentive schemes are often thoroughly unsystemic in their operation. Just like quick fixes in golf, they are conscious moves that may give only temporary relief.

Feedback Is Critical

One of the problems that golf and management share is that the feedback commonly available is both too complex to interpret and too late to make any difference to the current activity. Of course, this criticism applies to all formal appraisal systems where the feedback is always too late to change behavior. It's easy to see the problems in poor financial results and errant golf shots, but very difficult to discover their true causes. The traditional budgeting process does nothing to resolve this.

Worse still, the feedback situation can change as organizations and their technologies grow in size. A well-known European manufacturer of digital switches for telephone systems experienced this problem as the software code in their switches grew in length and complexity. Digital switches have to be ultrareliable, with standards much higher than conventional hardware and software; it is not acceptable for them to "crash" while in use. In addition, total system failures can be very difficult to learn from because of the complexity of the interactions.

In the early days, when the software was a few hundred thousand lines of code, there was no problem. The managers could both anticipate and solve problems in an afternoon by bringing all the programmers together in one room. In other words, they could operate like Herbert Simon's first watchmaker. As the code grew to several million lines, however, this was no longer possible; there were too many programmers, and no one could get his head around the system anymore. They were forced to change to the second watchmaker's strategy, chunking the code into modules and ensuring that all the modules fitted together seamlessly—a much tougher proposition than fitting together the hardware for watches! But once the design of the architecture, interfaces, and standards had been specified, they could get meaningful feedback, make changes, and test within each module, confident that the system as a whole would not crash. As one can imagine, the discipline required to do this on a regular basis is considerable.

Harvard Business School professor Kim Clark has argued that modularity in the design and manufacture of products and their use in organizations is central to their ability to innovate. As long as they obey the design rules, designers within modules are free to experiment independently of one another. In organizations, modules in the form of project teams can handle multiple, interrelated tasks far more effectively than a bureaucracy can. This is largely due to the clarity of goals within the modules, the independence of action they permit, and the rapidity of the feedback generated.

Focus on Execution, Not Outcomes

The need for timely, relevant feedback in management suggests that financial outcomes are quite inadequate as a guide to effective action and improvement. It's the correct execution of the individual tasks that matters and that requires practice. But for effective practice, a manager has to identify, measure, and create feedback from activities that take place much earlier in the web of cause and effect. One of the major obstacles to this is traditional cost accounting.

In their seminal book, *Relevance Lost: The Rise and Fall of Management Accounting,* first published in 1987, Thomas Johnson and Robert Kaplan contended that the information derived from traditional management accounting systems was too late, too aggregate, and too distorted to be helpful in making planning and control decisions. They argued that the root of the problem was that management accounting systems, particularly in public companies, had been overwhelmed by the firms' need to make financial reports to outsiders. This demanded that profits and sales be allocated to monthly and quarterly time periods, no matter what the scale of the underlying transactions, some of which might last for years. Harvard Business School professor Robert Kaplan and his colleagues went on to develop a framework to address this problem, which they called "the balanced scorecard" (BSC). The BSC directs a manager's attention away from an exclusive focus on lagging indicators of performance such as financial results. Financial results are important, but using them as your only measure of management performance is as helpful as thinking about your golf score during the swing—it's a desirable outcome of good performance, but a very poor guide to action. In golf, such thoughts may actually interfere with getting things done.

Instead, the BSC framework encourages managers to look at leading indicators of performance such as innovation and learning and the quality of business processes. These factors are difficult to measure, but this is precisely why firms default to the easy financial metrics. The retailers Sears, Roebuck & Company have used a variation of the BSC to track the web of cause and effect connecting employee attitudes through customer experience to financial results. They have been able to establish a fairly precise, cause-and-effect relationship between employee attitudes to their jobs and the company, on the one hand, and customer satisfaction and revenue growth on the other. The lag between the first variable (employee attitudes) and the financial outcomes is five quarters. Sears people can now train, drill, and work on the execution of tasks early in the value creation process, confident that they will lead to desirable results later in the process. Of course, for superior performance, these well-executed tasks have to be blended into a seamless whole.

To Develop Skills, Use Drills

When it comes to building an organizational culture and developing skills, the military boot camp is one of the most effective training programs ever devised. Although it's fashionable these days to decry the mind-numbing drills and the often repressive and intimidating behavior of the traditional drill instructors, the fact is that the method works, at least in the military. Indeed, it is a testament to its effectiveness that it is found in substantially the same form all over the world. And its form has changed little over the centuries, other than to adapt slowly to changing community standards. Milder versions of the boot camp are ubiquitous outside of the military and law-enforcement communities.

In the classic model, raw recruits with widely differing motivations and from a broad variety of social backgrounds are taken into the program. Here they are stripped of all the trappings of individuality and under intense social pressure are compelled to cooperate with each other. Studies of men in combat have established the fact that few men fight and die for high-minded ideological goals. Rather, they fight for their buddies, the members of the small squad to which they belong. The purpose of the boot camp, then, is to create the necessary heat and pressure to form such bonds among individuals who normally might have nothing to do with one another. Their bodies are trained and disciplined, and they are drilled so that they will act together, automatically and without the need for conscious thought. A few months later, most of the recruits will graduate as skilled individuals who have been molded into a coherent community with a distinctive culture. The effect of the program is to inculcate (from the Latin "to trample in") a few habits that will form the foundation upon which graduates can build skills for the rest of their lives. Together with the social network developed during their basic training, the new soldiers are ready to perform at a basic level and are equipped to learn new skills as they pursue their careers.

The benefits of inculcating such basic skills and building an esprit de corps in a business are strikingly illustrated in the success of Andersen Consulting (now Accenture), the consulting offshoot of Arthur Andersen, the tax and audit firm. Arthur Andersen, the founder of the firm, was a strong believer in extensive professional training for his people and in the extra productivity that a comprehensive understanding of the business gave to them. Andersen Consulting inherited this philosophy, and its training infrastructure is one of its distinctive features: the firm spends a stunning 10 percent of its revenues on professional training. Worldwide, every new employee has to take a six-week course,

"Computer Application Programming School" (CAPS), taught by members of the firm. The weeks are eighty hours long, and with business attire required at all times, the program is designed to simulate a project on a client site. Its objective is to teach liberal arts majors and engineers alike the Andersen methodology of systems design and implementation, but it does much more than that, for the program builds a community of practitioners at the same time:

> CAPS is a real shock at first . . . you wonder how you'll be able to keep up, it is very intense . . . but then you find that everyone is in this together and you begin working as a team, helping each other to pull through. And since then, this group has been my main network within the company. The experience created a career-long bond with these cohorts.*

The standardized techniques taught by practitioners and illustrated and updated by current experience from the field make for a powerful common language among the people at Andersen Consulting. Embedded in networks of people with intense shared experience—communities of trust—these techniques make organized behavior—getting things done—much simpler than they would be in other organizations. Andersen, of course, starts the process not with raw recruits, but with highly motivated college graduates, and after the CAPS program their people can carry out complex tasks based on single-sentence directions. A tough evaluation process (only about 10 percent of the recruits make it to partner) ensures that only those best suited to the firm are retained. The recruiting, training, and retention of highly motivated, self-disciplined people ensures that the correct skills are built in at the lowest possible level of the organization. The effect of this shows up clearly in the supervisory ratios. As the diagram shows, the typical professional service firm has a partner:manager:consultant ratio of 1:2:5. Andersen Consulting's ratio is 1:6:30!

---

*Andersen Consulting senior partner, quoted in *INSEAD Case*, p. 5.

Leveraging People in Personal Service Firms

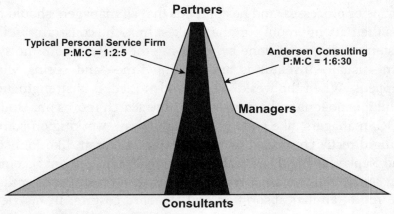

Partners

Typical Personal Service Firm
P:M:C = 1:2:5

Andersen Consulting
P:M:C = 1:6:30

Managers

Consultants

Source: Andersen Consulting (Europe) *INSEAD Case* 392-055-1.

Clearly, the Andersen partners can obtain huge leverage from the low "center of gravity" created by this broad, skilled base. One might say that their people are empowered through working in a flattened hierarchy to use the modern buzzwords, but this is clearly not a trivial achievement. Andersen's single-minded focus on professional competence in a community of practice is central to the process.

Work on Only One Thing at a Time

The shortage of conscious mental-processing capacity at all levels in an organization is a much more serious problem in human organizations than it is in golf. At least in golf the task remains fixed—it's the precision with which it has to be executed that's the real problem. In management, however, the tasks are changing all the time, and management attention is continually becoming fragmented. The setting of priorities is critical, and as we will see, this is the central task of leadership.

One approach from outside the mainstream is that of maverick management guru Eli Goldratt and his "theory of constraints" (TOC). Goldratt's theory of constraints views business as linked chains of processes, and he contends that all managers should focus their attention only on the weakest link, the constraint in the system. This can be done by removing the buffers from the system—usually inventories and waiting time—and seeing what happens. When the weakest link is identified, it is strengthened until it is no longer the weakest, and the search moves on. Under TOC, managers, like good golfers, are always working on something directly connected to performance. Goldratt, like Johnson and Kaplan, is highly critical of traditional management accounting, and TOC companies typically use variable costing rather than the more familiar absorption and standard costing. In his view, variable costing is desirable because it does not encourage the building up of inventories, is more useful in decisions, and is closer to the cash flow concept of income. But the central and most helpful feature of his approach is his focus on doing one thing at a time, through a monomaniacal preoccupation with finding and fixing *the* constraint.

What to Do

The annual corporate budgeting routine is so deeply embedded in most mature firms that the thought of changing it is daunting—exactly like changing something deep in the golf swing. But the question is, what should one change to? If an effective budget and planning process should perform the same functions for an organization that effective practice and training performs for a golfer, what would it look like? The most important requirements are to get into depth and to tie together the many elements of a plan into webs of cause and effect. Two corporations illustrate how to approach each of these issues: Emerson Electric, one of the most consistent profit producers in the history of business; and 3M, one of the most innovative.

Emerson Electric

Two brothers, Alexander and Charles Meston, who developed applications for the (then) new alternating current electric motor, founded Emerson Electric in 1890. Ever since then, Emerson has made a range of electrical, electromechanical, and electronic products. Although the corporate name may not be familiar to the general public, the products made by their divisions usually are: Skil, Dremel, and Craftsman power tools, Copeland compressors, Rosemount instruments, and in the power transmission market, Morse, Sealmaster, and U.S. Electric Motors. From this apparently unglamorous set of businesses, Emerson had, until 2001, produced forty-three years of consecutive increases in earnings per share. It is a record matched by only four other public companies in the United States, none of which are in Emerson's line of business.

Emerson's management approach under the leadership of long-time CEO Chuck Knight (who recently retired) is distinguished by its focus on the "fundamentals"—intensity, discipline, and persistence in the pursuit of continuous cost reduction and growth. Emerson concentrates on getting to the roots of the webs of cause and effect that drive financial results. They are highly decentralized, focusing on their sixty-plus divisions and their operators, who are responsible for both planning and execution of their strategies. Although they will group divisions together to exploit shared functions and technologies, they will *never* aggregate financial reports for planning or controlling purposes at any level other than that of the individual division or the corporation as a whole. The reason for this is that they feel that the use of aggregate financials makes the link between cause and effect too tenuous. Just as we experienced in Federal Industries, the budgeting process can easily become too abstract and remote from the everyday realities of running the business. Operators become unable to track results back to their own actions, and accountability is lost.

Emerson uses an ABC approach to budgeting, where the A budget reflects the most likely scenario, B is a possible lower level of activity, and C is lower still. Associated with each level of activity is a comprehensive action plan. In the case of the A budget, it will be directed at both cost reduction and growth. Every year for the past forty, in good times and in bad, Emerson has set cost reduction goals at every level in the organization and required plant personnel to develop detailed actions to reach those goals. Typically, Emerson targets and achieves a 6–7 percent reduction per year in cost of sales. In the past five years, as the potential for cost reductions has declined, this push has been supplemented with an increasing emphasis on innovation and growth. In 1998, almost one-third of sales came from products developed in the past five years, up from 18 percent ten years earlier. And by the year 2000, Emerson aims to have it up to 35 percent.

The B and C budgets together with their associated action plans contain more drastic yet specific actions aimed at making financial targets despite the lower revenues they contain. When it is clear that an A budget revenue plan is no longer attainable, the managers have to implement either the B or C cost reduction actions. They are not allowed to travel on hopefully. In short, the budgeting process at Emerson, like intelligent golf practice, is geared toward the examination of alternative methods of achieving acceptable outcomes.

3M

3M is one of the greatest innovative success stories of business. The firm was founded in 1902 to mine corundum in Minnesota, but the venture soon collapsed, and in desperation the managers turned to making sandpaper and grinding wheels. Under the direction of the legendary William McKnight, the company developed into a highly innovative organization—and the rest, as they say, is history. 3M has demonstrated time and again that it has been able to innovate even as it has grown in size. The stories of 3M innovations and the curious, unplanned ways in which many of them emerged are legion. For 3M functions in many ways as a complex ecology, and the precise webs of cause and effect are difficult to track except through stories. Perhaps it is the presence of so many stories in their history that led 3M to approach planning as a problem in story composition.

Their use of story began with their dissatisfaction with the traditional bullet-point presentation. A typical business plan might contain points like these:

- Increase our market share from 40 percent to 50 percent.
- Regain product development leadership position.
- Increase sales closings by 50 percent.

The reader will recognize instantly from chapter 12 that the verbs in these points are achievement verbs. That is, they refer to desirable outcomes and suggest no method for their achievement. While bullet lists are economical of space and time, that strength is also their weakness. For bullet lists cannot specify detailed relationships and assumptions. As a result, the points come across as generic—they could apply to any firm.

Stories, on the other hand, deal with particular events and define relationships between events and actions to reveal complex webs of cause and effect. Stories that convey drama (from the Greek *dra,* meaning "to do, act, or make") are particularly compelling. Central to the plot of any dramatic story is the character of the actors. Strong characters are not logic machines; they are passionate creatures who want and need and act—people who will commit themselves obsessively to a goal. And surely that's what one is looking for in most undertakings? It is all too easy to massage the assumptions in a spreadsheet forecast to meet corporate return on investment criteria. Forecast financial returns are "hygiene" factors—there has to be enough, but more is not necessarily better. As a result, investment decisions are rarely made on purely financial criteria.

So how does one decide which projects to approve? All things being equal, it makes sense to support the people who appear most committed to their projects, the ones who can "embody" them and make them come alive in the form of story. In a stage play, early in the performance, strong characters let the audience know that there are powerful forces at work within them. In musicals, within the first fifteen minutes the lead character usually sings what lyricist and playwright Oscar Hammerstein II calls an "I want" song. This identifies the character's hopes and aspirations and hooks the audience into what is to follow. So 3M people now try to write their plans as narratives. They set the stage or context within which the action is to take place, telling the history of the strategic unit and outlining the key factors that would make for success in their marketplace. Next, a dramatic conflict is presented, the challenge that they face, the gap that exists between what they are and what they would like to be. These are the kinds of challenges that can compel participation and attract resources from those making funding decisions. Last, there is the resolution—exactly how the challenge will be met and the results expected. Aristotle believed that drama was the "imitation of action." If a good play is read backward, it is said, the reader should be able to see how each action leads to every other action. A business plan written and presented as a dramatic story should have that same capacity to link multiple chains of cause and effect.

The "likely" story is a condensed vision, a desired "memory of the future." This is, of course, exactly the same process we saw being used by Jack Welch to mobilize the people at GE, but at 3M it is being used at the much more detailed level of individual units and programs.

Summary

This chapter began with the recounting of the dysfunctional dynamics of a typical annual corporate planning and budgeting session. The problem was illustrated by translating the budget discussion into a dialogue between a golfer and his coach. A preoccupation with final outcomes can lead only to the manipulation of scores of the kind we find in the public reporting of corporate results. The traditional budgeting process violates all of the systemic advice for improvement derived from golf: it is rife with quick fixes, as exemplified by incentive plans; the focus is on outcomes when it should be on execution—an approach encouraged by performance management systems such as the balanced scorecard; the role of drills is rarely understood, but their value is clear in the practice of Andersen Consulting—firms rarely focus on one thing at a time, as recommended by Eli Goldratt's theory of constraints. Last, the chapter examined two examples of sensible approaches to budgeting—Emerson Electric and 3M.

No. 14

Coaches and Caddies

Par-4	477 yards

Loneliness . . . This is the scythe of the game, its midnight heart and terror. The utter, excruciating isolation which attacks the player under pressure. . . . Forget all else but remember this: You are never alone. You have your caddie. You have me.
—STEVEN PRESSFIELD, THE LEGEND OF BAGGER VANCE

Now do not think that we use imagination *in teaching golf to evolve new theories . . . [w]hat we use imagination for is to translate theory into* feeling. . . .
—PERCY BOOMER, ON LEARNING GOLF

It is still dark just before dawn in the foothills of the Rockies, and it looks as though the day will start off overcast. In the east, however, far away across the vast plain, the sky is clear, and as the sun comes up it casts a fiery red glare across the giant landscape. In the west, the vertical faces and towers of Cheyenne Mountain respond to this advance by blushing a deep pink. The glow starts on the heights and travels slowly downward toward the canyons, growing in intensity until it touches the high walls of the Broadmoor Hotel, setting them afire. The small group of executives, gathered for breakfast in a high penthouse, has watched the unfolding spectacle in silence, held spellbound by the glory of it.

Now the red light is turning golden as it starts to catch the tops of the aspens and light up the fairways and greens of the Broadmoor's golf courses. One by one, the members of the group turn away to resume their meals, and the conversation picks up again.

Playing golf at the Broadmoor is always fun—the thin mountain air allows every shot to travel farther, and the combination of slope and hard fairways allows even mediocre golfers to hit the ball prodigious distances. Today, however, the golfers among the group can only look longingly at the courses. For they have come to the Broadmoor not to play golf, but to attend the weeklong Leadership at the Peak (LAP) course at the Colorado Springs facility of the Center for Creative Leadership.

Leadership Development

The late Donald Schon, a respected management academic at MIT for many years, once wrote:

> In the varied topography of professional practice, there is a high, hard ground overlooking a swamp. On the high ground, management problems lend themselves to solution through the application of research-based theory and technique. In the swampy lowland, messy, confusing problems defy technical solution. The irony of this situation is that the problems of the high ground tend to be relatively unimportant to individuals and society at large, however great their technical interest might be, while in the swamp lie the problems of greatest human concern. The practitioner must choose. Shall he remain on the high ground where he can solve relatively unimportant problems according to prevailing standards of rigor, or shall he descend to the swamp of important problems and nonrigorous inquiry.[*]

In the teaching of management, at least since the 1950s, many business schools have occupied the high, hard ground of rigor, al-

[*]Donald A. Schon, *Educating the Reflective Practitioner*, p. 3.

most as an extension of their location within the academic silos of their universities. In recent years, however, albeit reluctantly, almost all of them have had to edge closer to the swamp of relevance. This movement, which has dismayed many of the management academics, is testimony to the power of feedback to shift entrenched institutional attitudes and behaviors. For the primary catalyst for this change, at least in North America, has been the annual publication of B-school rankings, a process begun by *BusinessWeek* magazine in 1988. Prior to then, the various "customers" for qualifications such as the MBA were poorly identified and their views were rarely heard, let alone solicited. Now corporations, alumni, students, and deans all get their say, and their views are published in closely scrutinized reports that allow focused criticisms and provide regular indications of progress toward goals.

In the topography of professional practice, the Center for Creative Leadership is probably sited closer to the swamp of relevance than any of the recognized business schools. The swamp is the lair of the wicked problems, problems that defy clear definition and whose natures change as soon as we think we understand them. The nature of leadership is itself a wicked problem. Leadership cuts across boundaries; it has to do with relationships rather than objects, with synthesis rather than analysis, and it has to be learned as a process rather than taught as a product.

Leadership at the Peak sets out to do this. It is one of the center's most highly rated courses, and like all of their programs, it is feedback intensive. The structure of such programs is quite different from the traditional head-down courses found in many business schools, with their emphasis on lectures and cases. For if leadership behavior is to be authentic, then the knowledge has to be embodied, and this is best achieved by a combination of experience and feedback. Over the next five days, the executives will receive nonstop, intensive feedback from their bosses, peers, subordinates, and coaches on their personalities, their behaviors, all aspects of their leadership styles, and even their physical fitness and health. For the person to be developed is the whole person, and LAP is a proverbial "hall of mirrors," where participants continually catch sight of themselves in a huge variety of posed and unposed situations. Some of the managers in a period of five days will receive more feedback than they have in the past ten years. Some of the feedback will be about preferences and competencies that are difficult to change—basic personality traits, for example. All the feedback will take place within the center's coaching framework of assessment, challenge, and support: assessment to evaluate where they are in developing their capacity to lead; challenge to provoke them to set clear goals for improvement; and support on their pathway to the perfection of their art.

All of those who come to LAP are in search of personal change of some kind, although this realization may not have come to them unaided. Some may have been sent by their organizations for a variety of purposes, ranging from grooming for a bigger job to the need to "fix" a problem, although the center does not encourage the notion of quick fixes. Sometimes the course is a reward for a job well done. Whatever reasons have brought them there, however, none of those attending is exactly sure what it is they are looking for.

This paradox creates a dilemma that is familiar to all learners, including golfers and managers:

1. We know that we would like to change our behavior.
2. We recognize the desired behavior in others when we see it.
3. We can recognize, with help, when we are not producing it.
4. We do not know where to go from here.*

The center's approach to "where to go from here" is to immerse the learner in feedback. Apart from paper tests and reports from work, the primary vehicle for this feedback is a set of structured experiences that model a variety of important management activities. These structured situations are virtual worlds, safe halfway houses between abstract concept and real-world performance. They are places and occasions where the executives can act and

*Adapted slightly from Donald A. Schon, *Educating the Reflective Practitioner,* pp. 263–64.

react in real time and then review their behavior afterward. On the first day of the course, for example, each starts off with an unrehearsed, live interview in a TV studio replete with director, grips, and gaffers, while peers and coaches sit in the audience. After a pleasant beginning, the interview quickly takes on the character of a media ambush. For the news reporter has dug into the backgrounds of each executive's organizations and has some tough questions on specific, hot issues that are not general knowledge. "Last week the Oklahoma authorities accused your Tulsa plant of dumping chemicals into the local water supply," she might say, "How can your company allow such things to happen?" The executive then has to do the best he or she can in real time.

Later, each individual, together with peers and coaches, will go through the videotape, picking out the key points. Often participants are stunned to see how ineptly they have performed and the poor impression they have made. The impression that they create has little to do with what they say and much more to do with their behavior. Do they look tense or relaxed? Do their eyes move from side to side when tough questions are asked? Are they really listening to the questions? And so on. Communication experts suggest that as much as two-thirds of the content of communication is transmitted by this nonverbal body language. As a species, our communication skills have been honed over the millennia to help us decide whether we can trust another person or not. Without being consciously aware of it, we are able to detect deception quite easily by being acutely sensitive to facial muscle tone and expression, pitch and timbre of voice, and the myriad small clues to a person's real intentions. We even have muscles in our faces that are not under our conscious control and work only when we smile spontaneously—even a baby can detect a forced smile from the genuine expression. Indeed, it has been argued that the detectable display of emotions is essential for cooperation and our survival as a species. If people could cheat without revealing such clues, one would never know whom to trust.

Clearly a structured situation such as the TV interview, while safe, is not necessarily comfortable for the LAP participants. For the most part, they are managers who work at senior levels in large hierarchical organizations. As such they are used to being in well-structured situations and continually "on top" of events, briefed and primed for all contingencies. Nevertheless, in the simulations, with rare exceptions, they experience a loss of control, competence, and confidence, accompanied by unpleasant sensations of vulnerability and enforced dependency. Perhaps this is why relatively few CEOs are found on LAP—the feelings of discomfort are just too severe for all but a few to face. This is a pity, for it is with this surrender of traditional control, unilateral *power-over*—that the process of learning can begin; through the discovery of emergent control, of synergistic *power-with*. (Both these terms, "power-over" and "power-with," will be described in more detail in the next chapter.) For the participants on LAP, only their special relationship with peers and coaches makes this transition bearable. For they are all in it together—there are no judges, no critics, no shareholders, only partners in inquiry, fellow seekers on the path. For a brief week, they are part of a community of practitioners, learning from the know-how of others and sharing their own in return.

Outcomes

CCL's research suggests that there are a number of beneficial outcomes for the participants in feedback-intensive programs such as LAP. At the most superficial level, there is the content delivered by the various personality inventories—people learn about the skills of effective leaders and how personality affects leadership behaviors. At another level, there is a new sense of self-awareness that is often sparked by the gap between their self-assessment and the assessment of them given by others. The 360-degree feedback instruments are particularly helpful in this regard. Such instruments are anathema in hierarchies of command-and-control, where they are often seen as subversive of established authority. I can still remember the shock and incredulity of one of our senior managers when the principles of 360-degree feedback were explained to him: "You mean that *they* rate *me*?" Of course, he may have been under the mistaken belief that his compensation would depend upon his rating. One of the aggravating factors in many organizations is that no clear distinction is drawn between uses of performance appraisal for either development or administration. In many industries, performance ratings are often used for administrative purposes—pay, promotion, and the like—and every manager knows how this warps the appraisal process. CCL recommends and uses 360-degree feedback *only* for development purposes; their research suggests that ratings become far less reliable if raters know their responses are going to be used administratively.

LAP participants also report a change in their perspective, usually as a result of their exposure to the views of others and the better understanding of the contexts in which they live and work. The outcomes for participants in programs like LAP can be summed up as an expansion in their capacity to use their emotional intelligence.

The concept of emotional intelligence has been popularized by Daniel Goleman, a psychologist and journalist for *The New York Times*. He identifies its components as follows:*

Self-awareness: the ability to recognize and understand your moods, emotions, and drives, as well as their effect on others.

Self-regulation: the ability to control or redirect disruptive impulses and moods; the propensity to suspend judgment before acting.

Motivation: a passion to work for reasons that go beyond money or status; a propensity to pursue goals with energy and persistence.

---

*Adapted from Daniel Goleman, "What Makes a Leader?," *Harvard Business Review* (November–December 1998): 93–102.

Empathy: the ability to understand the emotional makeup of other people; skill in treating people according to their emotional reactions.

Social Skill: proficiency in managing relationships and building networks; an ability to find common ground and build rapport.

The Coaching Challenge and the Learner's Dilemma

It's worth taking the learner's dilemma outlined a few pages earlier and rephrase it as a golfer's dilemma:

1. I would like to change my swing to produce more consistent results.
2. I can recognize the desired swing features in others when I see them.
3. I can recognize, with help, when I am not producing them.
4. I do not know where to go from here—instruction doesn't seem to help.

From a systems perspective, the answer to the "where to go from here" question has to be to immerse the learner in timely, specific feedback at as many of the levels of the system as he or she can handle. Golf is usually thought of as an individual sport, but today the professional golfer is at the center of a team of feedback specialists. The most important members of this team in the golfing context are the coaches and the caddies, although it is estimated that a third of professional golfers now use a sports psychologist. The primary role of these specialists is to provide timely, specific feedback to their golfer, although usually at different systemic levels. In terms of the quality of feedback, the professional golfer is far better equipped than the average professional manager, who rarely gets feedback that is timely, specific, or disinterested.

To understand the coaching challenge and learner's dilemma, it's helpful to bring back a modified version of one of the diagrams used earlier in the book:

The Challenge of Teaching and Learning a Competence

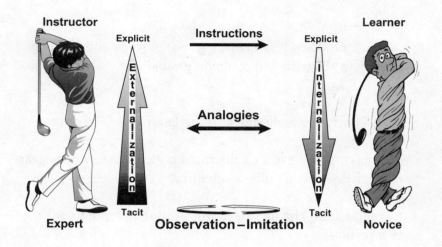

The diagram above identifies some of the systemic issues en-countered in teaching and learning golf. On the left-hand side we have the expert, whose knowledge is largely tacit—embodied and personal, as all true expertise must be. To teach what he knows, he has to be able either to transfer the tacit knowledge directly (at the bottom of the diagram) or to convert it into explicit knowledge through a process of externalization, where it can be conveyed in the form of instructions (top of the diagram). There's a range of techniques in between (I will discuss the role of analogies shortly), and in practice, the effective teacher will use a combination of them. On the right-hand side, we have the learner to whom the skills have to be transferred. The learner has to be able either to as-similate tacit knowledge directly or to take in explicit knowledge and then convert it into tacit knowledge. This latter process, which is essential in the development of competence, is labeled as a process of internalization.

The vertical arrows are shaded to represent the richness of the communication process between the expert and the learner. Com-munication is rich and "thick" at the bottom of the arrows (dark shading) and poor and "thin" at the top (light shading). Indeed, the quality of communication deteriorates as we move upward until we reach the level marked "instructions." Here the knowledge is completely explicit—the information contained in a "how to" golf book, for example—but the communication process has been progressively impoverished (denatured, one might say) by the translation of the skilled body's know-how into a verbal know-what.

The best learning takes place at the bottom of the arrows via the loop labeled "Observation-Imitation." Here there is a one-on-one, face-to-face, master-apprentice relationship with rich two-way feedback in real time between the expert and the learner. All the physical senses of both parties are engaged, and the delay between action and feedback is very short. The learner observes the expert, imitates his moves, and receives immediate feedback on his efforts. Enhanced by modern technology, such as real-time video, these are the ideal conditions for learning. The role of the expert teacher or coach is critical here—research suggests that typically one-on-one tutoring from an expert results in performance on the part of the learner two standard deviations above that produced by teaching in a general class.

Analogies

In the middle of the diagram I have put the label "analogies." Analogies and metaphors can carry us across the otherwise unbridgeable gap between ineffable, tacit know-how and the precise articulations of explicit know-what. Indeed, this concept is embedded in the derivations of both words. Analogy means literally "gather up," and metaphor comes from the combination of the Greek words *meta* ("beyond") and *pherein* ("carry"). The latter word is where our English word *ferry* comes from. Images and diagrams, which are also types of analogies, also have this ability to ferry us across gaps in our experience. Perhaps this is the reason a picture is worth a thousand words!

Thus, effective teachers of golf have an endless supply of analogies—images, feelings, and exercises—that allow the learner to both understand and feel what the swing should be like. The challenge for the teacher is that not any metaphor will do: it has to resonate in the mind of the student. Even great golfers are continually searching for a "trigger" image or feeling to evoke the right muscular actions. People vary greatly in their preferences for different ways of taking in and using information. "All good teachers must repeat," wrote Percy Boomer, "but never in exactly the same words or with just the same connections. . . . I do not mind if I have to say the same thing in a dozen different ways so long as one of the twelve gets home with you."

This ability to externalize tacit knowledge, to articulate the fundamentals of an activity, is a powerful skill in its own right. It may be the primary reason the best golfers are often not the best teachers. Top golfers who play entirely by feel—Fred Couples and Paul Stankowski come to mind immediately—admit that they are almost totally incoherent when it comes to explaining what they think or feel as they swing a golf club. It usually takes their coaches to help them put it into words. The converse is also true— the best teachers are rarely the best players. Their ability to put so much into words may actually interfere with their capacity to perform the activity unconsciously—they think too much. This may apply to management as well as sports, and it may be the systemic truth behind the adage that those who can, do, and those who can't, teach! But it takes nothing away from the art of the teacher, whose skill, though different from that of the performer, may be just as great. This capacity, however, to make explicit what an expert can only feel, and then turn it into a thought that can be used by a learner, is one of the most important functions of a coach.

Confidence

Coaches, caddies, and sports psychologists may work at different levels, but all of them try to sustain a good level of self-confidence in their players. The impact of self-confidence on performance and its susceptibility to both stress and the expectations of others is widely acknowledged but poorly understood. The relationship is usually illustrated as an inverted "u," with too little self-confidence being as destructive of performance as too much. This precarious balance on a rounded peak captures the dynamic nature of the processes involved, for there are slippery slopes on either side of the peak that lead either to a total lack of confidence or to arrogance and complacency.

Self-confidence is an expectation that we develop of our own capacities, but it seems to be nurtured by the expectations of others. In medicine it is the well-known placebo effect; in management it has been called the "Pygmalion effect." There is solid evidence that

- what a manager expects of his subordinates and the way he treats them largely determine their performance and career progress.
- a unique characteristic of superior managers is their ability to create high performance expectations that subordinates fulfill.
- less effective managers fail to develop similar expectations, and, as a consequence, the productivity of their subordinates suffers.
- subordinates, more often than not, appear to do what they believe they are expected to do.*

The manager/subordinate language reflects the era in which this article was written and contrasts sharply with the trendier coach/associate terms used today. Yet evidence continues to accumulate that the Pygmalion effect is real and that it works at group and organizational levels as well as that of the individual. The question remains, however, how does the effect work?

It must be that our actions are continually channeled by our anticipations—our memories—of the future. As psychologist George Kelly puts it, organisms come into the world "alive and struggling"; we are processes, not inert objects waiting for stimulation. Kelly conceives

---

*J. Sterling Livingston, "Pygmalion in Management," *Harvard Business Review* (July–August 1969): 81–89.

... of a person's processes as operating through a vast network of pathways rather than fluttering about in a vast emptiness. The network is flexible and is frequently modified, but it is structured and it both facilitates and restricts a person's range of action ... man seeks prediction. His structured network of pathways leads toward the future so that he may anticipate it. ... It is the future which tantalizes man, not the past. Always he reaches out to the future through the window of the present.*

The most coherent expression of this process, of course, is the story. It is the ongoing narrative within every individual that creates and sustains their identity. Shared among individuals, narratives can build and sustain higher-level organizations—families and teams, companies and communities. Sports psychologists and coaches and caddies, when they work at levels above that of basic technique, are continually trying to construct positive stories for the players. As we shall see in chapter 17, in this respect their role is no different from that of leaders.

Essentially, the participants on LAP have come to CCL to revisit and revise their own stories—to punctuate the past and frame the future. Like every participant on every course given at the center, they are asked to keep a private daily journal in which they record and reflect on all aspects of their experience. The role of diary is to focus attention and preserve learnings. On the Leading Creatively program described in chapter 12, participants are encouraged to draw and paint in their diaries, using whatever medium best allows them to capture their experience.

This discipline of keeping a journal can be enormously effective for golfers and managers alike. For golfers intent on improving their games, it is essential to maintain continuity between practice sessions and lessons, to remember what you were working on, how it felt, and so on. For managers, such journals are ideal for documenting events and keeping track of an agenda. John Kotter has identified the development and implementation of a broad-

---

*George A. Kelly, *A Theory of Personality*, p. 49.

based agenda as the central activity for effective general managers. Some highly effective managers make their daily notes public, circulating them among their colleagues so that they stay abreast of what's happening.

The Swedish Golf Model

The successful application of a coaching model that contains the elements of assessment, challenge, and support can be seen in the stunning success record of Swedish golfers, especially their women players, over the past decade. Golfers such as Helen Alfredsson, Liselotte Neumann, and Annika Sorenstam have become familiar figures on Sunday afternoons in U.S. tournaments. All three, together with their compatriots Maria Hjorth, Carin Koch, Sophie Gustafson, and Catrin Nilsmark, rank high in the lists of the tour's money winners. On the men's tour, with the exception of Jesper Parnevik and perhaps Gabriel Hjerkstedt, the Swedes are better known in Europe, where they perform consistently well. With a population of less than nine million, about $3\frac{1}{2}$ percent of whom play golf, Sweden has a climate that meets few of Daniel Chambliss's requirements for an environment conducive to sporting excellence. Sweden's land area is a little larger than California, but the regular golf season lasts from April to November at best. How do they do it?

The Swedish Golf Federation is a government-sponsored volunteer organization through which the game is coordinated in what they call an "elite golf programme." Organizationally the program is decentralized and consists of three layers—club, district, and national levels. Like a baseball farm system, the program is designed to identify and train likely-looking prospects, then expose them to challenges that escalate steadily in severity. They describe their tournament program as a "finely meshed net" in which all talented players can be caught and monitored. At the national level the best one hundred or so juniors, fifty adults, and twenty-five professionals are gathered into eight national squads for special attention and training. They put a great deal of emphasis on learning as a team, striving to create communities of learners who can help each other.

Once you are selected for a top team, the scrutiny becomes intense. The Swedish conception of coaching in golf is definitely not a head-down approach. It covers technique, personality development, mental strength, physique and health, diet, and technical knowledge of equipment. Pia Nilsson, former LPGA player and current head coach of both men's and women's teams, has articulated a comprehensive philosophy. In its broad approach to the game, it is reminiscent of violin teaching pioneer Shinichi Suzuki's objective, to teach not just the violin, but the acquisition of virtuous habits: a disciplined approach to life. "Our vision is that we develop as human beings through the game of golf," says Nilsson. "[The vision] is a tuning fork and a reminder to us that you are a human being that plays golf and not a golfer who also happens to be a human being. For us, the person is always more important than the result on a scorecard."

They do express their goal of a perfect outcome, however, in scoring terms:

> We have our 54-vision. To go around in 54 means birdying every hole on a par-72 course. Almost all of you have birdied each hole on your home course at some time or another. You can see yourself doing it on every single hole. You haven't done it yet in the same round. What would be needed to do it? Golf has existed for many hundreds of years. Since the origins of tournament golf two putts per green has been considered "normal." What would have happened if a single putt had been considered natural instead from the start? What the 54-vision says is: dare to go beyond the limits.*

Yet coupled with this difficult, challenging goal is a series of softer beliefs—that every person is unique and with unlimited potential and that golf should be fun. Importantly, they believe mind

*Pia Nilsson, Swedish National Golf Team.

and body are one system and that one's attitude, both physical and mental, affects the activity of the brain. Perhaps that's why they affirm in their beliefs that Swedes are good putters:

> Many believe dogmatically that we can't be good at putting because of our short season. There aren't many weeks in the year when the greens are up to international standards. But instead, we posed the question: What do we need to be a good putting nation? The answer we arrived at is that of course it is possible, even though we need to do it differently. Many aspects of putting are better practiced indoors on a good carpet. All the theoretical knowledge is found in this country. Also we need to be more disciplined when we have the opportunity to putt on good surfaces, always to undertake practice of the highest quality.[*]

As we saw in chapter 4, there are good systemic reasons for the correctness of this belief!

In the Swedish coaching model, the achievement of perfection requires the integration of many different skills, each of which has been developed by intensive, disciplined practice with constant, timely, specific feedback. The secret lies not in the skills, but in the balance with which they are blended:

> You need a way to access all your abilities when you need them. To play better than anyone has ever done requires being in ideal balance more often. . . . It means finding the equilibrium between different abilities. . . . The important thing is to get to know yourself about how balanced you are right now. Then you must find the best way of balancing yourself. Find your best way of playing in the moment. . . . As part of our work for making you better at playing golf and developing as a human being . . . we want you to be your own best coach.[†]

---

[*]Pia Nilsson, Swedish National Golf Team.
[†]Ibid.

Summary

This chapter has outlined a model of coaching that seems to apply to both golf and management. The LAP program at the Center for Creative Leadership was used to illustrate a coaching framework of assessment, challenge, and support. When a learner is confronted by a wicked problem of the kind that lurks in complex systems, the best approach seems to be to place them in a community of learners and immerse them all in rich feedback. The special skill of the coach is to be able to articulate to learners what the expert may only feel. Metaphors play a major role in allowing us to convey images—pictures and feelings—of the correct moves. The highly successful Swedish golf program was used to illustrate this coaching process at work in golf. The ultimate objective is to develop every learner so that he can become his own best coach.

No. 15

Flow

Par-5	548 yards

*Rhythm and timing are two things that we all must have, yet
no one knows how to teach either.*
—BOBBY JONES

*This is the meaning of effective decision—the control of the
changeable strategic factors, that is, exercise of control at the
right time, right place, right amount and right form so that
purpose is properly redefined and accomplished.*
—CHESTER BARNARD, FUNCTIONS OF THE EXECUTIVE

Early in his career as a management consultant, Peter Drucker observed:

> A well-managed plant . . . is a quiet place. A factory that is "dramatic,"
> a factory in which the "epic of industry" is unfolded before the visitor's
> eyes, is poorly managed. A well-managed factory is boring. Nothing
> exciting happens in it because the crises have been anticipated and
> have been converted into routine. Similarly a well-managed organiza-
> tion is a "dull" organization.*

Drucker is right: a well-managed factory runs smoothly because
the responses to the crises have been tested and embodied—

*The Effective Executive, p. 42.

transformed into routines and combined to make for superior performance. The routines that make factories boring are the very same routines that make sports played at the top level so exciting. We see it in the effortless swings of expert golfers and the un-canny coordination of a football, basketball, or hockey team that is really "on" its game. As spectators we don't find such perfor-mances boring or dull because we can see the actions easily and comprehend it at our own scale; we can identify closely with the players and, in the case of golf, can compare their smooth moves with our own less coordinated efforts. The phenomenon has even been observed in the workplace in the shape of the so-called super-workers or star performers who seem to accomplish work fast and produce results effortlessly.

Sometimes we can experience the same excitement watching an organization perform in situations where the activity is close to our own scale—on the smooth-running flight deck of a modern air-craft carrier, for example, or in the synchronized movements of a crack military unit. British writer John Masters captured this feel-ing during the time he commanded a Gurkha regiment in Britain's Indian army. Drawn from the hardy hill tribes of Nepal, these sol-diers have been described as the best infantrymen in the world:

> We were fast, flexible, and fit. We were a delicate instrument that re-acted to the rustle of a feather. Nothing ever had to be said twice and no word could be recalled, for with the breathing of it action was com-pleted. The discipline of skill was so ingrained that in the field there appeared to be no discipline. There were no stiff ranks, only carelessly grouped men, but all in the best places for doing whatever they had to do. Every man nourished in himself a part of the single, driving confi-dence of the regiment, which would not brook delay or incompetence, which tore into obstacles and pushed aside difficulties.*

We know these achievements when we see them, but we may struggle to define exactly what it is that sets them apart from other, less expert efforts. For what distinguishes all such accom-

*John Masters, writing about the Fourth Gurkhas Regiment, in *Bugles and a Tiger* (New York: Viking Press, 1956), p 302.

plishments is the effortless power and the amount of time that seem to be available to the performers to get things done; there are no glitches, hurry, or tension, just a smooth flow of activity. Even the performers themselves remark on the plastic quality of time when they are "in the zone." Top hitters in baseball say that everything seems to slow down so much that they can see the stitches on the ball as it hurtles toward them. Yet even they are powerless to explain where this effect comes from or how it works. Indeed, it may defy analysis altogether, for superior performances seem to have an integrative quality, a certain togetherness or harmony, that astounds and awes us—elegance, timing, synchronicity—we struggle with the language. *"Je ne sais quoi,"* say the French—"I don't know quite what." Of all the words we use to describe such performances, perhaps grace (from the Latin *gratia*, meaning "gratitude"), with its associations of forgiveness and even divine sanction, best sums up our state of wonder.

Although it may defy description, as we saw in chapter 6, excellence *is* mundane—the graceful integration of many component skills, each of which has been drilled individually and reduced to an automatic routine. That is why it is so difficult to analyze excellence, to put one's finger on "the" secret—for there is no one "thing" to put one's fingers on, only a set of disciplines and the processes that integrate them. Nevertheless, in this chapter I want to look at the systems dynamics of excellence, the smoothness of performance, that we call flow.

High-Performance Systems

Relatively few managers have the opportunity to see a high-performance business operation, let alone work with one. I was fortunate in that we had one or two of them hidden in our gritty, commodity business of steel distribution, and I could watch them develop. I have already violated one of the rules of a high-performance business by describing steel as a "commodity." This is a no-no in the business, especially on the sales desk, where salespeople who think of the product as a commodity typically sell it for prices that are too low to be profitable. The best of them learn that every day and for every customer there was no such thing as a price "point," that market-clearing fiction beloved of the economists. Rather, in real time there is a price band, and the challenge every day for the sales force is to find the top of that band. The key to doing this is in-depth knowledge both about their customers and about their products.

Norm Katzman, my mentor in the art of selling steel, himself a grizzled veteran, put it this way with a simple example: "When the phone goes and the customer asks our price for two-by-two-by-quarter-inch angle [a generic size and shape of steel], you have two choices. You can tell him 'twenty-three cents a pound,' in which case he can shop your price all over town, or you can ask him 'What do you want to use it for?' And he may tell you that he is a farmer who wants to make fence poles eight feet long. And if you know your inventory and how steel can be used, you may be able to substitute some other shape and dimension and quote a price of 'seven dollars a pole, including cutting.' Now you have shown an interest in his business, addressed his real, deeper need, and given him a price that is much more difficult to shop around."

Norm Katzman's advice to me was, of course, the managerial equivalent of a golf tip. In the steel business, it would not be enough even to have an entire sales desk made up of Norm Katzmans. The whole system has to be tuned. But one has to be careful what one tunes it to. For years, for example, we had encouraged the taking of small orders in our branches. For if you, a customer, call up a steel distributor asking for a small amount of steel, it's likely that you are a casual buyer. Steel is probably not a very large component of the cost of whatever it is that you are doing. You will find yourself giving us a much higher margin than we could earn in a high-volume deal with (say) an auto company, for whom steel buying is a science and price is critical. Margins on small orders are high, and as far as we were concerned, the more we had of them the better.

Then one day, as a by-product of the total quality management movement that was sweeping our industry, we began to measure our on-time delivery performance—were our customers getting their steel when we promised it to them? They were not. Our performance was abysmal—we discovered that our deliveries were late nearly 50 percent of the time. The top seven reasons for this were instructive:

1. Salespeople promised the steel early so that they could get the order.
2. The credit department could not approve the credit in time.
3. The processing department couldn't make the schedule.
4. The quality of the product was not up to standard.
5. We were unable to locate the product in our inventory.
6. The trucks were unable to deliver on schedule.
7. A third party let us down.

We formed teams to look at each of these reasons and to search for the systemic causes behind them, drilling into the bowels of the system in the process. Reason one was no surprise in the steel industry—salespeople paid on commission in many industries tend to take orders without checking on availability. The fact that it was no surprise to us does not mean, of course, that it is not a problem—the disconnection between sales incentive schemes and factory production systems is a major obstacle to effective performance. Reason two (credit delay) did surprise us—surely credit approval was a mechanical, by-the-numbers job? How could it be a major source of delay? The team discovered, as some readers may already have guessed, that the problem lay with all those small orders. Small buyers aren't followed closely by the major credit-rating agencies, and in the steel industry they often tend to be highly leveraged borrowers from their banks. Credit approval under such circumstances cannot be done "by the numbers." It requires discussions and sometimes face-to-face meetings, and those take time. Granting credit to small customers in the steel industry is closer to making an unsecured personal loan than it is to taking a business decision. At about the same time, another team working in the warehouse on reason three (production delay) found that the primary source of production delays was the time spent waiting for cranes. After another investigation, a team of warehouse people found that the main reason for that was—you guessed it, small orders: the cranes were busy carrying small quantities of steel all over the warehouse while the processing machines needed to run the big orders waited to be fed.

This was a shocking revelation, because up until then and since time immemorial we had allocated our warehouse costs on the basis of weight. It was dead simple for the cost accountants: heavy orders picked up heavy costs; light orders picked up light costs. Small orders were profitable because while they carried large gross margins, they were burdened with only light costs. Yet here they were tying up our cranes. The cranes didn't mind how much weight they lifted—the limiting factor was time—and small orders took as long to lift as big orders. And when you allocated costs based on crane time (a much tougher variable to measure) and took into account the problems with credit, the small orders didn't look at all profitable. Management was stunned—our small-order strategy had been an article of faith throughout the corporation. Yet here our strategy was creating a fundamentally unprofitable operation for systemic reasons that we had never understood.

Now the reader may well feel that management must have been asleep at the switch to miss something as obvious as this. But as we saw in chapter 3, the logic of complex systems is neither obvious nor intuitive, and it became clear to us only in hindsight. And even then it was the people who worked in operations every day who had to point out to us that the real cost drivers on a warehouse floor are finding and handling the product. It's a common problem in large organizations—the people on the front lines have all the answers, but senior managers never ask them the questions, at least in a form they can understand.

There is a happy ending to this story. At the suggestion of our operations people, we approved the placement of pigeonhole racks in lean-to sheds on the sides of the warehouses. Inside every shed there was a counter where we could handle cash, checks, and credit cards. At one stroke this eliminated both the credit and crane problems, and the small customers loved it: they could get in and out with the minimum of delay. Retail steel became one of the fastest-growing areas of our business. Eventually the retail stores moved out of the industrial sites to be closer to their retail customers.

Opening the Books

The effect of the "drill down" into operations had been to take a fairly simple concept—on-time delivery—and transform it into a host of changes and adjustments to our operations. We transformed the concept of on-time delivery from a boardroom bullet point into a coherent system of activities conducted at all levels of the organization, but with intense involvement on the part of people on the shop floor. During the change process, people in every branch operation became much more familiar with the whys and the hows for change, as we supplied them with detailed performance statistics in every location, including branch financial results.

During this process of making information freely available, we rediscovered something that seems to be continually discovered and then forgotten in human organizations. Work is performed best when the people doing it have a comprehensive understanding of the goals of the organization, are skilled in the appropriate methods and techniques, and receive regular feedback on their progress—both toward reaching the goals and perfecting their skills. During the last twenty years in North America there has been yet another rediscovery of this principle under the banner of "open-book management."

Open-book management is a philosophy rather than a single system—that is, there is no comprehensive framework or set of techniques that can be implemented. Indeed, it is not a substitute for any set of techniques such as total quality management (TQM) or business process reengineering (BPR). The philosophy is that it makes good sense to turn firms into "companies of business-people," firms where everyone, repeat *everyone,* acts and thinks like an informed, self-disciplined businessperson. This philosophy, of course, is just the opposite of Frederick Taylor's, with his view that workers were "heavy both physically and mentally" and incapable of planning. Open-book management approaches the challenge first, as its name suggests, by opening the books—making the detailed financial results of the firm generally available. Next, everyone in the firm is taught business literacy, so that all employees can grasp the implications of the numbers. They are then given the responsibility and held accountable for improving those numbers, a move that will be accompanied by further training in improvement techniques. Last, everyone has a stake in the success of the business via a number of incentive schemes. *The result is a concerted effort to push down decision making in the organization to as low a level as possible, so that decisions are made and integrated as close to the facts as possible.*

Often, open-book companies try to break themselves up into as many self-contained units as possible to enhance people's feelings of autonomy. Effectively, the people doing the work of the firm are invited to make the causal connections between the work they do every day and the financial consequences that have previously been hidden from them. During the process it becomes clear that the interests of management and workers are the same—they are both in the same predicament—and the workers are now being asked to focus and organize their own experience to respond to this shared situation. There is a systemic wisdom to this approach, for the aim of management, as management writer Mary Parker Follett pointed out over seventy years ago, is ". . . to unite those concerned in the study of the situation, to see what the situation demands, to discover the law of the situation and obey that."*

Orders come from—authority is generated by—our shared appreciation of what the situation demands. Here's Follett again: "When you and I decide on a course of action together and do that thing, you have no power over me nor I over you, but we have power

---

*Mary Parker Follett, *Freedom and Coordination*, p. 22.

over ourselves together."* Follett called the power that emerges from this process "power-with," to contrast it with the more common concept of power, "power-over." As will become clear, these concepts of power are directly relevant for golfers. Power-with is synergistic power that emerges from a "tuned" system, where every element of the system works together in support of every other to deliver a continuous flow of effortless power. It is cumulative power that builds as the process flows: the more it flows, the more you have. Power-with is the power of Self 2, whose discovery by Timothy Gallwey was mentioned in chapter 8. Power-over, on the other hand, is the power of Self 1. It is the familiar top-down concept of power, of power as a stock or store that lies outside and above the system and is imposed upon it. Power-over is the kind of power that IBM employed in "Deep Blue" to defeat Gary Kasparov at chess—they just beefed up the processor.

Like many managers, golfers know intellectually that to be consistently successful, what they really need is the synergistic power-with, the power that builds smoothly as all the elements of the swing work progressively together. But they are often unwilling or feel unable to take the time to develop this power. In their impatience they default to the use of power-over—raw, effort-full power—hierarchical domination in the case of management, muscular strength in the case of golf. Power-over can work for a while but leads eventually to a breakdown in coordination. And that spells disaster in both golf and management.

The open-book approach is particularly helpful in building synergistic power in an organization by ensuring that the application of incentives is systemic. As we saw in chapter 13, the haphazard use of incentives is a popular managerial "quick fix." John Case, the best-known documenter of open-book practice, sums up the criticism of traditional incentive plans:†

1. The plan is discretionary with management determining the payout each year.
2. The plan is incomprehensible—people can't understand it.

---

*Mary Parker Follett, *Creative Experience*, p. 186.
†Adapted slightly from *Open-Book Management*, pp. 100–01.

3. The payment is always the same—and becomes regarded as part of regular pay.
4. The plan is invisible—it becomes part of the background routine conducted long after the relevant events.
5. The employees typically have no clue as to whether, or how, what they do day in and day out affects the payout.

The last point is by far the most important, but an additional feature of traditional plans that aggravates all five points is the constant tinkering that goes on. Corporations seem unable to resist fiddling with their incentive plans, searching for the magic formula that will solve all their problems. As Case makes clear, however, there is no magic formula; each system has to be tailored to the individual firm's needs and situation. One swing doesn't fit all.

Open-book companies typically get their people's attention by scrapping the across-the-board annual increase. This highlights the connection between performance and rewards. It also makes it clear that top management will no longer sit in judgment on the performance of the workers, awarding merit or cost-of-living increases. If people want a pay raise, it's up to them—the role of management is to help them create a meaningful framework and reach the goals. A few clear goals are set involving as many people as possible so that they understand why they are important. Progress toward the goals is tracked in public using measures that everyone understands. A fiscally responsible (and everyone understands the reason for that) bonus is paid if and only if the goals are reached.

One problem with all monetary incentives is the lag between the actions and the payout. John Case tells of two interesting ways of dealing with this. The first is Springfield ReManufacturing's (SRC) 10-20-30-40 system, which works like a skins game in golf! If the employees make their targets for the first quarter of the fiscal year, they get 10 percent of the bonus payout; making it in the second quarter, too, garners 20 percent; and so on. If they miss targets for any quarter, the relevant percentage of the bonus pool is carried over to the remaining quarters. Provided the cumulative targets are met by the end of the fiscal year, the full payout is made. Like a skins game, this scheme builds excitement even when there isn't a payout, holding everyone's interest to the final moments of the year. The second approach is Mid-States Technical's "bucket plan," which almost ignores the calendar completely—each time the firm makes $75,000 in pretax earnings (called "filling a bucket"), a bonus is paid. Buckets filled later in the year pay out larger bonuses than earlier ones.

Both these techniques are games that sustain the employees' interest and keep their attention focused on their goals. Indeed, SRC runs its whole open-book approach as a game, and many open-book firms use games both to train and to perform. But unless these techniques are embedded systemically in the transparent world of the open-book approach, they are little more than quick fixes. For the incentive process can go well beyond the paying of bonuses to groups of individuals. As people strive toward the overall goals, various constraints are sure to emerge. Some may be technological, but more often they are skill related. The operators will have to be taught to use a variety of methods and measures to track events and create the feedback loops necessary for learning to take place. Johnsonville Foods, one of the pioneers in the field, is famous for having dispensed almost entirely with its traditional human resources function. Workers conduct their own performance appraisals and make all the hiring and firing decisions on the factory floor. The only way to get an increase in one's basic pay rate at the firm is to become more effective by learning a new skill—budgeting, training, or marketing; nearly two-thirds of its people are involved in formal learning programs.

The thought of "opening the books" to anyone, let alone the workers, is abhorrent to many managers—they think they are giving up control. Like so many golfers who turn to their professionals only when they are in trouble, many open-book companies come to the philosophy only when they are in crisis. Often their financials are so bad that no one would believe them unless they saw them for themselves. Thus, SRC began its conversion to open-book in 1983 in the aftermath of a highly leveraged (debt-to-equity ratio of 90:1) buyout of a factory from International Harvester. Its subsequent success was astonishing—sales grew by 40 percent for several years, while the stock price went up to 186 times its initial value—and drew widespread comment and admiration. It also drew a flood of visitors to Springfield, Missouri, bands of business pilgrims who wanted to visit the shrine and emulate the company's performance. It's likely, however, that many of them saw the techniques but could not appreciate the systematic way in which they were used and the long process of trial and error it had taken to get there. This problem afflicts both managers and golfers. In 1986, Jack Nicklaus won his sixth Masters using an ugly, oversize aluminum-headed putter. On the day after, McGregor sold over five thousand of them. It's a testament to our tendency to reach for the relics—the bones of the system, tools, and techniques—rather than take the time to understand the disciplines behind them that make them work, that put flesh on the skeleton. In business, nowhere is this foible more apparent than in our ongoing attempts to understand the essence of the Japanese lean production system.

Lean Production

Open-book management is a philosophy that aims to push discipline downward in an organization to the lowest levels of the formal hierarchy. Lean production goes several steps further. It is both a philosophy and a system, and it works systemically in both space and time.

The emergence of lean production and its implications for American manufacturing have been chronicled and examined by Jim Womack and Dan Jones in two books, *The Machine That Changed the World* and *Lean Thinking*. The Japanese originators of lean production worked from the bottom up and focused tightly on specific production situations and problems. They had little interest in contrasting it with Western mass production, and as a result, the knowledge behind their system has been mostly tacit. It has required Western writers like Womack and Jones to fill this gap and make the conceptual framework explicit.

As Womack and Jones make clear, the system was developed not as a theoretical exercise, but in response to the enormous challenges faced by all elements of Japanese society in the aftermath of World War II. With their manufacturing facilities devastated and their markets reduced to poverty, firms such as Toyota and Honda had to make do with highly limited resources. For example, the large American auto producers could afford multiple transfer presses and spread their costs across production runs of five hundred thousand units or more of a single model. With capital and foreign exchange in short supply, the Japanese could afford far fewer presses, and they would have to make them flexible with fast die changes so that they could produce different parts for multiple models. In the process of doing this, they found that making small batches of a few parts had unsuspected advantages—inventories and manufacturing errors could be reduced or even eliminated. It took them twenty years to turn these insights from their experience into a comprehensive manufacturing system that reduced the scale of manufacturing from "mass" to what has come to be called "lean." Exemplified by the Toyota Production System (TPS), the system continues to evolve, for like golf and indeed life itself, it is a process of learning, a journey rather than a destination.

Lean production is a vast, complex topic that requires an intimate knowledge of production systems, not to mention an expanded vocabulary of Japanese words. Many volumes have been written on it, and even an outline of the system is beyond the scope of this book. The purpose of discussing it here is to get a flavor for the approach by highlighting some of its features. For lean production, as exemplified by TPS, is a profoundly systemic approach to improving the performance of complex systems. As such it has implications for both management and golf.

The key images in a lean production system are those of "flow" and "pull." The "flow" is the flow of products and information in time, and "pull" means that information flows in the *opposite* direction to that of the products. Products flow from the suppliers of raw materials through the manufacturers and distributors to the final consumer. In a pull system, information flows in the opposite direction, from the consumer backward.

In the ideal lean system there are few, if any, buffers in the form of inventories or delays. These are regarded as *muda,* the evocative Japanese word for waste, and the ultimate goal of lean production is to eliminate *muda* completely. Inventories and delays in a production system function systemically in the same way as perimeter weighting and oversizing in golf clubs—they forgive mistakes and allow the maintenance of an existing level of performance, but at the expense of learning. By systematically removing the buffers from the system, lean production stimulates the learning process. Thus, the buffers such as work-in-process inventories in the production line are reduced until a glitch appears in the flow. The inventories are then restored and the glitch is fixed so that the buffers can be lowered again until the next glitch emerges. Each time the buffers are restored, they are at lower levels than they were before. The ideal is a so-called single-piece flow, where the consumer orders one unit and the system produces one unit, on time, with perfect quality and no waste.

If we apply this approach to golf, one's immediate thought is that one should practice with more demanding clubs than one plays with—say, forged blades for practice and perimeter-weighted oversize irons for play. Thus, one could learn on the practice tee and yet be forgiven on the course! Apart from the more complex logistics of two sets of clubs, however, it might be difficult to maintain precisely the same feel for the two sets of clubs. Many pros say that they can "work" the ball better with blades, so perhaps this approach wouldn't be effective at the top level. The best candidate for it would be the putter, and indeed short-game guru Dave Pelz has actually built a putter with folding "prongs" that make it more demanding in practice mode than it is on the course. I'll return to the implications for golf in a few pages, but first we need to explore lean production a little more.

In contrast to the pull systems of lean production, conventional mass-manufacturing systems are push systems. Each stage in the production chain is instructed what and when to produce by a centralized authority—both products and information flow in the *same* direction. Although such systems may work well in theory, in practice they are too inflexible to perform well in anything but the most benign conditions.

As if to underline the concept of flow and the differences between pull and push systems, the proponents of lean production talk of a value *stream* rather than a value *chain*. If we contrast the two metaphors, the essential differences become clear:

VALUE CHAIN	VALUE STREAM
Mechanical	Organic
Artificial	Natural
Forged	Evolved
Links	Bonds
Imposed dynamic	Natural dynamic
Push	Pull

In traditional mass manufacturing, the production system is viewed as a machine-based process that has to be controlled from the outside. There is a paper or data-based system that tracks the physical processes at each link of the chain. The objective is to create a real-time, abstract model of the production process that managers can use both for simulations and decision making.

The head-down philosophy behind the mechanical approach is identical, of course, to that of good old-fashioned artificial intelligence (GOFAI) discussed in chapter 3—make a symbolic representation of reality, manipulate the symbols, and transfer the results of the calculation in the form of instructions to the operators. In the organic, lean production model, however, the approach is systemically similar to the construction of Rodney Brooks's mobots. Intelligence is embodied in the system from the ground up. The whole idea is to avoid making abstract representations of the world and to deal with it as it actually is—in real space and real time—using the people who are closest to it: the people on the shop floor. Coordination is accomplished by making the process transparent, so that all can see what is happening and get instant feedback on their actions. There are a number of visual means to this, including the ubiquitous *andon* boards, displays that show the status of production at any time. This implies that all machines are manned, and indeed they are. The Japanese are distrustful of automation—the substitution of machine for man— and prefer to talk of *autonomation:* the supplementing of man with machine. Typically, lean production systems use semiautomatic processes that allow the operator to bring intelligence to the operation of the machine.

Manufacturers around the world, including other Japanese automakers, have struggled to understand the essence of the Toyota Production System, let alone reproduce it. This is despite Toyota's extraordinary openness, allowing hundreds of thousands of visitors through its plants. To an outside observer, it's almost as if the TPS were an alien spacecraft to which we earthlings have free access, but whose workings we are powerless to understand. For TPS succeeds in using rigidly scripted procedures and methods to run operations that are enormously flexible in their ability to adapt quickly to change. Toyota builds better cars faster and uses fewer resources to do so than anyone else in the world. In a way, the alien spacecraft analogy is not so farfetched. For TPS is an evolutionary product, and Toyota has been developing it for longer than almost anyone else. It's rather like the development of talent discussed in chapter 7. Those who start young put in the required minimum of ten thousand hours of deliberate practice before those who start later. As an aside, it's interesting to note that people at Toyota say it takes them ten years to develop an effective engineer.

TPS is an evolutionary product, and both it and its associated product development processes require the use of evolutionary techniques for their ongoing elaboration. Like nature itself, the people at Toyota are continually conducting multiple real-world experiments on the shop floor and ruthlessly discard those that don't work. It's not random experimentation, however, for Toyota uses its people's experience (for example, their own stories) as building blocks. The rigidities in methods and procedures are not imposed from above, but are encoded experience. Toyota realizes Frederick Taylor's objective of making the "great mass of traditional knowledge" explicit (see chapter 7), but the scientific managers are the workers themselves, not specially selected overlords. This makes all the difference to the quality of cooperation and commitment on the shop floor, and it allows the procedures and methods developed to be subject to further testing and improvement.

Experimentation requires that options be left open for as long as possible in the production process. Typically, Toyota produces far more design options than its U.S. counterparts and pursues them much further down its funnel-shaped design process. They build more one-fifth-scale clay models, for example, but they keep their options open in other, more surprising ways. Take the length of the automobile, for example: unlike U.S. manufacturers, Toyota does not fix an exact length at the start of the design process and then demand that all the subassemblies conform to it. They reason that within limits the customer does not care about the length of the car, only about the quality of the fit—the integrity with which all the parts relate to one another. So they allow the length of the designed vehicle to vary by as much as two centimeters, as the various subassemblies (each represented by its engineers) jostle with one another in the design stage to achieve the best trade-offs among multiple constraints. When the length is finally set a long way down the evolutionary "funnel," there is great confidence that they have achieved the best adaptation of current operating practices to customer demands.

The systemic wisdom of doing this is very difficult for many of us to grasp; like many systems concepts, it's neither obvious nor intuitive. Indeed, the logic of setting design parameters early seems unassailable. But in the topsy-turvy world of TPS, the situation is quite reversed. Toyota will set fixed tolerances for suppliers, but only for those they do not think are capable of playing this evolutionary game. It's true, of course, that setting detailed specifications early is one way of coordinating people's activities, and in its absence other methods have to be used. At Toyota they have myriad techniques for doing this, ranging from the discipline of writing and reading standard-format, one-page reports to the art of holding specialized single-purpose meetings all within a community of professionals with a shared destiny. The disciplines are drilled into the engineers during their training, training that Toyota regards as a key competency. As we saw in the case of Andersen Consulting, it's a huge advantage to have cadres of people who are technically expert, proficient in the basic disciplines, and imbued with the same values. So the need to freeze design early may actually reflect a weakness—the fact that you cannot coordinate your people's activities if you don't. And surely it is the absence of multiple integrating skills that causes so many firms to hold endless, general-purpose meetings.

Golf and Flow

The goals and methods of lean production would seem to be systemically identical to those of golf. Perhaps we should be talking of a lean swing, a *pull* swing without glitches or wasted effort, a swing where every element performs its function at just the right time, pulled by its image. Such a swing would have to be created in the same way as any other pull system—by dropping the locus of control to the lowest possible level in the system. In a golf swing, this would mean lowering the center of gravity of most swings. As PGA professional teacher Dr. Jim Suttie has pointed out, most recreational golfers believe that the center of gravity of the swing is in their chests. In fact the center of gravity ought to be at the bottom of their spines, behind their hips. Here the big, slow muscles of the hips, back, and shoulders can move to create the contexts within which the smaller, faster muscles of the arms and hands can do their proper job in the right place and at the right time. A pull swing relies on power-with:

You will . . . feel that you have been the source of a controlled explosion through the ball. All the forces have come together at the exact appropriate moment. . . . All of these forces coalesce at the ball. It's a fantastic feeling that I am always striving for. It is an ideal state. This is the feeling that brings us back to the course day after day.[*]

In contrast with this vision of perfection, many golfers (and most businesses) seem to employ *push* swings, swings where instructions come from the top, pushing people to push products, pushing the club to push the ball. The smaller, faster elements are always jumping at the target, out of sync with the bigger, slower elements. Such swings are full of hitches and glitches—pure *muda*, with some components being produced too early while others are produced too late, if at all. The result is a weakly coordinated slap at the ball that only enrages us; we resort to power-over to get something done.

A pull swing, with perfect tempo and rhythm, would flow toward the target with effortless power. It would seem as if the target pulled the ball! Come to think of it, isn't that what a memory of the future (chapter 9) is all about? Compelling visions of the future pull our current activities toward them—they act as powerful attractors. When Jack Nicklaus and other top players "go to the movies," their images of their shots—pictures and feelings—have the power, via their effect on the mind (body and brain), to pull the ball toward the flag.

And when a golfer is "in the zone" isn't that the same as being "in the flow"? Mihaly Csikszentmihalyi, a psychology professor at the University of Chicago, has worked for years on the psychological concept of flow. He describes it as the psychology of optimal experience; it is about the control of our inner lives, about the control of consciousness. In his view, it is the focusing of attention that determines the shape and content of life, making it either rich or miserable. He quotes an expert rock climber:

It's exhilarating to come closer and closer to self-discipline. You make your body go and everything hurts; then you look back in awe at the self, at what you've done, it just blows your mind. It leads to ecstasy, to

[*]Nick Price, with Lorne Rubenstein, *The Swing*, p. 117.

self-fulfillment. If you win these battles enough, that battle against your self, at least for a moment, it becomes easier to win the battles in the world.*

Csikszentmihalyi contends the organization of the psychological self is more complex after a flow experience. That is, it is both more differentiated—capable of paying attention to more detail—and more integrated—capable of synthesizing the details into a seamless whole. Thus, flow is an experience that takes place just on the ordered side of the "edge of chaos." After a flow experience, a person is a little more unique, possessing rarer skills. This often happens when golfers overcome injuries and challenges of the kind mentioned in chapter 6. It is the same process of challenge and adversity that develops leaders as we saw in chapter 10. The development process works in the same way at other levels of organization. When we came out of the takeover and turnaround experience in the steel industry, briefly related in chapter 10, the camaraderie and esprit de corps among our management team was palpable. There was nothing we feared, no obstacle that we could not overcome, and the quality of our cooperation was outstanding. We had new skills and an ability to integrate our activities that outsiders marveled at. At yet another, higher level of organization, that of the corporation as a whole, we see the same process at work in the evolution of the TPS—as it develops, the people at Toyota become more capable and more skilled in exactly this way.

Summary

This chapter has looked at how systems run smoothly, at how they flow. We marvel at flow when we see it, but often we are powerless to describe it, let alone understand it. I recounted my own experience of seeing a business flow and how it involved drilling down to the deepest levels and supplying the right information at the

*Mihaly Csikszentmihalyi, *Flow*, p. 40.

right places for the people on the front lines. We explored open-book management and showed how it helped to develop power-with and how it could be used to make incentives systemic. We examined briefly the concepts of flow and pull from lean production and how they are achieved. Last, I looked at the concept of flow and its implications for golf, of our need for lean swings that flow toward the target as if they were pulled by it.

No. 16

Walking the Walk

Par-4	315 yards

Since there can be no common measure for the translation of the physical, biological, economic, social, personal, and spiritual utilities involved, the determination of the strategic factors of creative cooperation is a matter of sense, of feeling of proportions. . . . This general executive process is not intellectual in its important aspect; it is aesthetic and moral.
—CHESTER BARNARD, FUNCTIONS OF THE EXECUTIVE

A round of golf partakes of the journey, and the journey is one of the central myths and signs of Western Man. It is built into his thoughts and dreams, into his genetic code. The Exodus, the Ascension, the Odyssey, the Crusades, the pilgrimages of Europe and the voyage of Columbus, Magellan's circumnavigation of the Globe, the Discovery of Evolution and the March of Time, getting ahead and the ladder of perfection, the exploration of space and the Inner Trip; from the beginning our Western World has been on the move. We tend to see everything as part of the journey.
—SHIVAS IRONS, MICHAEL MURPHY'S MENTOR,
IN GOLF IN THE KINGDOM

It's the spring tournament for the members at Bryan Park in Greensboro, North Carolina, and on this beautiful day there's a charge in the air. Everywhere on the Champions course the sweet, cool tingle of fresh-mown grass wafts through the air.

The 150 or so members of the Bryan Park Men's Golf Association are distributed around the clubhouse and environs, preparing for their nine A.M. shotgun start. For many of them, it's their first competitive outing of the year. On the practice tee, the earth seems to be in motion as golfers earnestly warm up, sending showers of grass and soil flying. Their skills cover a vast range of expertise. Here is the effortless grace of a fine player who sends the ball boring through the air, ripping a thin dollar-bill divot from the grass. There is the herky-jerky lunge of another, whose ball is gouged from the deep red earth complete with its attached clod of grass and roots. Behind the line of those hitting, others wait their turn, either watching those hitting or standing in small knots, talking softly to each other. Dressed in their golfing best, they tell of their recent activities, and some show to others any new weapons acquired over the winter.

On the putting green many men are hunched over, checking the ballistics of their missiles, testing their roll over the humps and hollows—you don't want to leave your ball above the hole very often on this course! Others still are cleaning cleats or rummaging in their golf bags, checking their equipment and selecting gloves, tees, markers, and all the varied paraphernalia they will need during the round. As departure time approaches, the players gather round their carts and golf cars to find out who is playing with whom and wait for the final announcements. It is a time of introductions and greetings, of the telling of jokes that probably should have not been told, of gusts of laughter. And then—"Hit it well!" and we're off.

Historians believe that golf was probably invented by Scottish shepherds, using the handles of their crooks to wack rounded pebbles into rabbit holes. It conjures up a relaxed, pastoral scene, where work and play go hand in hand. We imagine them honing their skills as their flocks slowly wend their way across the hills, following the contours of the land. Shepherds have probably been hitting pebbles with sticks for thousands of years, and certainly we can see that the game might have evolved that way technically. But there is increasingly solid evidence from the burgeoning field of evolutionary psychology that golf, as both a physical and a social

activity, may be a distant echo of an even earlier mode of living—
that of the hunter-gatherer. As a species, we have spent most of
our existence as hunter-gatherers, so it stands to reason that we
still carry many, if not all, of the adaptations that allowed us to survive and grow in those environments. Some of these skills and
preferences may not be helpful in the modern world, but it is
a world that we have created using minds founded on Stone Age
adaptations.

The Hunters

On the savannas of Africa, where *Homo sapiens* is thought to have
emerged as a species a hundred thousand years or so ago, the resources are ephemeral and scattered across immense spaces. For
the plants are seasonal in their yield and most of the animals are
migratory: predators and their prey are always on the move. Thus
the hunter-foragers, and their ancestral species for eons before
them, were of necessity nomadic. From the study of societies such
as the Kalahari !Kung bushmen, who still live in this way, we know
that they probably organized themselves into networks of small
bands spread out over the vast landscape. There were no fixed territories; indeed, band territories often overlapped, because there
were no concentrated resources to defend and no one could live in
one place for any length of time. Each band consisted of seven to
fifteen people held together by family ties or even bonds of friend-
ship. There was considerable flux and flow in the membership of
the bands, and there were few barriers to membership of any
band. In the rare times of plenty, when the resources could support a larger gathering, several bands might come together briefly
in what anthropologists call a "carnival." Here they would exchange news, search for spouses, find friends to hunt with, and
celebrate in story, song, and dance the great myths and visions
that sustained them in their wanderings. After a few days, the carnival would end and the bands would head back into the wilder-
ness.

This flat, mobile structure of the hunter-gatherer society maximized their chances of collecting food and encouraged cooperation and teamwork, for no one could survive alone in that environment. Indeed, the hunter-gatherers were acutely sensitive to any signs of rejection, for expulsion from the group meant death. At the same time, everyone within the band had to be trustworthy. Anyone who showed signs of desiring personal power, for instance, was regarded with suspicion, for that could lead to dissent, with fatal consequences for the band. For this reason, there was no permanent hierarchy, and leadership rotated among the members of the band depending upon the situation faced. Since everyone was multiskilled, anyone could lead and all would follow. Sometimes the leader might be an expert tracker who could follow spoor across stony ground; at other times it might be an experienced forager who knew where to find buried vegetables. Although there were role differences between the genders—men did most of the hunting, women did the foraging—there were few status differences. Women were not regarded as possessions— they could marry whom they liked and divorce if they wanted to.

Although about 80 percent of the hunter-gatherers' food intake consisted of vegetables, fruits, and nuts, meat was highly prized because of the flavor it brought to an otherwise bland diet. It also supplied essential vitamins, and it's thought that our marked appetite for fat developed in this context. The hunters traveled light and fast, armed with personal weapons that they had made and maintained expertly. A hunt might last several days, even after a herd had been located, for the effective range of the hunter's small bow with its poisoned arrows was not much more than thirty yards. If the cover was thin and the game wary, the hunters might have to wait for hours or even days for the herd to move close enough for a shot. Even then, although the poison was deadly, a hit was not instantly fatal and the hunters might have to track the animal for up to three days. Afterward, if the animal was a large one—a big eland might exceed one thousand pounds in weight— the hunters and their families would camp around it for a week or more, eating it down to the bones.

Everyone in the region was invited to the feast, for the hunters shared their good fortune with the neighboring bands against the day when others would kill and share with them. Interestingly, the hunter did not distribute the meat; the maker of the arrow that killed the animal did this. Since arrows were borrowed and lent and given as gifts, the distributor of the meat might not even be on the hunt. The rewards of the hunt belonged to a team rather than to an individual, and allowing successful hunters to distribute the meat might have allowed them to accumulate too much personal power. Thus, the sharing of meat maintained community, and as one can imagine, the hunt itself built an intense camaraderie among the participants. Seated in a circle around their cooking fires, the hunters would reminisce and relive their experiences. They would tell and retell the stories of their exploits and of the fat bucks they had killed. Minor incidents would be recalled and recounted with endless repetition and detail. Small children, too young to hunt, would also be gathered around the fire, listening and learning. The hunters would use the same campfire dialogue to plan their future activities, daydreaming about hunting, remembering what had happened on previous outings, and then, through mental rehearsal, creating a shared vision of where they might search for the herds.

The Golfers

Bryan Park is a municipal course, a public facility, not a private club, and the members of the association receive no special privileges. Young and old, they come from every walk of life. Some are blue-collar workers who appreciate the two fine courses available for play at modest cost. Others are professional or corporate nomads whose diaries and travel schedules do not allow them to book regular games in a regular foursome. All are united by their shared love of this game that at its roots is profoundly egalitarian. Stepping onto the 1st tee with three people one has never met before, one feels that the evolutionary psychologists must be on to something. There's that feeling of relaxation and openness, of goodwill and reciprocity. Of course, it's also fun to play with people you know, but the fact that these effects are generated when we are with strangers is quite amazing. Somehow, standing in a small group overlooking an open fairway, weapons in hand, evokes some ancient instinct that we are at a loss to explain. At a loss, that is, until the evolutionary psychologists came along.

According to evolutionary psychologists, "the savanna hypothesis of habitat preferences" suggests that our minds are specially tuned to recognize landscapes that can provide all the resources a nomadic hunter-gatherer might need. We like to be close to good water in fertile terrain, where we can move around easily. We like trees to protect us from the sun, but we need to be able to see game from a long way off, so we don't like our view to be obscured. Experiments suggest that we like particular kinds of trees, with moderately dense canopies and forks near the ground so that they can be climbed. Dense canopies make us feel shut in—claustrophobic—sparse canopies too exposed. We need shelter, but we are wary of being trapped, of being unable to get out. The mix of grass and woodland characteristic of savanna meets all these conditions and, it takes only a moment to realize, so do most golf courses. Courses are usually designed to present a pleasing mix of hunter-gatherer resources in savanna-type settings, with vistas and distances at which the movement of game animals and predators could be usefully recognized.

It has been shown that people in stressful situations relax when they are shown pictures of natural landscapes, especially those with trees and vegetation. We are especially sensitive to greenness and the signs of fruitfulness characteristic of spring. The savanna hypothesis has even been invoked to explain our responses to flowers and the fact that hospital patients respond positively, physically and psychologically, to the presence of fresh flowers in their rooms. So our responses, even to TV pictures, of resource-rich Augusta National in April or Pebble Beach on a fine day are rooted in that same sense of relaxation we feel when we step onto the tee. Perhaps it's a little unconscious sigh of relief—the feeling that we are safe, that we are "home."

Walking the Walk

In North America these days, it's rare to find many players walking on a golf course outside of a top-level amateur or professional tournament. On some of the newly designed courses, motorized golf carts seem to have all but replaced caddies and handcarts. This is a pity, because there is something about walking together that builds a sense of community among a group of people. As far as I know, the evolutionary psychologists have not yet studied this phenomenon, but it too probably stems from our hunter-gatherer roots. Today, from parades and processions to mass marches of protest and even our charitable "walkathons," the act of a group of people walking together still expresses solidarity and commitment to a shared purpose.

Leaders seem to have known this since the beginning of time and have often both organized and participated in marches in order to generate solidarity with their followers and commitment to their cause. They still do so in modern times. In 1930, at the age of sixty, the Indian leader Mahatma Gandhi chose to walk the 240 miles from Ahmadabad to Dandi on the Arabian Sea to protest the taxes on salt. He planned to walk with less than a hundred of his followers but was accompanied by thousands of people, gathering support as he moved through the villages. The march acted as a catalyst for the popular struggle against British rule. The strategy was copied thirty-five years later by his student Martin Luther King, in the march from Selma to Montgomery, which led to the rapid passage of the Voting Rights Act of 1965. Many of those who took part in the march went on to become leaders in the civil rights movement.

Both these walks are dwarfed by the six-thousand-mile Long March made by Mao Zedong and his followers in 1934 to escape the surrounding nationalist forces of Chiang Kai-shek. Eighty-six thousand men and women began the march, but a year later only a tenth of that number survived to reach the remote sanctuary of the mountains in the north of the country. The march was a retreat, but it developed leadership and built a core of supporters who would follow Mao anywhere. When the Communists finally took power in 1949, most of his associates around him had been on the march, and its mythology, boosted by regular celebrations of the key events on it, sustained him in power to the end of his life.

Why is the walk so effective as an activity for mobilizing commitment? It must be because it demonstrates genuine, collective purpose over an extended period of time. A person on a march shows by his or her behavior that the cause is the priority. The commitment is physical, not just intellectual, for little else is to be accomplished while on the move. To walk with others is a mark of respect for them and their cause. This is surely why, in times of war, visits to the front lines by senior officers have such a powerful effect on the morale of soldiers. They build a notion of a shared fate and common purpose among both leaders and followers. On a smaller scale, the same effect is noticeable when senior executives visit the shop floors and front lines of business enterprises— the actions make an unambiguous statement about management's priorities. It often helps if they, like Toyota auto executives, wear overalls on the floor rather than bankers' pinstripes. That says unequivocally "I am one of you—we are in this together."

As an executive in the steel industry, I used to enjoy going out on the trucks at five A.M., riding with the deliveries. You learn an enormous amount about how the business actually works. I discovered, for example, how our drivers were at the mercy of the customer's yard boss and what a huge difference it made to our delivery schedule if we could get in and out of a customer's yard quickly. In the steel business, it's usually the sales managers who hand out the hockey tickets to the customers' purchasing agents. But it helps if your drivers can also do something for the customers' yard bosses. Communication through other means just doesn't yield these insights. Of course, I was also sending a message in "body language" to our people in the front lines. Technoevangelists extol the virtues of converting "atoms" to "bits," because bits can be duplicated and multiple copies of the original can be made. But when it comes to behaviors that build commitment and trust, it's the atoms that count. Unlike bits, atoms can't be copied—you have only one set of them. So where you put your atoms through your behavior is the very best guide to your priorities and intentions. This is surely why even the most technologically sophisticated firms say that it takes "face time" to build commitment and trust.

Close observation of people while they engaged in a purposeful activity gives us a good deal of information about their character. Leaderless group tests, in which a group is assigned a difficult task with joint responsibility for the outcome, have long been used to assess leadership behavior. Perhaps a game of golf performs the same function at several levels. After all, it assigns an individual and often a team to a challenging task in a context where there is plenty of scope for observation of a person's responses to both success and adversity.

For golf, with its ups and downs, its strokes of good fortune and runs of bad luck, is in many ways a small-scale simulacrum of life. We can easily see whether a person is boastful or overbearing when things are going well or whether he wears his good fortune lightly. It's obvious if he takes responsibility for his actions when things go badly or whether he storms at the unfairness of the game. I once played a round with a senior executive, a chairman of several corporate boards, who played incredibly quickly, rarely waiting for others to see if it was his turn or whether they had found their balls. The quality of his play deteriorated during the course of the round, and he began to rail at his caddy (we had them on this occasion), accusing him of giving the wrong advice on clubs and being a distraction in other ways. Later I learned that he was a holy terror in the boardroom, continually invoking *Robert's Rules of Order* and generally abrading people. It's a sample of one, but it makes one wonder.

There are no scientific studies that I am aware of, but it does seem reasonable (especially to a Stone Age mind!) that a people's behavior on the golf course is probably a fairly reliable guide to their behavior off it. People who cheat on the golf course will probably cheat in life. *The New York Times* went so far as to describe the mulligan as "the perfect metaphor for [Bill Clinton's] Presidency." On the golf course, the former president apparently takes "mulligans," penalty-free repeat shots, at all stages of a round without asking for permission from his playing partners to do so. The *Times* suggested that this happened off the course, too:

> The voters have given the Comeback Kid more than one mulligan. Mr. Clinton was granted a second chance by the Senate . . . after the House impeached him for his behavior in the Monica S. Lewinsky matter. And it can be assumed that Hillary Rodham Clinton has given Mr. Clinton a few mulligans too.*

The Scots, of course, would be horrified by this practice in any context—there are no such things as mulligans in the home of the game.

True Company

The feelings of mutuality and reciprocity in golf are perhaps best experienced in that most popular of team formats, the fourball scramble. Four players, who may be strangers to one another, gather together as a small team. As many readers will know, the scramble format allows the team (with some restrictions) to pick the best of each series of shots and then have every team member play from that position. Recreational golfers enjoy the scramble format because it does not place too much stress on individual performance, and they get to play shots from positions on the course that they might not usually reach. Like the early hunters, they will have to cooperate, with leadership moving among them depending on the situation the team faces and the skills each player possesses. They will have to learn from one another's mistakes, and they will feel the pressure of having to perform when the team is relying on them.

In a scramble, various rules usually ensure that no single player can dominate and that the burden is shared roughly equally in a genuine team outcome. If a team is to do well, everyone has to contribute, and if they win, it will undoubtedly be a shared tri-

*"Taking Second Chances: Par for Clinton's Course," *The New York Times*, August 29, 1999, p. 1.

umph in which everyone's performance is recognized. Afterward, all the teams will repair to the modern equivalent of a campfire to celebrate success and regale one another with stories of their achievements, of the challenges they faced, and often of the disasters that befell them. There will be many good-natured exchanges and much joshing at the unexpected success of some and the failures of others. Whatever the individual outcomes, at the end of the day when the group splits up, its members will return to their own families with the feeling that they have again been part of a true company—a larger community that has broken bread together. For that is the original derivation of the word *company*—from the Latin *cum panis,* meaning "with bread."

It seems that our evolutionary past has equipped us to exploit dispersed, short-lived resources by working in small, egalitarian teams of 4 to 15 people who can come together on occasions to form larger groups of roughly 150 or so. This is probably the maximum number of people with whom we can be on an intimate "first name" basis, and it sets the size limit for "true company." Firms such as Hewlett-Packard (HP) and Magna International, the big Canadian car parts manufacturer, have tried to keep their facilities at "true company" size, but this can be difficult to do. HP found it relatively easy when they were only in the instruments business, but the computer systems business is inherently large scale. Indeed, it was the very different scales of the businesses that contributed to the 1999 decision to split them. HP's original instrument business is now an independent company called Agilent—the computer business uses the HP name.

In a huge, technologically complex organization, HP people still try to walk the walk—to show their respect for people in their practices, not just in words. The hunting-gathering dynamics are in all the small things, the mundanities that sustain us on our journeys: people who are accessible, face-to-face communication, the sharing of experience, pain, and profits, and the telling of stories that buoy our spirits in times of adversity and make us laugh. It's the journey, not the destination, that's important. Every golfer knows.

Summary

The findings from evolutionary psychology suggest that we still have Stone Age minds—bodies and brains adapted to functioning as hunter-gatherers on the savannas of Africa. These evolutionary mechanisms are reflected in our ability to work cooperatively as well as our acute ability to detect people who are untrustworthy. These embedded habits also help to choose congenial places to live in and account for our delight at being out on a golf course. Although hunter-gatherer dynamics are in tension with bureaucracy, they remain our default condition and essential for the exploitation of scattered, ephemeral resources and the sustaining of our commitment to a group.

The Left Hand of Leadership

| Par-4 | 447 yards |

But of course there is no secret; there is only the doing of those little things, each done correctly, time and again, until excellence in every detail becomes a firmly ingrained habit, an ordinary part of one's everyday life.
  —DANIEL CHAMBLISS, THE MUNDANITY OF EXCELLENCE

[T]he leader [is the] one who can organize the experience of the group, make it all available and most effectively available, and thus get the full power of the group. It is by organizing experience that we transform experience into power. And that is what experience is for, to be made into power.
  —MARY PARKER FOLLETT, DYNAMIC ADMINISTRATION

This book has explored the relationship between golf and management by looking at both of them as complex systems. I have used the emerging theory of complex adaptive systems as a lens, so that familiarities in one area can be used to illuminate mysteries in the other. If I had to condense the conclusions of this book into a single diagram, it would look something like the diagram on page 267.

Effective goals are formed when three aspects of mind interact. In the diagram, they are represented by three intersecting circles that can be thought of as both areas and "time zones":

Building Competence in Complex Systems

A Must Add in Presentation

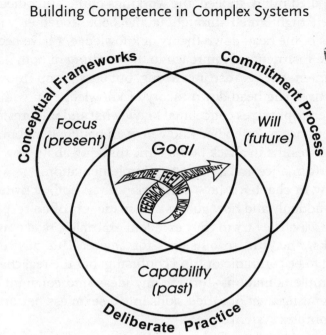

1. *Focus* addresses our mental orientation in the *present;* it is steered best by conceptual frameworks that help us pay attention to the right questions.
2. *Will* deals with our aspirations for the *future;* it is developed by a complex commitment process and enhanced by compelling images—memories of the future.
3. *Capability* reflects our abilities developed in the *past*—our experience—and it is developed best by deliberate practice.

At the nexus of the three circles, I have placed the "do loop." It reminds us that goals do not operate effectively in the abstract, they have to be made part of experience. The do loop also reminds us that action is just a moment in a process—a feedback process—and that, as Aristotle observed, excellence is not an act, but a habit. Abstract goals have to be transformed into images that generate timely, effective feedback in all three areas if they are to "move" the embodied mind. Indeed, the workings of the embodied mind have been highlighted throughout the book, together with the problems of the head-down theory of knowledge. I have been critical of the instructional approach to the teaching of both golf and management, not because it is wrong, but because on its own it is not effective. The head-down theory of knowledge on which it is based overemphasizes conceptual know-what and underestimates the importance of embodied know-how. In both golf and management, this results in a lack of systemic thinking about how to improve performance and a neglect of implementation.

We saw in chapter 2 how performances in both activities can decline suddenly and how golfers and managers often respond in the same way. They try to copy excellent examples, read authoritative books, and turn to outsiders for advice. This advice often turns out to be contradictory and confusing, but the real challenge is with implementation—turning any ideas into coherent action and integrating a set of varied skills into a seamless performance from a complex system.

The best examples of complex adaptive systems are our own bodies, and we saw in chapter 3 how the body has served as a model in the past. We tracked the evolution of the systems perspective from Cannon's work on homeostasis through the development of cybernetics and artificial intelligence. We looked at the multiple elements of complex systems and their organization into hierarchically structured layers. One key distinction was between hierarchies of command-and-control and hierarchies of control, illustrated by Simon's examples of the two watchmakers and two very different approaches to artificial intelligence. Command-and-control hierarchies are unstable because they require perfect knowledge and performance on the part of the "small, fast" elements that govern the actions of the big, slow ones. Hierarchies of control, in contrast, are extremely stable because they can be built from the bottom up in a modular fashion. Problems are contained within their modules and do not leak across the entire system. Cause and effect in complex systems is extremely difficult to disentangle, and intuitive solutions to complex problems are often wrong. Perverse outcomes often make implementation of solutions even more difficult: better-before-worse solutions can easily become addictive, and worse-before-better solutions are hard to sell.

In chapter 4 this complexity framework was applied to the golf swing. The perspective gives a rather different view of the swing from the usual analysis. We saw how the three major phases of the swing differ according to the role that *feedback* plays in control and the importance of the *ballistic move* in the downswing. The systemic reasons for the importance of the setup are clear—it's the biggest, slowest, earliest part of the swing. The complexity framework gave us important insight into the nested hierarchies of the backswing and the downswing. The legs, hips, trunk, shoulders, and arms create successively small and tighter constraints in which the hands must work. Because our bodies are general-purpose mechanisms, the constraints between the levels are relatively weak. We often end up making adjustments at later phases of the swing to compensate for a breakdown of constraints at an earlier stage. Our favorite instrument for making such adjustments is the right hand and shoulder. The systems approach supports the view that one swing does not fit all. People vary so widely in their physical shape, size, strength, and flexibility that it makes sense that they will need different swings. Casual attempts to copy the moves of unsuitable, albeit excellent, examples can lead only to trouble. *You have to find your own swing.*

The stunning collapse of Oxford Health Plans opened chapter 5, which applied the complexity framework to organizations. Although the dynamics of business enterprises are quite different from those of the golf swing, they are not systemically different; the systems perspective can be applied to them both. Complex adaptive systems can be seen as actors walking on the "edge of chaos." On this walk, discipline and freedom go together hand in hand. When an actor encounters a constraint in the environment, he or she overcomes it by incorporating—literally embodying—a technology or technique. These embodied routines then allow the actor the freedom to continue exploring. The disciplines must be sited as low as possible in the system and must be executed unconsciously; otherwise they will use up precious conscious capacity needed to pay attention to the external environment.

Dan Chambliss's in-depth study of top-level swimmers formed the backbone of chapter 6. He found that the usual explanations for excellence such as "talent" were unhelpful when it came to understanding top swimmers. They were descriptions that appeared only *after* the person's skills became apparent. We often find this in business, when the performance of excellent companies is described in terms that emerge only after they are successful. Chambliss discovered that excellence in swimming was mundane and depended on the disciplined repetition of multiple small actions, correctly, consistently, and all together.

Top-level swimmers lived in a different world, where they did things *qualitatively* differently from lesser performers. Technique differed in the infinite details of the movements; top-level swimmers were more disciplined in their practice, and they often had an inverse attitude toward practice. What lower-level swimmers found boring, they actually enjoyed. Natural ability did not seem to be a major factor, and many top swimmers, like many top golfers, often had to recover from a severe setback of one kind or another. Sometimes the setback actually seemed to help their focus and concentration. These findings appear to apply to golf, although the game has not been studied in nearly the same detail. Excellence is a result of the relentless attention to detail, the drilling of routines into habits, and their seamless integration into a flawless delivery.

In chapter 7 we saw how our concepts of excellence in sport are changing from a genetic bias toward a developmental emphasis. Expert performance results from the honing of technique through disciplined practice. Disciplined practice is characterized by a close attention to task, immediate, specific feedback on actions, and multiple repetitions of the correct moves. The so-called ten-year rule suggests that across a number of skills, it takes about ten thousand hours of deliberate practice to produce an expert. The power of timely, specific feedback is that it allows a practitioner to move from a conceptual understanding of what to do to an embodied feeling of how to perform—how to exercise dynamic control.

The requirements for effective practice are extremely demanding and rarely met in either golf or management. This places real limits on the uses of practice unless the practitioner can generate his or her own timely, effective feedback. One intriguing suggestion is that the purpose of practice should not be just to groove a single swing, but to experiment with multiple ways of achieving acceptable outcomes.

The exacting demands made by deliberate practice show us why putting is such a challenge for most golfers—it takes place in an impoverished feedback environment that often makes practice counterproductive. The only way to change the situation is to control the environment so that external influences are minimized and to crank up the feedback so that incorrect actions are detected immediately. The systems perspective allowed us to carry these insights across to that huge consumer of management time— meetings. Many meetings, particularly unscheduled ones, should probably be seen as "right hand" adjustments to the organizational "swing." They are symptomatic of a breakdown of a discipline somewhere earlier in the process—a high-level means of coordinating activities that should have been integrated at a lower, earlier stage. The only way to fix the problem permanently is to track the web of cause and effect back to that earlier stage and make the changes there. Rules for meetings that require detailed agendas and the like are a useful adjunct to this systemic approach, but in its absence, they are only a quick fix that will soon fade into disuse. Management time is our scarcest resource, but like putting, it takes a systemic approach to improve its use.

Chapter 8 opened with Benjamin Bloom's work on the development of talent in young people. There seem to be three broad phases in the development of talent—the nurturing of emotional commitment, the acquisition of technique through deliberate practice, and the transcendence of technique to produce true mastery. I then introduced the consciousness/competence model as a way of putting dimensions on this learning cycle. The consciousness/ competence framework is a way of organizing one's thinking about the acquisition of skills. The key distinction is between implicit and explicit learning and their knowledge counterparts— implicit or tacit "know-how" and explicit information or "know-what." We all start life as unconsciously incompetent. As implicit learners, we pick up basic skills as our inborn mechanisms encounter contexts that they have been "designed" (over evolutionary time) to handle; we become unconsciously competent at these basics. The acquisition of further, more advanced skills, however, such as reading and writing, requires explicit learning. We have to become consciously incompetent before we can learn them. Complex activities have to be analyzed into their components and individually drilled to perfection until we become consciously competent. The skills then have to be integrated—chunked and chained—into the effortless performance that characterizes unconscious competence.

The model was then applied to golf, where there is evidence for both kinds of learning. Four different kinds of feedback were identified as being essential to move from one quadrant of the model to another. Implicit learning seems to be the more desirable method, if it is possible. Skills learned explicitly and not drilled sufficiently have a nasty habit of becoming explicit under stress. In golf we call it a "choke." It happens in all sports, but it also seems to happen in management. Frederick Taylor's scheme of scientific management was an admirable attempt to make the tacit knowledge of skilled workers explicit, refine it according to the rules of logic, and then reinstall it back into the workplace. It often failed in that final step. Similarly, the field of strategic management can be seen as the attempt to make the tacit knowledge of successful entrepreneurs explicit, refine and teach the principles, and then implement the resulting strategies in the real world. It also tends to fail in the final step. The problem of implementation is largely unexamined by the head-down theory of knowledge, but it is the barrier to excellent performance in both golf and management.

In chapter 9 we looked at the increasing importance that is being attached to the role of images—pictures and feelings—as catalysts for action. I suggested that the sequence picture-feeling-action-feedback-adjustment constitutes the essence of a feedback loop—the "do loop"—that can serve any goal. In golf and management, images can act as "memories of the future" that function together with memories of the past to produce a desired action. Dysfunctional memories of either past or future can produce dysfunctional actions. It turns out that imagination is essential to all levels of voluntary action, ranging from simple body movements to the complex activities of top golfers and excellent companies. The chapter closed with the implications for goal setting. To be effective, abstract, high-level goals have to be broken down into their components, which have to be capable of being seen and felt in the imagination. Only then can they be used in combination with effective feedback to improve performance.

If constant repetition of the correct moves is essential for building different techniques, chapter 10 made it clear that diversity and adversity seem to be essential to the integration of those techniques—to achieve mastery. The best learning seems to take place "under fire." In the 1970s, a split developed in the management literature between the concept of management and the concept of leadership. There was a dawning recognition that the analytical techniques being taught in the business schools were all very well, but that a key dimension was missing. It showed itself in problems of implementation, the inability of well-schooled executives to turn ideas into action. This problem has its direct counterpart in golf. It is the inability that many golfers experience in taking techniques learned on the practice tee and turning them into performance on the course, particularly when under pressure. The reasons for this are intimately related to the structure of the "ballistic" mind.

In chapter 11 we looked at the evolution of the "ballistic" mind, beginning with the split in our brains between two halves that are similar but not identical. William Calvin suggests that this asymmetrical specialization developed as a by-product of hunting. The need to make ballistic (or preprogrammed) movements, he argues, also underpins our use of language as well as our ability to plan. Effective planning, decisions, and actions require the concentration of the general-purpose neurons in the ballistic brain. Who's in charge? The storytellers are in charge. Each of us creates an indivualized story, a narrative "center of gravity." Our identity emerges slung between our memories of the past and our visions of the future. We exist in that perpetual present, a still point in a turning world.

The *djembe* drums of the Leading Creatively program at the Center for Creative Leadership opened chapter 12. Here we saw how talented teachers and effective executives can restore people to their senses—help them to perceive their world more accurately. They use both verbal and nonverbal methods of communication to do this. Betty Edwards's work on art suggests that people are often poor artists not because they can't draw or paint, but because they have not learned to see. They tend to draw what they know from the past, rather than what is actually present. Golfers may play poorly not because they can't execute the shots physically, but because they can't feel where their bodies are in real time. In managers, this inability to gather real-time feedback has been described as a lack of self-awareness or emotional intelligence. The example of the unfortunate, brain-damaged Phineas Gage shows that it is impossible to stop the rational calculation of outcomes without making emotion-based judgments; emotion and logic are essential to effective decision making.

Chapter 12 closed with a discussion of our use of language, its foundation in our bodily experience of the world, and the power of stories to compel action. The split in the English language between its Germanic roots and its Romance superstructure parallels that between the body-up (R-mode) and head-down (L-mode) modalities of thought. Much advice in golf and management cannot be implemented because it fails to grasp these nuances of language. Either it is too abstract to generate feeling and commitment or it refers to achievements rather than to actions. The best approach is to immerse people who are eager to learn in the situation that contains the issue or problem. Stories are a powerful medium for coordinating such experiences because they invite their listeners and readers to participate in the experience.

Much activity in business organizations makes little systemic sense. Chapter 13 looked at the planning and budgeting process typical in many firms. An exclusive emphasis on financial results means that the webs of cause and effect that produce the results cannot be explored. The annual budget meeting ends up like a typical golf practice session, with players trying to bomb their drivers over the back fence. A more sensible approach to the annual budget dialogue was illustrated using as a model a golfer's discussion with his coach. Five actions were suggested that would make business processes more systemic: stop using incentives as a quick fix; build the organization and its subsystems in a modular fashion; use process approaches such as the balanced scorecard to highlight nonfinancial factors; use training to drill the shared skills that facilitate cooperative work; and always ensure that your efforts are focused on the key constraint. More systemic budgeting processes were illustrated using Emerson Electric and 3M. 3M's use of stories to dramatize their plans and specify the exact chains of cause and effect they intend to follow is particularly interesting.

Throughout the book, we encountered the apparent paradox that *competence can be learned, but it cannot be taught.* It cannot be transferred from teacher to novice by the transmission of pure content. The content may be useful, but only in a context where the learner can recognize its value. In chapter 14 we saw how such contexts are created in the Leadership at the Peak program in CCL's Colorado Springs facility. The purpose is to immerse the learner in feedback in a context featuring assessment, challenge, and support. A similar philosophy underpins the highly successful Swedish golf model. A team approach creates a community of practitioners who can give one another timely, specific feedback. The instructional challenge in coaching is to find metaphors that can help the learner put mind into muscle, ideas into action. The ultimate goal is to allow the learner to generate and learn from his or her own feedback, to become his or her own best coach.

The holy grail of every golfer and every manager is to achieve "flow." Flow occurs when a system runs effortlessly and the only conscious decision required is either to start it or stop it. Fine golf swings flow, great organizations flow, and people performing at their very best feel the flow. Flow takes place when minimal moves produce optimal results. The great enemy of flow is waste—wasted effort, wasted time—*muda,* as the Japanese call it. In chapter 15 we saw that the precondition for flow is that control—actions and their integration—be dropped to the *lowest* possible level in the organization. This is the goal of both open-book management and the lean production movement. Coordinated action at the lowest levels produces a synergistic "power-with" that emerges to replace conventional top-down, "power-over." In golf it results in effortless power and the feeling that the target is "pulling" the ball. The state of mindful awareness, relaxed concentration, necessary for this to happen creates psychological flow, the condition some have called "happiness."

Excellent performance in organizations requires cooperative effort in pursuit of a common goal. Chapter 16 used findings from evolutionary psychology to show why golf generates powerful insights into how this can be done. Although we live in a modern world, we have Stone Age minds: bodies and brains adapted to survival and growth as hunter-gatherers. On the savanna, resources are scattered and transient. We are adapted to working in small, cooperative teams that come together in communities numbering up to about 150 people. I called this community "true company." It takes true company dynamics to sustain people in their daily lives and create the commitment to cooperative activity. The challenge for managers is to somehow retain these dynamics in organizations whose size and technological complexity continually threaten to destroy them.

Leadership

Suppose the rules of golf were changed so that the equipment remained the same, but players were allowed to use only one arm at a time? Assuming that you were allowed plenty of time to practice your technique, which arm would you play with? Would you change hands for different shots?

After giving this question some thought, together with some experimentation, most right-handed players will say that they would play all the long shots with their left arms and all the control shots with their right. There is no doubt that Bobby Jones would have agreed:

> I think there can be no question that the golf stroke ought to be dominated from first to last by the left arm. . . . The right hand is a difficult factor to control in a golf swing, because it is working more or less "on the loose" with no anchor to hold it down.[*]

There may, of course, be a few ambidextrous golfers like current PGA star Notah Begay, whose decision whether to putt with the left or the right hand would depend on the break of the putt. Begay putts right-to-left breaking putts right-handed and left-to-right breaking putts left-handed!

The reason right-handed golfers choose a left arm power swing is that its pulling action allows all of the big muscles of the body to play a role in the swing, while maintaining the leverage of a wide arc. Some golfers can hit the long shots with a single left arm almost as far as two-handed golfers can. Alastair Cochran and John Stobbs in *Search for the Perfect Swing* cite the example of English one-armed golfer Bobby Reid, who can drive the ball over 280 yards using his left arm. He has to have a simple swing, because he has no right hand with which to make any adjustments. A one-armed golfer hitting power shots with the right hand has a problem. Although the right arm is physically stronger than the left (once again, in right-handed golfers), its pushing action means that it cannot deliver that power in a reliable direction; it is far too likely to be deflected. It needs the cooperation of the big muscles and the big arc that only the left arm can provide. The right hand does, however, have a great capacity for the small, fine motor movements demanded by chipping, which is why most golfers say they would use it for control shots.

This hypothetical situation (for everyone, that is, except one-armed golfers) illustrates the subtle differences in contribution between the left and the right hands in golf. There is no doubt that

[*]Bobby Jones, 1920s syndicated column.

golf is a two-handed game, but the contributions from each hand are quite different. To quote Cochran and Stobbs in defining the role of the right arm:

1. To reinforce and brace the swinging action of the [left arm] . . .
2. To provide additional clubhead speed into impact . . .
3. To add both control and sensitivity to . . . clubhead action through the ball.
4. To do what is required in 1, 2 and 3 without upsetting the pattern of the basic left-arm swing. To serve it, reinforce it; but not to change it, or impose any right-arm-based pattern upon it.*

I believe that the relationship between leadership and management in organizations is analogous to that between the left and the right hands in the golf swing (in a right-handed person). That is, they are two different kinds of power and control that have to work in a complementary fashion if good results are to be achieved. Like the left arm in golf, leadership is about the arc and leverage generated by the mobilization of the whole "body" of the organization.

In contrast, consider the following as the role of management:

1. To reinforce and brace the overall direction and momentum supplied by leadership.
2. To provide additional speed and urgency in the taking of action.
3. To add both control and sensitivity to implementation activities.
4. To do what is required in 1, 2, and 3 without upsetting the pattern of leadership. To serve it, reinforce it; but not to change it, or impose any management pattern upon it.

From some purely systemic point of view, leadership consists in the integration of a system's elements in space and time. Whether

---

*Search for the Perfect Swing, p. 63.

it's creating a true company or coordinating the muscles used in a golf swing, the process is the same systemically.

In the field of management, no one has expressed this view of leadership better than Mary Parker Follett, although she wrote about it over eighty years ago, at a time when leaders were predominantly male and personal power was still seen as central to the process. For she understood clearly that a leader's activities are not the expression of the lonely purpose of one individual. Rather, they are the interweaving of shared purposes, an integration of the experiences of many:

> The leader guides the group and is at the same time himself guided by the group, is always part of the group. No one can truly lead except from within. . . . The leader . . . must interpret our experience to us, must see all the different points of view which underlie our daily activities and also their connections, must adjust the varying and often conflicting needs, must lead the group . . . to a unification of its purpose. He must give form to things vague, things latent, to mere tendencies. He must be able to lead us to wise decisions, not to impose his own wise decisions upon us. We need leaders, not masters or drivers. . . .
>
> The power of leadership is the power of integrating. This is the power that creates community. . . .
>
> The skilful leader then does not rely on personal force; he controls his group not by dominating but by expressing it. He stimulates what is best in us; he unifies and concentrates what we feel only gropingly and scatteringly, but he never gets away from the current of which we and he are both an integral part. He is a leader who gives form to the inchoate energy in every man. The person who influences me most is not he who does great deeds but he who makes me feel I can do great deeds.[*]

---

[*]Mary Parker Follett, *The New State*, pp. 229–30.

A Few Good Questions

The trouble with the head-down view of knowledge is that it places too much emphasis on answers and not enough on the questions. As a result, managers often spend a good deal of their time trying to find solutions to the wrong problems—good answers to meaningless or unanswerable questions. *We have to find good questions before we can get good answers.* And indeed, this is the value of all good conceptual frameworks—they help us find such questions. The systems perspective cannot tell managers or golfers exactly what to do, but it does ensure that they focus on and tackle the key questions—it stops them from wasting their time and effort.

The specific answers—implemented responses—to such key questions will vary from organization to organization. But finding them is usually not the problem. As every consultant knows, people in organizations usually have most, if not all, of the answers. And they have the competence to implement them. The problem is that no one tells them what the important questions are or, at least, these questions are rarely posed in a form or language that they can handle. As a result, they spend much time on wasted effort. It is the posing of such questions, the translation of the great issues into a form that can be addressed here and now, and the mobilization of the corporate body to respond to them, the focusing of collective attention, that is the essential role of effective leadership.

No. 18

This Time I've Really Got It!

Par-3	165 yards

We have never mastered golf until we realize that our good shots are accidents and our bad shots, good exercise.
—BOBBY JONES

By archery . . . the Japanese does not understand a sport but, strange as this may sound, a religious ritual . . . whose aim consists in hitting a spiritual mark, so that fundamentally the marksman aims at himself and may even succeed in hitting himself.
—EUGEN HERRIGEL, ZEN IN THE ART OF ARCHERY

"How can you write about such an elitist game?" an acquaintance of mine asked when I told her I was writing a book about golf and management. I was shocked—I had never thought of golf as an elitist game. But she saw it as a frivolous pastime pursued by corporate fat cats (mostly white male) at exclusive clubs. In the great business centers of the world, golf may have this image, but I don't think it reflects on the game. We don't judge art by the motives and manners of some of those who bid for it at Sotheby's and Christie's; one just hopes that they buy it because they enjoy it. Even if they buy art purely for financial purposes, by living with it, they may come to love it. For art has a redemptive power. Golf, too, like any complex activity, if approached as an art, has that same power. The key difference between art and mere entertainment is that art demands the investment of our attention, and I believe that golf, like art, repays such an investment. "If you watch a game, it's fun," says Bob Hope. "If you participate, it's recreation; and if you *work* at it, it's golf."

Sociologist Todd Crosset, in his excellent book on the LPGA, *Outsiders in the Clubhouse,* describes the liberating potential of sport in this way:

> We come to know the world through the body. . . . Body movement is no more or less important than thought, sight, or touch. . . . [It] is a resource to understanding. . . .
>
> Each sport, with its particular rules, regulates the movement of the athlete. It is here at the intersection between body and sport, that we can catch a glimpse of the liberating potential of sport. The interaction between body and sport provides the athlete with ways of thinking about "self" in the world. . . . If we restrict movement, we restrict our ability to know the world.
>
> Controlling movement is an integral part of institutions whose principal task is to promote an ideology. Religions, cults, social protests, and military organizations all incorporate body movements to enforce or communicate belief systems or worldviews. . . . Denial of access to sport is nothing less than the denial of a resource. Restricting access to movement is not unlike restricting access to high-tech information, or restricted access to credit or capital. It hinders that group's ability to understand the world.*

The message that has been implicit for much of this book is now clear: Golf, pursued with diligence and application, makes for a fine corporal discipline. By corporal discipline, I mean that golf can be used to discipline the embodied mind at several levels of complexity—the individual, the family or team, and the community or true company—the building blocks of society. After a bad day on the course, many of us may think of golf as corporal punishment rather than corporal discipline. But this happens only if we fail to appreciate all the lessons the game can teach.

*Todd W. Crosset, *Outsiders in the Clubhouse,* pp. 185–86, original emphasis.

The Lessons Golf Teaches

Golf teaches systemic thinking—it helps us understand the complexity of cause and effect and the difficulty of making fundamental changes in complex systems. It teaches not through lessons and lectures, but through structured experience. We absorb the notion of a system by paying attention to the movements of our bodies; we grasp the meaning of synergy by feeling the controlled explosion through the ball. Golf teaches us to work with persistence and focus—even the top golfers are always "working at something." By acting in a disciplined way, one comes to think in a different way.

Golf teaches strategic thinking. We have to think ahead continually and construct "likely stories," memories of the future. What's the best way for me to play this hole? Where should I putt from? What kind of second shot must I play? Where should I put my tee shot? Golf encourages us to think of multiple scenarios and look at the downsides of our strategies. Every golfer knows that each strategy must have a contingency plan—suppose the ball doesn't slice; what if I hit it short, or straight? In golf, questions of strategy can never be separated from questions of competence and circumstance. The game requires analysis, but it will not yield to it. We know that we cannot risk getting too far ahead of our ability to execute our plans. When we do, disaster is at hand.

Golf teaches values—ways of behavior that are followed not for financial gain, but because they are intrinsically valuable. The rules of the game make these values plain. They are the common courtesies, ways of behaving that, as evolutionary psychology suggests, have proved essential to our growth and survival over hundreds of thousands of years. Many organizations, religious and secular, use rituals to teach values, to remind their members of the living presence of the past in the present. When members of the Society of Jesus, the Jesuits, seek renewal, they try to understand how the values of their founder can be realized in the new contexts in which they find themselves. To this end, they go through the "exercises" developed by Ignatius of Loyola over five hundred years

ago, either doing the exercises themselves or supervising someone else going through the process. By "walking the walk," by
stepping in the footsteps of their founder, they participate in the
activities that lead to the founding of their institution. This is not
an intellectual activity. They develop no logic, no "map" of how to
proceed. But the feelings, the appreciation of the founder's values,
generated by this participation act as a compass needle, giving
them a continual sense of the direction in which to head. One has
only to look at the exemplary behavior of someone like Arnold
Palmer, who seems to embody the values of the game, to realize
that the values taught by golf can supply that moral compass.

Golf can teach us the right attitude toward nature. Some observers, with good reason, see many golf courses as profligate con-
sumers of natural resources and destructive of natural habitat.
With a growing appreciation of complex systems, I believe that
this will change. In our society, we have and will continue to use
nature to take us where we would like to go, hitchhiking a ride on
its natural dynamics. But nature is a system, too, and the webs of
cause and effect are complex beyond our current understanding.
Small changes may have large consequences. The best approach
is a cautious one—the kind you'd take on a tough course you've
never played before.

Golf is not life, but golf is part of life, and it contains within it
some truths about living. So golf is really more than a metaphor, it
is perhaps a model, a miniature simulation of life. It is a replica of
the systemic way in which we may exercise control over the trajec-
tories of our own lives as well as those of our organizations. Complex systems cannot be consciously controlled in real time, so
control must be delegated to many subsystems and agents. And
many of the agents are themselves complex systems. They, like us,
must spin and move to stay steady; yet in that spinning, our personal and interpersonal dynamics, lie all the joys and the woes,
the achievements and the challenges. And in life, just as in golf,
we are often the architects of our own misfortunes.

Golf teaches us that life is a journey and that we can never go
back, only move on. Nature is neither cruel nor kind, neither
vengeful nor benign; it's just indifferent to our strivings. It doesn't

care. Only people care, and the people who care most are the small teams and communities around us, cheering our victories and commiserating in our defeats. It is their support and regard that sustain us on our journey.

The Secret of Success

Golf is a search for that mastery of paradox that gives us control over ourselves. It is a search for the sweet spot in space and time. Indeed, golf can teach us how to understand and use our time. For golf emphasizes the importance of staying in the present, of living in the moment and using goals and feedback to keep us there.

Many of us in management have trouble living in the present—paying attention to the here and now, getting feedback from what is actually happening. We spend too much time in the future, seeing the present only as a means and the future as an end. We scramble after objectives that we never seem to reach, for the future, as such, never comes—it always recedes from our grasp. It's true of life as well as of golf and management. Few have said it better than Fritz Roethlisberger. We met him in chapter 1 with his critique of "verbal wands." Over fifty years ago, he made a speech to a class at Harvard Business School, trying to put a different spin on the perennial question "What's the secret of success?" He felt that it was silly, meaningless, and unanswerable:

> Instead of asking the question "What is the secret of success?" it might be more sensible to ask . . . "What prevents me from learning here and now?" . . . It should be obvious that growth and learning take place in the present. One cannot adjust easily to the past or future. The past is gone and the future is uncertain. . . . Some of you, I fear, tend to think of the present as a means and the future as an end. . . . What if I suggested to you that the future is the means and the present is the end? Would that sound too silly? Before throwing it out as absurd, however, let's consider it for a moment. You can't live in the past or the future, can you? And when the future comes, it is "present," isn't it? When a businessman retires at the age of sixty-five he doesn't have the

same organism he had when he was twenty. Isn't it likely—or am I just dreaming—that he won't be able to enjoy some of the things he thought he would enjoy at the age of twenty? Why is it then that so many of us feel we can't settle down and enjoy the present until we achieve success? . . .

Are there not two different kinds of goals? . . . one kind which takes all meaning and significance out of the present, and . . . another kind of goal which makes the present more meaningful and significant. . . . By means of [the first kind] we make ourselves miserable in the present . . . we create a target just in order to shoot at it and we make ourselves miserable every time we fail to hit the bull's-eye. . . . In the case of the second kind of goal, we create the target to perfect our shooting here and now. This kind of goal works for us. It makes meaningful and significant the present. It facilitates growth, learning, the sense of adventure and exploration. In this frame of reference, hitting the bull's-eye isn't an end in itself. The bull's-eye merely becomes a means for correcting the source of error here and now. Are not such goals treating the future as a means and the present as an end? If so, what are these goals which allow us to retain our zest for growth and learning and adaptation until the day we die? This [is the] question.*

In my mind's eye I am standing again on the 18th tee at Harbour Town. It's a beautiful warm afternoon, but the wind is fresh into our faces. The sea oats sway and bend in the wind, and I can smell the sea marsh all around us; it reeks of life. Out in the Calibogue Sound, a school of dolphins is roving the shore, in search of dinner. Far away the flag flutters with the lighthouse as backdrop. It's my turn . . . no worries . . . relaxed in the shoulders, no tension in the arms, no thought of technique . . . just a smooth flow. . . . I am the target . . . and the ball flies like an arrow released from a bow, streaking across the marsh into the sunset, straight and true.

Hmm . . . this time I've *really* got it.

*Fritz Roethlisberger, "The Secret of Success," in *Man-in-Organization* (Cambridge, Mass.: Belknap Press, 1968), pp. 85–94.

Bibliography

Ackenhusen, M., and S. Ghoshal. *Anderson Consulting (Europe)* Case 392-055-1. Fontainebleau: INSEAD, 1992.

Adams, M., T. J. Tomasi, and J. Suttie. *The LAWs of the Golf Swing*. New York: Harper-Collins, 1998.

Adams, S. *The Dilbert Principle*. New York: HarperCollins, 1996.

Adler, P. S. "Time-and-Motion Regained." *Harvard Business Review* (January–February 1993): 97–108.

Ahl, V., and T. F. H. Allen. *Hierarchy Theory*. New York: Columbia University Press, 1996.

Allen, T. F. H., and T. W. Hoekstra. *Toward a Unified Ecology*. New York: Columbia University Press, 1992.

Allen, T. F. H., and T. B. Starr. *Hierarchy: Perspectives for Ecological Complexity*. Chicago: University of Chicago Press, 1982.

Amabile, T. M., and R. Conti. "Changes in the Work Environment for Creativity During Downsizing." *Academy of Management Journal* 42, no. 6 (1999): 630–40.

Armour, T. *How to Play Your Best Golf All the Time*. Greenwich, Conn.: Fawcett Publications, 1961.

Ashmos, D. P., and G. P. Huber. "The Systems Paradigm in Organization Theory." *Academy of Management Review* 12, no. 4 (1987): 607–21.

"Asia in the Rough." *The Economist*, December 20, 1997, 85–87.

Athos, A. G., and J. J. Gabarro. *Interpersonal Behavior: Communicating and Understanding in Relationship*. Englewood Cliffs, N.J.: Prentice-Hall, 1978.

Axelrod, R. *The Evolution of Cooperation*. New York: Basic Books, 1984.

Baldwin, C. Y., and K. B. Clark. "Managing in an Age of Modularity." *Harvard Business Review* (September–October 1997): 84–93.

Bandura, A. "Self-Efficacy: Toward a Unifying Theory of Behavioral Change." *Psychological Review* 84, no. 2 (1977): 191–215.

Barkow, J. H., J. Tooby, and L. Cosmides. *The Adapted Mind: Evolutionary Psychology and the Generation of Culture*. New York: Oxford University Press, 1992.

Barnard, C. I. *The Functions of the Executive*. Cambridge, Mass.: Harvard University Press (30th anniversary ed.), 1968.

Barten, S. S. "Speaking of Music: The Use of Motor-Affective Metaphors in Music Instruction." *Journal of Aesthetic Education* 32, no. 2 (Summer 1998): 89–97.

Bateson, G. *Steps to an Ecology of Mind*. New York: Ballantine Books, 1983.

Bertozzi-Villa, E. *Broadmoor Memories: The History of the Broadmoor.* Missoula, Mont.: Pictorial Histories Publishing Company, 1993.

Bloom, B. S. (ed.). *Developing Talent in Young People.* New York: Ballantine Books, 1985.

Boardman, A. W. *The Medieval Soldier.* Stroud, Gloucestershire: Sutton Publishing, 1998.

Boje, D. M., et al. "Restorying Reengineering: Some Deconstructions and Postmodern Alternatives." *Communication Research* 24, no. 6 (December 1997): 631–38.

Bonner, J. T. *The Evolution of Complexity.* Princeton, N.J.: Princeton University Press, 1988.

Boomer, P. *On Learning Golf.* New York: Alfred A. Knopf, 1997.

Boulding, K. "General Systems Theory—The Skeleton of a Science." *Management Science* 2 (1956): 197–208.

Brooks, R. A. "Intelligence without Reason." M.I.T. A.I. Memo No. 1293, 1991.

Brooks, R. A., and A. Flynn. "Fast, Cheap and Out of Control." M.I.T. A.I. Memo 1182, December 1989.

Brooks, R. A., et al. "The Cog Project: Building a Humanoid Robot." MIT Artificial Intelligence Lab, http://www.ai.mit.edu/projects/cog/publications.html.

Brown, J. S., and P. Duguid. "Organizing Knowledge." *California Management Review* 40, no. 3 (Spring 1998): 90.

Bryant, A. "Duffers Need Not Apply." *New York Times,* May 31, 1998, Section 3: 1.

Buss, D. M. *Evolutionary Psychology.* Needham Heights, Mass.: Allyn & Bacon, 1999.

Byrne, J. A. *Chainsaw: The Notorious Career of Al Dunlap in the Era of Profit-at-Any-Price.* New York: HarperCollins, 1999.

Case, J. *Open-Book Management.* New York: HarperBusiness, 1996.

Calvin, W. H. *Cerebral Symphony.* New York: Bantam Books, 1990.

———. *The Throwing Madonna.* New York: Bantam Doubleday Dell, 1991.

Cascio, W. F. "Downsizing: What Do We Know? What Have We Learned?" *Academy of Management Executive* 7, no. 1 (1993): 95–104.

Chambliss, D. F. *Champions: The Making of Olympic Swimmers.* New York: William Morrow & Company, Inc., 1988.

———. "The Mundanity of Excellence: An Ethnographic Report on Stratification and Olympic Swimmers." *Sociological Theory* (Spring 1989): 70–86.

Charan, R., and G. Colvin. "Why CEOs Fail." *Fortune,* June 21, 1999, 69–82.

Christiansen, E. T. Honda (A) and Honda (B) Teaching Note, Harvard Business School Case 5–386–034, Boston, Mass., 1985.

Cochran, A., and J. Stobbs. *Search for the Perfect Swing.* Chicago, Ill.: Triumph Books, 1996.

Collins, J. C., and J. I. Porras. *Built to Last.* New York: HarperCollins, 1994.

Coop, R. *Mind Over Golf.* New York: Macmillan, 1993.

Cosmides, L., and J. Tooby. "Better than Rational: Evolutionary Psychology and the Invisible Hand." *American Economic Review* 84, no. 7 (1994): 327–32.

Crosset, T. W. *Outsiders in the Clubhouse.* Albany, N.Y.: State University of New York Press, 1995.

Csikszentmihalyi, M. *Flow: The Psychology of Optimal Experience.* New York: Harper-Perennial, 1991.

Dale, Ernest. *The Great Organizers.* New York: McGraw-Hill, 1960.

Damasio, A. R. *Descartes' Error: Emotion, Reason, and the Human Brain.* New York: Avon Books, 1995.

Davenport, T. H. "The Fad That Forgot People." *Fast Company,* November 1995, 70.

Davenport, T. H., and J. E. Short. "The New Industrial Engineering: Information Technology and Business Process Redesign." *Sloan Management Review* (Summer 1990): 11–27.

DeGunther, R. *The Art and Science of Putting.* Indianapolis, Ind.: Masters Press, 1996.

Deming, W. E. *Out of the Crisis.* Cambridge, Mass.: M.I.T. Center for Advanced Engineering Study, 1986.

Dennett, D. C. *Consciousness Explained.* New York: Little, Brown & Company, 1991.

———. *Darwin's Dangerous Idea.* New York: Touchstone Books, 1996.

Dewey, J. *The Quest for Certainty.* New York: Minton, Balch & Company, 1929.

Diamond, J. *Guns, Germs, and Steel.* New York: W. W. Norton & Company, 1997.

Dodgson, H. "Management Learning in *Markstrat.*" *Journal of Business Research* 15 (1987): 481–89.

Dougherty, D., and E. H. Bowman. "The Effects of Organizational Downsizing on Product Innovation." *California Management Review* 37, no. 4 (Summer 1995).

Drucker, P. F. *The Effective Executive.* New York: Harper & Row Publishers, 1966.

———. *Adventures of a Bystander.* New York: HarperCollins, 1991.

Earle, M. D. (ed.). *Makers of Modern Strategy.* Princeton, N.J.: Princeton University Press, 1943.

Eccles, R. G., and N. Nohria, with J. D. Berkley. *Beyond the Hype.* Cambridge, Mass.: Harvard Business School Press, 1992.

Edwards, B. *Drawing on the Right Side of the Brain.* New York: Tarcher/Putnam, 1989.

Ericsson, K. A., and N. Charness. "Expert Performance: Its Structure and Acquisition." *American Psychologist* 49, no. 8 (August 1994): 725–47.

Ericsson, K. A., R. T. Krampe, and T. Tesch-Romer. "The Role of Deliberate Practice in the Acquisition of Expert Performance." *Psychological Review* 100, no. 3 (1993): 363–406.

Farnsworth, C. L. *See It and Sink It.* New York: HarperCollins, 1997.

Fishman, G. "Sabbaticals Are Serious Business." *Fast Company,* October 1996, 44.

Flick, J., with G. Waggoner. *On Golf.* New York: Villard, 1997.

Follett, M. P. *Creative Experience.* New York: Longmans, Green & Co., 1924.

———. *Dynamic Administration.* London: Pitman, 1965.

———. *Freedom and Co-ordination.* London: Management Publications Trust, 1949.

———. *The New State.* New York: Longmans, Green & Co., 1920.

Forrester, J. *Industrial Dynamics.* Cambridge, Mass.: MIT Press, 1961.

Frank, R. H. *Passions within Reason.* New York: W. W. Norton & Company, 1988.

Gallwey, W. T. *The Inner Game of Golf.* New York: Random House, 1981.

Gardner, H. *Frames of Mind.* New York: Basic Books, 1983.

Gazzaniga, M. S. *The Mind's Past.* Berkeley: University of California Press, 1998.

Geisler, P. "Kinesiology of the Full Golf Swing." *Sports Medicine Update* 11, no. 2 (1996): 9–19.

Gist, M. E., and T. R. Mitchell. "Self-Efficacy: A Theoretical Analysis of Its Determinants and Malleability." *Academy of Management Review* 17, no. 2 (1992): 183–211.

Goldratt, E. M., and J. Cox. *The Goal* (rev. ed.). Croton-on-Hudson, N.Y.: North River Press, 1986.

Goleman, D. *Emotional Intelligence.* New York: Bantam Books, 1995.

Golf Research Associates: http://www.shotbyshot.com.

Gomes, L. "New CEO Aims to Brighten Silicon Graphics' Picture." *Wall Street Journal,* April 15, 1998, B6.

Hammer, M., and J. Champy. *Reengineering the Corporation: A Manifesto for Business Revolution.* New York: HarperCollins, 1993.

Hammer, M. "Reengineering Work: Don't Automate, Obliterate." *Harvard Business Review* (July–August 1990): 104–112.

Hampden-Turner, C. *Maps of the Mind.* New York: Collier Books, 1982.

Hatcher, J. *The Art & Craft of Playwriting.* Cincinnati, Ohio: Story Press, 1996.

Haultain, A. *The Mystery of Golf.* Sandwich, Mass.: Serendipity Press, 1997.

Hayes, R. H., and W. J. Abernathy. "Managing Our Way to Economic Decline." *Harvard Business Review* (July–August 1980): 67–77.

Herrigel, E. *Zen in the Art of Archery.* New York: Random House, 1971.

Hofstadter, D. R. *Gödel, Escher, Bach.* New York: Random House, 1980.

Hogan, B. *Power Golf.* London: Corgi Editions, 1965.

Hogan, B., with H. W. Wind. *The Modern Fundamentals of Golf.* London: Corgi Books, 1965.

Holland, J. H., *Hidden Order.* Reading, Mass.: Addison-Wesley, 1995.

Hurst, D. K. *Crisis & Renewal: Meeting the Challenge of Organizational Change.* Cambridge, Mass.: Harvard Business School Press, 1995.

Imperato, G. "You Have to Start Meeting Like This." *Fast Company,* April 1999: 204–10.

Ingvar, D. H. "Memory of the Future." *Human Neurobiology* 4 (1985): 127–36.

Janis, I. L., and L. Mann. *Decision Making.* New York: Free Press, 1977.

Jaques, E. *The Form of Time.* New York: Crane Russak, 1982.

Jaynes, J. *The Origins of Consciousness in the Breakdown of the Bicameral Mind.* Boston, Mass.: Houghton Mifflin Company, 1982.

Jerome, J. *The Sweet Spot in Time.* New York: Breakaway Books, 1998.

Johnson, H. T., and R. S. Kaplan. *Relevance Lost: The Rise and Fall of Management Accounting.* Cambridge, Mass.: Harvard Business School Press, 1987.

Johnson, M. *The Body in the Mind.* Chicago, Ill.: University of Chicago Press, 1987.

Jones, J. G., and L. Hard (eds.). *Stress and Performance in Sport.* Chichester, Eng.: John Wiley & Sons, 1990.

Kaplan, R. S., and R. Cooper. *Cost & Effect.* Cambridge, Mass.: Harvard Business School Press, 1998.

Kaufman, S. *At Home in the Universe.* New York: Oxford University Press, 1995.

Keller, M. *Rude Awakening: The Rise, Fall, and Struggle for Recovery of General Motors.* New York: William Morrow & Company, 1989.

Kelley, H. *The Golfing Machine.* Seattle, Wash.: Star Systems Press, 1982.

Kelly, G. A. *A Theory of Personality,* New York: W. W. Norton & Company, 1963.

Kelly, K. *Out of Control.* Reading, Mass.: Addison-Wesley, 1994.

Kermode, F. *The Sense of an Ending.* New York: Oxford University Press, 1967.

Kim, K. H. S., N. R. Relkin, and K-M. Lee. "Distinct Cortical Areas Associated with Native and Second Languages." *Nature* 388, no. 10 (July 1997): 171–75.

Kimble, G. A., and L. C. Perlmuter. "The Problem of Volition." *Psychological Review* 77, no. 5 (September 1970): 361–84.

Kirsh, D. "Foundations of AI: The Big Issues." *Artificial Intelligence* 47 (1991): 3–30.

Kosslyn, S. M., and O. Koenig. *Wet Mind.* New York: The Free Press, 1992.

Kotter, J. P. "What Effective General Managers Really Do." *Harvard Business Review* (November–December 1982): 156–67.

Kruger, J., and D. Dunning. "Unskilled and Unaware of It: How Difficulties in Recognizing One's Own Incompetence Lead to Inflated Self-Assessments." *Journal of Personality and Social Psychology* 77, no. 6 (1999): 1121–34.

Lakoff, G., and M. Johnson. *Metaphors We Live By.* Chicago, Ill.: University of Chicago Press, 1980.

Lakoff, M., and M. Johnson. *Philosophy in the Flesh.* New York: Basic Books, 1999.

Langer, E. J. *Mindfulness.* Reading, Mass.: Addison-Wesley, 1989.

Leadbetter, D. "Your New Swing Starts Here." *Golf Digest* (January 2002): 54–64.

Leadbetter, D., with J. Huggan. *The Golf Swing.* Lexington, Mass.: Stephen Greene Press, 1990.

Leadbetter, D., with R. Simmons. *Positive Practice.* New York: HarperCollins, 1997.

Leavitt, H. J. "Beyond the Analytic Manager: Parts I & II." *California Management Review* 17, nos. 3–4 (Spring 1975): 5–21.

Letters, *The Economist,* January 17, 1998, 6–8.

Lewin, R. *Complexity.* New York: Macmillan Publishing Company, 1992.

Lindsley, D. H., and D. J. Brass. "Efficacy-Performance Spirals: A Multilevel Perspective." *Academy of Management Review* 20, no. 3 (1995): 645–78.

Locke, E. A., and G. P. Latham. "The Application of Goal Setting to Sports." *Journal of Sport Psychology* 7 (1985): 205–22.

MacRury, D. (ed.) *Golfers on Golf.* Ladbroke Grove, London: Virgin Books, 1997.

Mahoney, T. S., and J. R. Deckop. "Y'Gotta Believe: Lesson from American- vs. Japanese-run U.S. Factories." *Organizational Dynamics* (Spring 1993): 27–38.

Mandelbrot, B. B. *The Fractal Geometry of Nature.* New York: W. H. Freeman & Company, 1977.

Marvin, D. D., and L. M. Hough (eds.). *Handbook of Industrial and Organizational Psychology* (2nd ed.). Palo Alto, Calif.: Consulting Psychologists Press, 1990.

Masters, R. S. W. "Knowledge, Knerves and Know-how: The Role of Explicit Versus Implicit Knowledge in the Breakdown of a Complex Motor Skill Under Pressure." *British Journal of Psychology* 83 (August 1992): 343–57.

Matthew, S. L. (ed.). *Secrets of the Master.* Chelsea, Mich.: Sleeping Bear Press, 1996.

McCaffrey, N., and T. Orlick. "Mental Factors Related to Excellence Among Top Professional Golfers." *International Journal of Sport Psychology* 20 (1989): 256–78.

McCall, M.W., Jr., M. M. Lombardo, and A. M. Morrison. *The Lessons of Experience.* Lexington, Mass.: Lexington Books, 1988.

McCall, M. W., Jr., and R. E. Kaplan. *Whatever It Takes.* Englewood Cliffs, N.J.: Prentice-Hall, 1985.

McCauley, C. D., R. S. Moxley, and E. Van Velsor (eds.). *The Center for Creative Leadership Handbook of Leadership Development.* San Francisco, Calif.: Jossey-Bass Publishers, 1998.

McClelland, D. C. *The Achieving Society.* Princeton, N.J.: D. Van Nostrand Company, 1961.

Miller, G. A. "The Magical Number Seven, Plus or Minus Two: Some Limits on Our Capacity for Processing Information." *Psychological Review* 63, no. 2, (1956): 81–97.

Minsky, M. *The Society of Mind.* New York: Simon & Schuster (Touchstone ed.), 1988.

Mintzberg, H., and L. Van der Heyden. "Organigraphs: Drawing How Companies Really Work." *Harvard Business Review* (September–October 1999): 87–94.

Mintzberg, H. *The Rise and Fall of Strategic Planning.* New York: The Free Press, 1994.

Morris, J. R., W. F. Cascio, and C. E. Young. "Downsizing After All These Years." *Organizational Dynamics* (Winter 1999): 78–87.

Neisser, U. *Cognition and Reality.* San Francisco, Calif.: W. H. Freeman & Company, 1976.

Nicklaus, J., with K. Bowden. *Golf My Way.* New York: Simon & Schuster, 1974.

Nilsson, P. "Swedish National Golf Team." Publication of the Swedish Golf Federation.

Nilsson, P., and L. Evertsson. "Balance." Publication of the Swedish Golf Federation.

Noer, D. M. *Healing the Wounds.* San Francisco, Calif.: Jossey-Bass Publishers, 1993.

Nolan, R. L., and D. C. Croson. *Creative Destruction.* Cambridge, Mass.: Harvard Business School Press, 1995.

Nonaka, I., and H. Takeuchi. *The Knowledge-Creating Company.* New York: Oxford University Press, 1995.

Nonaka, I., et al. "The Concept of 'Ba': Building a Foundation for Knowledge Creation." *California Management Review* 40, no. 3 (Spring 1998): 40 (15).

Ohno, T. *Workplace Management.* Cambridge, Mass.: Productivity Press, 1988.

Orlick, T. *In Pursuit of Excellence.* Champaign, Ill.: Leisure Press, 1990.

Ornstein, R. *The Right Mind.* New York: Harcourt Brace & Company, 1997.

Packard, D. *The HP Way.* New York: HarperCollins, 1995.

Paivio, A. "Mental Imagery in Associative Learning." *Psychological Review* 76, no. 3 (May 1969): 241– 63.

Pascal, B. *Pensees.* London: Penguin Books, 1995.

Pascale, R. T., and A. G. Athos. *The Art of Japanese Management.* New York: Warner Books, 1982.

Pascale, R. T. Honda (A), Case 9-384-049. Boston, Mass.: Harvard Business School, 1983.

———. Honda (B), Case 9-384-050. Boston, Mass.: Harvard Business School, 1983.

———. "Perspectives on Strategy: The Real Story Behind Honda's Success." *California Management Review* 26, no. 3 (Spring 1984): 47–72.

———. *Managing on the Edge.* New York: Touchstone Books, Simon & Schuster, 1990.

Pelz, D., with J. A. Frank. *Dave Pelz's Short Game Bible.* New York: Broadway Books, 1999.

Pelz, D., with N. Mastroni. *Putt Like the Pros.* New York: HarperPerennial, 1989.

Peters, T. J., and R. H. Waterman. *In Search of Excellence.* New York: Harper & Row, 1982.

Pfeffer, P., and R. I. Sutton. "The Smart-Talk Trap." *Harvard Business Review* (May–June 1999): 135–42.

Polanyi, M. *Personal Knowledge,* corrected ed. Chicago, Ill.: University of Chicago Press, 1962.

Polkinghorne, D. E. *Narrative Knowing and the Human Sciences.* Albany, N.Y.: State University of New York Press, 1988.

Popper, K. R. *Objective Knowledge.* Oxford: Oxford University Press, 1979.

Powers, W. T. *Making Sense of Behavior.* New Canaan, Conn.: Benchmark Publications, 1998.

Price, N., with L. Rubenstein. *The Swing.* Toronto: Random House Canada, 1997.

Reber, A. S. *Implicit Learning and Tacit Knowledge.* New York: Oxford University Press, 1993.

Report of the Presidential Commission on the Space Shuttle *Challenger* Accident at http://science.ksc.nasa.gov/shuttle/missions/51-1/docs/rogers-commission/table-of-contents.html.

Riccio, L. J. "Statistical Analysis of the Average Golfer," in Cochran, A. J. (ed.). *Science and Golf.* London: E&F.N. Spon, 1990, 153–57.

Richardson, G. P. *Feedback Thought in Social Science and Systems Theory.* Philadelphia, Pa.: University of Pennsylvania Press, 1991.

Ridley, M. *The Origins of Virtue.* London: Viking, Penguin Group, 1996.

Rother, M., and J. Shook. *Learning to See,* version 1.2. Brookline, Mass.: Lean Enterprise Institute, 1999.

Ryle, G. *The Concept of Mind.* London: Penguin Books, 1990.

Schoenberg, R. J. *Geneen.* New York: W. W. Norton & Company, 1985.

Scott, D. N. C., and J. S. Brown. "Bridging Epistemologies: The Generative Dance Between Organizational Knowledge and Organizational Knowing." *Organization Science* 10, no. 4 (July–August 1999): 381–400.

Simon, H. A. *The New Science of Management Decision.* New York: Harper & Row, 1960.

———. *The Sciences of the Artificial.* Cambridge, Mass.: MIT Press, 1969.

Smith, L. "Can Oxford Heal Itself?" *Fortune,* December 29, 1997, 238–40.

Snead, S., with D. Wade. *Better Golf the Sam Snead Way.* Chicago, Ill.: Contemporary Books, 1989.

Sobek, D. K., J. K. Liker, and A. C. Ward. "Another Look at How Toyota Integrates Product Development." *Harvard Business Review* (July–August 1998): 36–49.

Sobek, D. K., A. C. Ward, and J. K. Liker. "Toyota's Principles of Set-Based Concurrent Engineering," *Sloan Management Review* (Winter 1999): 67–83.

Sommer, R. T. *Golf Anecdotes.* New York: Oxford University Press, 1995.

Spear, S., and H. K. Bowen. "Decoding the DNA of the Toyota Production System." *Harvard Business Review* (September–October 1999): 97–106.

Springer, S. P., and G. Deutsch. *Left Brain, Right Brain.* New York: W. H. Freeman & Company, 1989.

Stein, L. A. "Imagination and Situated Cognition." *Journal of Experimental and Theoretical Artificial Intelligence* 6 (1994): 393–407.

Steinbreder, J. "Handicapping America's CEOs." *Golf Digest,* June 1998, 99–101.

Stewart, T. A. "Reengineering: The Hot New Managing Tool." *Fortune,* August 23, 1993, 41–48.

Strassman, P. A. "The Hocus-Pocus of Reengineering." *Across the Board* 31, no. 6 (June 1994): 35(4).

Taylor, F. W. *Scientific Management.* New York: Harper & Row, 1947.

"The *Challenger* Disaster," at http://onlineethics.org/moral/boisjoly/RB-intro.html.

The Swedish Golf Model—Elite Programme, publication of the Swedish Golf Federation.

Toski, B., and D. Love Jr., with R. Carney. *How to Feel a Real Golf Swing.* New York: Times Books, 1997.

Updike, J. *Golf Dreams.* New York: Ballantine Books, 1996.

Vaill, P. B. *Managing as a Performing Art*. San Francisco, Calif.: Jossey-Bass Publishers, 1989.

van Creveld, M. *Fighting Power*. London: Arms and Armour Press, 1983.

Van Natta, D., Jr. "Taking Second Chances: Par for Clinton's Course." *New York Times*, August 29, 1999, 1.

Von Bertalanffy, L. *General Systems Theory*. New York: George Braziller, 1968.

Wagman, M. *The Ultimate Objectives of Artificial Intelligence*. Westport, Conn.: Praeger, 1998.

Waldrop, M. M. *Complexity: The Emerging Science at the Edge of Order*. New York: Simon & Schuster, 1992.

Ward, A., et al. "The Second Toyota Paradox: How Delaying Decisions Can Make Better Cars Faster." *Sloan Management Review* (Spring 1995): 43–61.

Weick, K. E. *The Social Psychology of Organizing*. Reading, Mass.: Addison-Wesley, 1979.

Wildavsky, A. "If Planning Is Everything, Maybe It's Nothing." *Policy Sciences* 4 (1973): 127–153.

Willingham, D. B. "A Neuropsychological Theory of Motor Skill Learning." *Psychological Review* 105, no. 3 (1998): 558–84.

Wilson, F. R. *The Hand; How It Shapes the Brain, Language and Human Culture*. New York: Pantheon Books, 1998.

Winslow, R., and S. J. Paltrow. "Ill-Managed Care." *Wall Street Journal*, April 29, 1998, A1.

Wiren, G. *The PGA Manual of Golf*. New York: Macmillan, 1991.

Womack, J. P., and D. T. Jones. *Lean Thinking*. New York: Simon & Schuster, 1996.

Womack, J. P., D. T. Jones, and D. Roos. *The Machine That Changed the World*. New York: HarperPerennial, 1991.

Index

Page numbers in *italics* refer to illustrations.

About the Author

David K. Hurst is a speaker, consultant, and writer on management, with extensive experience both as an effective manager and educator. He has been a sole practitioner since 1992, and has worked with numerous educational institutions, most recently with the Center for Creative Leadership in Greensboro, North Carolina, and the Richard Ivey School of Business in London, Ontario. He is currently a Research Fellow at the University of Western Ontario's National Centre for Management Research and Development. David was born in England but grew up in South Africa. He now lives with his wife and family in Oakville, Ontario. He has played golf since the age of twelve.